Hidden in Mist

Penina Keen Spinka

authorHOUSE

AuthorHouse™
1663 Liberty Drive
Bloomington, IN 47403
www.authorhouse.com
Phone: 1 (800) 839-8640

Published by AuthorHouse 01/05/2016

ISBN: 978-1-5049-6905-5 (sc)
ISBN: 978-1-5049-6880-5 (hc)
ISBN: 978-1-5049-6904-8 (e)

Library of Congress Control Number: 2015920787

Print information available on the last page.

Any people depicted in stock imagery provided by Thinkstock are models, and such images are being used for illustrative purposes only.
Certain stock imagery © Thinkstock.

This book is printed on acid-free paper.

Dedicated to my friend, Lysis, author of excellent Alexander the Great fan fiction, for her belief in me and my stories.

Acknowledgements:

Since I read Mary Renault's *The King Must Die*, I have been fascinated at how novelists turn legends and history into novels. I studied the oral tradition of the Iroquois. The Five Tribes founded what might be the first representative government in North America. Women ruled the houses and families. I had to love that. I hope the reader gains an understanding of the time period and an appreciation for the people who became the legends. There are several versions of the Creation and the Unification story. I chose the versions that most helped the narrative. Names differ in spelling.

My husband Barry Spinka should be commended for his patience while I edited Hidden in Mist endlessly. Thank you for fixing my computer every time it did something strange. Great thanks to my dear friend Bella Romain for reading and proofing. I accept total responsibility for any errors. Thanks to Stew Romain for my author photo and help with Windows 10. Thanks to my friend and Sun City neighbor, Jacques Condor (Maka Tamai) for his recommendations. Being part Algonquin, he knows the stories, but without my additions. To my friends at Writers Round Table, of Phoenix, (John Safin, our founder, KC, Walter and the rest) for their reading and suggestions. To my dear readers who read the first two books of my Norse/Mohawk trilogy and especially to those who wrote to me at my website HYPERLINK "http://www. peninakeenspinka.info" www.peninakeenspinka.info to ask for the third. Please write again.

Thanks to Karen Stansberry and Allie Ireland, Coordinators at Author House, for helping me bring this project to you.

Suggested reading - *The League of the Iroquois* by Lewis Henry Morgan. "The Iroquois" from *The Indians of North America* series by Barbara Graymont, Frank W. Porter III, General Editor. *Wildwood Wisdom* by E. Jaeger.

Chapter 1

Saiyen-gu

Saiyen-gu's father died. After the burial and mourning, his sisters went home to their husbands, leaving Saiyen-gu alone with his mother in her tipi. "Well, Saiyen-gu," said his mother, narrowing her eyes as though dried buffalo dung smoke irritated them. "All I have now is you." He suppressed a sigh and turned his wide leather armlet, a remembrance of his father, over and over on his forearm. It was studded with copper and turquoise beads in a design of the moon and the sun. "Your sisters take care of their husband's mothers and their children. With your father gone and no children in his tipi, who will take care of me? You need to marry a hard-working wife who can cook and clean and give me grandchildren to fill my tipi."

Despite his father's trading and the wealth he had brought them, his mother deemed him a failure. "I learned to trade. Father has customers from the Mississippi to the Great Lakes. They are mine now. When was I to find a wife?"

"If you weren't such a dreamer, you would have one by now."

Father had confided to his son that he first took up trading to escape his wife's nagging. "Iowan girls want a warrior, not a trader." It went without saying that he would never make a warrior. He supposed he would kill in defense of his family and village, but to go out raiding and kill? That was not in his nature. In fact, he was disgusted that it was in anyone's nature.

His mother snorted. "A wise maiden might see the good points of a trader husband. I could tell her how I enjoyed being married to your father. For one thing, you won't be home to pester her except when Father Winter closes the trails. For another, you will return with copper

1

and turquoise trinkets from the south, and quill work and cakes of maple sugar from the east. With enough sons and daughters, your wife could be happy." There was no arguing with his mother. He was already feeling sorry for his wife-to-be. Mother was all business now, not giving him time to think. "How many maidens have you asked so far?"

"Every available maiden in this village and several nearby." Father would have walked out by now, but he'd only have to come back. The snow was nearly gone. He wondered how his father managed the months he had to spend with Saiyen-gu's mother until he could leave again. "What do you suggest?"

"Ask your sisters." It was late already. His brothers-in-law would be welcoming their wives home under the blankets. It could wait until the morning.

After breakfast, Saiyen-gu went to his younger sister's tipi. She offered him a bowl of black walnuts and a mug of mint water. "What do you want, Brother?" she asked.

"I came to get your sage advice. Mother wants me to marry, but as you know, no Iowan maiden will have me. What should I do?"

She chuckled. Her brother was hopeless, but he was family. One must try. "You know why they refuse. You've never raided. There are no notches on your coup stick. You don't have a coup stick. What kind of status will you give your wife? The girls think you're a coward and who can blame them?"

He decided not to lose patience. "You know I'm not a coward. I don't like to fight. I want to be like father. You wouldn't have called him a coward."

"Father was seldom around. If you want to marry, my advice is to be the kind of man a woman wants. Join my husband on the next raid. Then, I'll find you a wife."

He told her he would think about it and went to ask his second sister. She had no better advice, but she recounted his good qualities. "Little brother, you are tall and you have broad shoulders. You're not exactly ugly. You can give a wife pretty children. That is something. Come back tomorrow and I'll give you an answer." Her children, his nieces and nephews, climbed onto him and asked him to tell them what the rest of the world was like for they never left the world of the prairies.

He told them about the high mountains in the west and the cities in the south, and the woodland of the east. "With trees so close together, you can't see if there is a bear hiding and getting ready to swallow you. You won't know anything until you're inside him." They giggled and tickled him, liking his deep laugh. His sister nodded, thinking he would be a decent husband and father, telling stories all winter, not around to annoy a wife the other three seasons.

The next day, his second sister said, "Saiyen-gu. A girl from the plains is unlikely to want you. A prospective wife will share your status. Unfortunately, you have none."

"I know that. What can I do to have status besides killing someone?"

"Why not look where people don't know you? Go somewhere else. Bring obsidian points and bracelets east. Come home with cordage and supple wood for bows, sugar and quill work, and a wife. Mother can teach her to keep house as she wants. Get her pregnant. You'll have a baby in less than a year. What do you think?"

"Your suggestion is reasonable," he said.

He told his mother he was going east to trade and look around. He made her no promises, but to Mother, the issue was settled. "She should not be lazy. She should be fertile. Be sure she comes from a large family. You might stay a month to be sure before you bring her home. I want grandsons who will be men and do the things men should do. My tipi used to be full of children and food." She continued her demands and complaints until he went outside for fresh air.

The next day, he put together his father's travois and packed his trading goods. With his mother's packets of jerky and parched corn in his backpack, he visited his sisters to say goodbye. He told his family goodbye and set out for the eastern forests. He didn't like them much. One felt closed-in all the time. One couldn't see the ancestors' campfires in the sky through the trees, except over rivers and lakes.

At the first woodland village, he did not mention his quest. With his copper bracelets, skinning blades and obsidian points, he made good trades. He kept his eyes open, but the maidens were too young or already married. One day, between villages, he came to a wide lake and decided it was a good place to camp and fish. He had picked berries on the way and had a supply of dried beans.

The lowering sun was the color of his turquoise. It touched the low clouds with pink and orange. Reflections from the lake were pretty and upside down. The ripples made the sky and clouds seem to sway. Flocks of grey and white seabirds bobbed between wavelets. Otters romped and teased in the shallows, enjoying the last of the light. A fish tugged at his line and woke him to his task. He cooked his supper and sat back to watch the stars appear over the lake as he ate.

He set up no shelter that night. The stars seemed friendly. The constellations were the same as at home above the lake. Lakes were like the plains. The spirits were closer. He wondered which campfire was Father's and wondered if Father was looking down, watching him looking up. He threw twigs and spruce cones on his fire. He didn't care for hunting, but the bears couldn't know that. Humans and animals were not meant to be friends, but it would be nice. He wasn't opposed to eating meat in principle, but ending a life chilled him. "Sorry fish," he said to the bones of his supper and buried them under a pile of spruce needles. "Maybe next time, you'll be the human and I'll be the fish. We can take turns." He agreed with his mother that he wasn't like other men. He wondered if a woman could actually like him.

At last, he wrapped himself in his hide blanket and closed his eyes. Solitude led to thoughts. For a while, he listened to loons calling to the moon and tried to picture his future wife. Maybe she was looking at the same sky and wondering with whom she would share her tipi. He tried to imagine her residing with her large, hard-working family. Would she have a nice voice? Would she nag? Would she get along with his mother? Smiling because he decided she would be just talkative enough, but not too talkative, he drifted off.

He came to a larger village – more people, more trades, more maidens, perhaps. The chiefs and faith-talkers welcomed him and the women brought him a bowl with chunks of venison in a stew of beans, corn and squash. The broth was fragrant with herbs. Satisfied, he thanked them and extended greetings from his Iowa People. There being much of the day left, he set out his wares.

The men admired the black points that had traveled so far. The maidens admired the copper and turquoise. Some of them admired Saiyen-gu's strong shoulders and broad back. He heard their musical whispers and tried to understand. He had learned some of the Erie speech with his father several years before. The girls were speaking of his eyes with their exotic tilt. They supposed it was because he came from the mysterious Plains. His accent was like music when he spoke their words.

He wondered if one might leave her home for him. Some were too young, others had children and several were big with child, but there was one. A chief watched her vigilantly. "Red Wing," he said, "get back."

"Where did these black, shiny rocks come from?" asked a youth.

"Be careful," said Saiyen-gu. "The edge is sharp. It would make an excellent skinning knife."

The boy smirked. "Or a dagger or the point of a spear." He stepped high in a war dance, the knife in his hand. "I could skin my enemies. Go on, Trader. Tell us where the blades came from."

Saiyen-gu smiled to his audience. Red Wing smiled too and pretended she was not looking at him. "Once, long ago, a mountain west of the prairies exploded. It made a great noise. Rocks jumped from its throat like corn kernels popped on a hearth. Some said a monster lived in the mountain and he was angry." Saiyen-gu did not know all the words he used, but he acted out his story. Everyone was entranced. He was an entertainer as well as a trader. Red Wing could not take her eyes off him.

He talked about the large cities near the Father of Rivers, Mississippi. "These are very popular in Cahokia. Have you heard of Cahokia?" They had not. "It is a city." He used the Cahokian word since neither the Iowan nor the Erie people had such a word. He described it like many towns gathered round a great mound with a house on top for the king. "King?" asked the chief.

"High chief. Ordinary chiefs bow to him and touch his feet to their heads." He wasn't sure of this, but it made a good story. "City houses are built of clay and rock and sun bricks made of mud and straw. The Cahokians ride in boats day and night on Father Mississippi. They bring each other flowers and beans, copper and turquoise and clothing made of woven cotton instead of skins. They keep turkeys right in the city, and use the feathers and skins to make beautiful robes. Sadly, I have none to show you."

"Will you come back with some?" asked Red Wing's father" "Will you tell us more stories?" asked her mother. "Do the people make music and dance?" asked Red Wing. Her mother pulled her back. It was not proper for a maiden to speak boldly.

"Oh, yes," said Saiyen-gu. "They wear these beautiful robes to dances. They make music with copper bells and clay flutes. This is how they dance." He showed them a portion of a dance spreading his arms out like wings and pretending to glide on a current, twisting and turning, singing an Iowan marriage song for luck.

Red Wing gave him a shy smile. He met her eyes longer than was seemly. She hoped her mother had not noticed. Red Wing's mother said men did not like bold women, but she could not help wondering if the handsome trader could like her. She was more than ready for a husband, but none of the Erie men were so interesting or well-proportioned, and Saiyen-gu could sing. His voice gave her happy shivers.

After the trading, they ate and went to their curved wigwams which smelled of wood and were nothing like tipis. Red Wing confided to her friends and sisters that she was going to seduce the trader so he would take her home with him.

"Don't do it. We'll never see you again," they cautioned.

"Don't tell Mother," said her sister. "She'll tie you to the lodge pole so you can't go to him."

"Shush then."

They continued to try to dissuade her. "You don't know his customs. Maybe he already has a wife or two."

Red Wing thought her sister might be envious. "I'll ask him. If he doesn't already have a wife, I will make him want me."

Smooth bowstrings, supple wood for bows, and lumps of maple sugar were given to Saiyen-gu in exchange for the obsidian points. Also sacks of parched corn and beans for his return journey. He kept his last bracelet as a bride gift. Perhaps he had found one in the chief's daughter, but he needed to ask her parents.

Red Wing's father invited him to visit with them until he was ready for sleep. He liked to watch the fire sink to glowing coals. Everyone was a silhouette, but Red Wing's eyes reflected the glow. He talked to all of them, but had his mind on Red Wing. "You should see the sun set over the prairies and the wide-winged condors that soar on the morning wind," he said. "I could show you the Mississippi." He could be happy with her. He knew he could. He would ask her father for her tomorrow.

He wished his hosts good night and slipped into his blankets in the small guest wigwam. He was half asleep when Red Wing slipped under his blanket. Startled, Saiyen-gu sat up. "Who is there?" he asked in his own tongue.

"Me. Red Wing," she replied, guessing at his question. She touched his fingers to her mouth to show him that she was smiling. He smiled back and lifted her fingers to his lips to show that he was pleased. "Do you already have a wife?" she whispered.

"No, but I am looking for one." Before they slept, she had convinced him that they belonged together. One thing, though, he must tell her, even if it decided her against him. "We will live in my home on the plains with my mother. I will defend you as well as I can, but I don't raid. I have killed no one. Will you think me a coward and be ashamed to be my wife?"

"Never," she whispered. Her dreams were coming true. "I will always be with you." He did not understand how that could be. She must mean as long as they both lived, but it was good enough.

The next morning, he offered her parents his copper and turquoise bracelet in exchange for Red Wing. They did not object so after breakfast, her mother summoned the village's faith keeper to invoke Corn Mother's good will on the new couple and wished them well. Saiyen-gu tied his bundles onto his travois, secured his back pack and looked to his wife. Red Wing embraced her parents and sisters, and they began.

They stayed in villages where they traded stories for supper and a warm place to sleep. The trees gave out until there were only willows and slim birches beside brooks, and the grasses grew higher. Red Wing saw her first plains bison. They made camp on a rise and watched a hunt. An Iowan band drove them forward with yells and spears. Others were waiting behind the tall grass. They killed several, enough to supply meat for a month or more.

They found Saiyen-gu's village. It had moved several times in following the herds. He introduced Red Wing to his mother and sisters and his nieces and nephews who were soon all over him, demanding treats. Everyone liked Red Wing. They lived with Saiyen-gu's mother who took to her at once. Red Wing did not mind the work as long as she could share her husband's blanket at night. His sisters showed her how to erect a tipi and how to find and dry buffalo dung for fuel. The women shared tanned hides to cover the lodge poles of the new couple's home and helped them enlarge their tipi as their family grew.

Saiyen-gu brought Red Wing to the Mississippi. They and their children picnicked on its banks. The wild flowers were bright beautiful spots of red and blue in the sea of long grasses. Red Wing never accompanied Saiyen-gu on his trade journeys to Cahokia. She was too busy caring for the children, tanning hides, gathering dry dung, and sewing, but she found friends and took joy in her children and her tall husband. She was happy.

The peaceful years ended when Omaha tribesmen raided. The Iowans raided back, stealing meat, women, and boys to replace those killed. Saiyen-gu was derided for urging peace. "Weakness makes you a target," said his friends. "Wouldn't you defend your family?"

"I would, but I won't go looking for war."

"What if they killed or took away your children? Wouldn't you want revenge?"

"If others felt as I do, it wouldn't happen." His brothers-in-law and cousins said he was a dreamer. They raided. Fewer returned.

Saiyen-gu's boys grew up and took the warrior way from their uncles. They began to look down on their father. Saiyen-gu's daughters married warriors. Only Red Wing understood. When their last daughter took her place in her mother-in-law's tipi, Red Wing told Saiyen-gu she wanted to visit her family in Erie.

They did not know Erie was at war with Seneca, the most western Longhouse tribe. The middle-aged couple camped for the night when a band of Seneca took them for enemies. Saiyen-gu shouted that they were neutrals and took no part in any war. Before his words reached them, an arrow found Red Wing's heart. She lifted her pained eyes sadly to Saiyen-gu and her spirit left her body.

The warriors apologized, but regret would not bring her back. Saiyen-gu wanted to follow her so she would not be alone, but the warriors refused. "You can have my widowed sister to warm you at night and cook for you," one offered.

"I don't want another woman," Saiyen-gu said. "Kill me too so Red Wing won't by lonely." He opened his arms to welcome death. When the warrior made no motion, Saiyen-gu thought he was undecided. "If you don't want to waste an arrow, you can crush my head with your tomahawk. If that doesn't suit you, stab me or cut my throat. Your blade is obsidian. I'm a trader. I probably sold it to you."

"You are mad," suggested the warrior.

"Probably, but Red Wing is waiting. Be quick. I'm ready."

The warrior grew angry. "Your wife's death was a mistake. Are you trying to get me cursed? The Creator protects the insane. Go away." When Saiyen-gu would not move, the warriors pushed by him and left him standing there. He heard them muttering angrily about strangers getting between enemies and camping in their forest.

Saiyen-gu wrapped Red Wing in her blanket and held her in his lap. "I'm so sorry," he said. "I meant to go with you, but the warrior would not kill me. I will bring you home so your people may bury you in your native earth and mourn you."

He heard her voice in his head. *They can have my body, but I won't be far from you, dearest,* it said. *I keep my promises.*

Red Wing's family buried their sister tenderly, but regarded him with displeasure since the one and only time he brought her home resulted in her death. He told them she had six children on the Plains, all married. She had been a grandmother. "What good are her children to us? We will never see them? Go away," said Red Wing's sister.

Saiyen-gu would not go home, nor stay in Erie. Having nothing left to trade but stories, he traveled from village to town to village in Huron country. An elder advised told him to visit a holy place to ask its spirit for advice. "It is called Niagara. It is very powerful. Lake Erie becomes a river and flows east. The river becomes stronger. An island splits the current, but even then its power grows. The river falls over two great cliffs where it joins again in a lake far below. The water flows to a new river. At the end, the water joins the ocean river that encircles Turtle Island which is the world."

Saiyen-gu listened reverently. "I would like to see Niagara," he said.

"People say Niagara is a place of peace. If you reach the Falls, its spirit might pity you and advise you what to do."

Word spread about the crazy man. People offered him food and a place to rest because it was well known that spirits protect the mad and curse those who offer them injury. He spoke often to a spirit that seemed to accompany him. At last he found the river called Niagara. He followed it to an island where he camped, wanting to approach the holy place by daylight.

The next day, he found the Falls. In awe, he dropped to his knees to praise the Creator for such splendor and power. Instead of widespread flooding and trees torn and flung by winds, as on the prairies, the river's power was condensed into two mighty torrents. It seemed there was a message in this.

Saiyen-gu descended a footpath beside the falling river. Mist rose in clouds from the depths and hung in the air. The sun touched the mist and rainbows appeared. Then, he saw the spirit of Red Wing. She held out her arms, appearing young again. "Is my madness complete or are you really here?" he asked.

He was too close to the rushing water to hear above it, but she spoke directly to his mind. "What do you think, love? The Huron elder said spirits live here."

"Shall I climb up the trail and leap so my spirit can join yours? Life without you is too lonely."

"You don't have to die to be with me. I'm with you now."

"But what will I do with the rest of my life?" It seemed perfectly normal to him that they should have this conversation.

"Learn the secrets the mist keeps hidden. What do you see?" He saw power flowing like magic. He saw a love that survived death, his and Red Wing's. "Stay here with me," she said. "I'll teach you more."

So Saiyen-gu stayed. Red Wing showed him a cave beneath the falls as if it had been waiting for him. He sat on the shelf of rock before his cave and looked out. Here in this holy place he would never be alone. Red Wing might join with other spirits when he slept, but she always returned. He could see her best against the mist. The surging water took most of his hearing, but he learned to hear with spirit ears and see with spirit eyes. People said Saiyen-gu was insane, but he didn't mind. He had Red Wing. In dreams, they could even touch. If he was mad, it was a gentle madness, and he held it close.

His long hair turned gray as the Falls under cloudy skies. Instead of trading goods, he traded prayers. Huron and Seneca children brought him furs, snowshoes, corn meal and more for his appeals to the spirits of harvests, hunts and health. The Hurons called him Father Mist; the Seneca called him Hidden in Mist for it was said he appeared only to the innocent. When they entered his domain, he stepped out of the mist.

His presence hovered around Niagara. The children taught him both Huron and Longhouse words. He discovered how to exert his influence over his domain and compel tribesmen to be peaceful. He might remove his favor if one lifted a weapon against another. Niagara became known as a place where power and peace merged.

Children approached the Falls with awe calling for Father Mist. Saiyen-gu stepped out behind them and said, "Here I am. Why did you come?" His hair was gray now, but he walked as straight and tall as before.

One child said, "Father Mist, the Tribes are at war. Make them stop before my father gets killed." The boy was perhaps ten, not yet a youth. He wanted to stop war. Perhaps there were more like him. It would be good if he could promote peace even beyond his domain. The breeze lifted his long hair to blow about his face.

"Let me think what I can do," he said. "This may take some time." When he said no more, the children thanked him and gave him their gifts as one does with a god.

When he was alone again, he began to wonder why children changed their nature as they matured. Animals changed when it was time to breed. Buck deer that once grazed and slept together now clashed with antlers and hooves over females. Humans did not clash over females often, although they did. He wondered if he would have fought for Red Wing, if she had chosen another. He doubted it, but he would have fought to defend her. Youths clashed to prove they were brave and gain status.

Saiyen-gu wondered how he kept men who entered his domain peaceful. The power of the Falls seemed to have become a part of him, or he a part of them. They amplified his will. If only there was a way to extend the power. He stowed the tobacco, cornmeal and dried beans in storage baskets inside his cave. His work done, he filled his pipe and went to his ledge to pray. Spirits were more attentive when he conveyed requests in fragrant smoke. It curled from his lips and nostrils and mingled with the hovering droplets.

Perhaps there could be a boy with power, who could influence the others. Saiyen-gu had withdrawn from the Tribes. The boy would have to be part of them. Now, if there were to be such a boy, how would he find him? He spoke his prayer. *Let me find such a child so my influence may extend beyond this place.*

Red Wing shimmered into view and sat beside him, young, strong and beautiful. Her smiling eyes filled him with joy. "Saiyen-gu," she said. "Be young again and come join me in a memory so we can talk."

Chapter 2

Saiyen-gu's dream self rose to join her. Both were dark-haired again and neither showed signs of care or age. They came to rest on a hide cloak in a flowered field overlooking the eastern bank of the wide Mississippi. Their children swam in the shallows after their picnic. Saiyen-gu pointed toward them. "You do realize that outside our dream, they are grown. They probably think we're both dead."

"It is best. They no longer need us." The dream lovers embraced on the buffalo robe, hidden by the fragrant long grass until the dream seemed more real than the cold mist of Niagara. When they separated, their hands remained joined. He held her to his chest. The clover and wildflower smell of her hair filled his nostrils. "I miss you. If only we could live in dreams forever, always young and happy."

"It is not time for that to happen so you must wait. I'm glad you remember how it is to be with a woman. Soon, memories won't be enough."

"What do you mean? Surely you do not mean I will marry again?" She sat up, very serious. Her breasts were high as when they were first discovering each other, but he knew it was a dream. He always knew, but it didn't matter. "No one can replace you."

"I do not want to be replaced, but you, dearest, must soon involve yourself with others. A lost and unhappy Huron maiden will come into your life. You will care for her and give her what she requires."

Red Wing liked riddles. "What can a maiden require of an old man that she would not prefer from a younger man?" In reality, he knew he slept rolled in a deer hide in the cave behind Niagara. He knew his hair was gray and crows had given his skin wrinkles. His children were far away with children of their own. He knew Red Wing was dead.

"You'll find her near my people's lake, foraging. She may seem ordinary, but the Creator has taken a special interest in her. Go fishing and you will see her. Remember to protect her."

Protect her from what? As though he had spoken aloud, Red Wing shook her head and smiled slyly. "I'm too old for anyone but you," he reminded her.

"No; you're not." She clasped his hand and lifted it to show him. It had turned smooth, supple, and strong. Was that part of his dream or was it real? Anything was possible if the Creator willed it. A warm damp breeze blew off the river. It was Mississippi, not Niagara. Saiyen-gu inhaled the smells of flowing water, willows and prairie flowers. He fell asleep within his dream to the sound of Red Wing's gentle laughter. When he opened his eyes, he was back in his dark cave and alone.

After breakfast, Saiyen-gu left food in his cook pot beside the coals for later and set out for Lake Erie. He walked the trail beside the swiftly flowing Niagara. It did not take long for him to find his favorite fishing hole. He wondered what he would catch this time, salmon, trout, or yellow perch. Before he cast his line, he collected purple and white quahog shells from the sandy shore where the small waves left them, folded them in a rag and set the package in his basket. Then he dug for worms, baited his shell hook and cast his line.

He did not see the Huron maiden that day, but he built a narrow tipi to smoke his catch and bring it home. He laid damp hickory branches over his coals. While he waited for the smoke to draw out the moisture from his catch and harden it to last, he strung the quahog shells on sinew thread. The villages valued them and were willing to exchange them for more fishing lines, corn meal and beans. He needed warm boots for winter and other necessities he could not make for himself. Away from his river and Falls, he was simply an old man, and nearly deaf.

When his fish was dry enough, he wrapped it and set the band of his burden basket on his forehead to return home. He waited three days. Being dead, he supposed Red Wing had little concept of time. If and when he found the Huron maiden, he would give her what she required, once he figured it out.

A few days later, Saiyen-gu followed the river path again. He baited his hook and had just cast his line when a slender girl stepped out from behind the trees. He pulled in his empty line and watched as she stooped to gather mushrooms and cress. He strolled closer and waited her for to notice him, but she didn't. She nearly bumped into him.

From her emotionless face, he might have been a tree. She began to walk around him. "Wait, girl," he said, taking her arm. She tugged, annoyed, as if she were caught by a bramble or a branch. "Where are you going?"

She looked at him blankly, but then her eyes focused on him and a simple sort of understanding came into her. "Aren't you a man?" she asked.

"Of course I am." Something was wrong with her. "Surely, I'm not the first man you ever saw?"

The girl grinned bashfully. "I'm not sure. I didn't know there were any around here. Mother says men are spiteful and impolite. She took me away from them to live alone. There might have been a man in our house when I was small. Men are tall and they have flat chests, like yours." She touched Saiyen-gu's chest. "Flat," she observed.

She seemed to live more in her mind than in reality, something they had in common. This must be the right girl. Now he must learn what she wanted and how to fill her request. He decided to begin by speaking gently so she would lose her fear of him. "You must have had a father and fathers are men. A woman can't make a baby by herself. A man must help."

"Oh?" She scrunched her eyes. What could she be thinking? He did not have to wait long. "You don't know my mother, but I can tell you. She has nothing new to talk about. If I had a baby, it would be something new. Babies grow, don't they? We could talk to each other. You're a man. Could you help me make a baby?"

"Not right now," he replied. "Well, this is a little odd," he mumbled to Red Wing. "You're laughing at me, aren't you?"

"Who are you talking to?"

"My wife. She's a ghost. Let us go to my house. I'll show you my rainbows and give you lunch."

"You don't seem spiteful and impolite," she said. "All right. I'll go with you." As they walked, Saiyen-gu continued his conversation with Red Wing. The girl didn't pay attention, but looked around at the new trees and the stream that grew more tumultuous as they progressed. He took her hand to be sure she did not attempt to touch it.

"She is a child in a young woman's body. Did you know she was going to ask me for baby? Well. I suppose it is good that I found her. A young man would take his pleasure and leave her to deal with the result. Even if the man wanted to protect her, the mother who hates men would drive him away."

She knelt to try to pick watercress. "Not there, girl. It's too rough and will sweep you away. What is your name?"

She stood up. "Tree Frog." She suddenly wanted to talk. "I don't remember the last time I saw someone. Mother says we are safer without other people." She giggled. "She was wrong. You are nice. Are we almost to your house? I will have to go home after lunch. Mother will worry."

The girl still had her baby name. "You would think the mother would have changed it as the girl matured," he commented to Red Wing. "Then again…"

"What is that noise? Where is the river going?" He helped her down the path and swept the vines away from the entrance to his cave. Tree Frog looked over the rushing waterfall and back at him. "You can't live here," she said. "The Falls will wash your wigwam away."

"I don't have one. Come in and see."

The roar of the falls did not seem to bother her. She stood on the ledge. "Look at the white drops that hang in the air. Look at the rainbows." The mist bathed them in gentle moisture. "What is making it happen?"

"Move back a little. It can be slippery there. The rainbows were hidden in the mist. The sun makes them come out and play. My name is Saiyen-gu."

"I like it." She studied his face. The white hanging drops drifted around him like clouds. "You are hidden in mist, too. Only I can see you." They ate smoked fish and beans and drank fresh water. "I wonder what I will do when my mother dies. Old people do that, don't they?" She studied him again. "Of course, you don't. You must be old. Are you real or a spirit?"

"Both," said Saiyen-gu, handing her a plum. "What do you think you will do if your mother dies?"

She chewed thoughtfully and saved the pit. "I don't know. I'd be afraid to find people and ask them to take me in. People will laugh at me."

Tree Frog was vague and childlike, but her conjecture about her future was real. He wondered how he could improve her chance for happiness. "I could protect you," he suggested. Perhaps an introduction was all she required. He could do that. He smoothed back her long hair until their eyes met.

"That would be nice. Your hair is grayer than my mother's, like dark clouds before a storm." She was not a fool, only a very innocent girl with extremely limited experience.

"My wife says I am not very old. I can take you home to your mother and then bring you both to a village."

Tree Frog frowned. "Mama would not like that," she said. "I'm too strange and Mama is too angry. No one would want us. That is why I want you to help me make a baby, so I can have company. Will you?"

He thought she had forgotten about that. He hoped she had. "It would be better for you to find a young man who can hunt for you and protect you and the child."

She gazed down sadly. "Mama would chase a man away." Then she looked up and smiled eagerly. "Do you know how to make babies?"

A normal girl speaking such words would be rude, but convention and modesty were unknown to her. If he did as she asked, would he be wronging her? Wouldn't endangering a mad person anger the Creator? And yet, Red Wing had encouraged him to give her what she requested. "What do you think?" he asked Red Wing. The ghost floated beside them, sitting as if on something solid. She did not reply, but continued to smile encouragingly.

He turned to Tree Frog, hoping to make her request clear to her. "Making a baby is not as easily done as handing you a piece of fish. We would need a summoning ceremony and the Creator has to agree. It takes nine moons time. A new baby can't do anything for itself. You will have to feed it and keep it clean and safe."

Tree Frog walked to the ledge and washed her hands in a puddle. She turned back, her face dripping with condensed mist. "Mama can help. How do we summon the baby? Show me."

Saiyen-gu grimaced. "Do you really want me to make a fool of myself for this poor girl?"

Tree Frog seemed to know when he was addressing his wife. She waited a moment for Red Wing to reply. "What does she say?"

"She says to give you want you want. Come here." He was not sure he was capable of fathering a child after so long, or performing the summoning ceremony. Perhaps that is what impregnating a woman was, but he had never expressed it so before. Red Wing had been a modest wife, summoning him with her eyes. He smiled. She had done so now, for another. Tree Frog came to him. He spoke as a teacher. "This may seem strange." If the girl was as she seemed, she had never since she was quite young, experienced the touch of a man. "I will need to touch you."

"I'm ready."

At just the wrong moment, she asked if he were too old for the ceremony to work. He sighed. "Perhaps I am. Let us try this again." Saiyen-gu did the best he could, then leaned back and waited for his breath to slow. "You shouldn't tease me like this, Red Wing," he scolded, turning to her.

"Did you do this ceremony with your wife?" asked Tree Frog.

"As often as possible," he replied. "She told me to look for you by the lake."

"She is smart for a ghost. When do I get the baby?"

"In the winter, if the Creator approves. Come with me now, and we'll bathe." He helped her to her feet.

She did not object when he brought her to a calm pool and washed her, although the cold water raised bumps on her skin. He cupped his two hands to splash some onto her face. "Oh!" she cried out fearfully. "Where am I?"

"You're with me," said Saiyen-gu. "I'm washing you."

Tree Frog shook her head, the earlier strangeness settling over her again. She backed away from him, suddenly frightened. "Who are you? My mother will be angry. I've been gone all day. There's no one but me to take care of her."

Saiyen-gu shook her shoulders. "I'm Hidden in Mist," giving her back the name she had bestowed upon him. See me!"

She looked at him and through him. "There is only mist here. I'm wet. I must get dry and hurry home. Where did I leave my dress?"

"Red Wing," Saiyen-gu implored. "What is wrong with the girl?"

She needs protection.

"I can see that." He took Tree Frog's hand and led her out of the water, where he dried and dressed her. The dress was well stitched. Chances were her mother made it. What kind of care could Tree Frog give a baby? Was once even enough? He answered his own question. If the Creator willed it, it was, but the babe would need more than a deranged mother and a cranky grandmother.

"I will watch over you and your child, Tree Frog," he said. "We will get my supplies and then you will show me where you live."

They camped in the forest that night. Saiyen-gu did not touch the girl, but during their trek, he tried to befriend her once more. She seemed to accept him as her protector, so he did not speak of their intimacy. She was disturbed enough.

As Tree Frog foresaw, her mother had been frantic. As soon as she saw them, she ran to assure herself that the girl was well, taking a moment first to give Saiyen-gu a malevolent glare. She tried to ignore him, but Tree Frog would not allow it. "This is Saiyen-gu, Mama," she said. "I got lost and he brought me home. He lives with his wife who is a ghost."

"Where is this ghost now?" the mother asked.

"There." The girl pointed to Red Wing's faint ghost as if she could see her. Perhaps she could.

"Another mad one," muttered the mother. She finally recalled her manners enough to thank Saiyen-gu for bringing Tree Frog home. "I have her safe now. She doesn't need you any more so you may go."

The girl protested. "Not yet. We should feed him at least."

"Come in then," the mother said reluctantly.

They ducked into a low, bark-walled wigwam that did not look sturdy enough to keep out the cold. He would have to do something about that. "I found the girl foraging." His few words were enough to make her suspicious.

"You're a foreigner," accused the mother.

"I am, but you have not shown the good manners of telling me your name."

The mother handed him a bowl of beans and a cup of water. "I'm called Big Sister. Eat and go away. I do not want a man in my house." As soon as he was able, he rose to go, promising to look in on them. Tree Frog smiled. Big Sister frowned, and he left the meager excuse for a house.

He found the nearest village and waited for someone to welcome him to bid him leave. He did not call himself Father Mist when he was away from Niagara. An elder invited him in. He gave his name as

Saiyen-gu and was made welcome. "You may stay as long as you like," the elder said. "Winter is coming."

"Thank you. While I'm here, may I learn from your healer how to set bones and prepare healing droughts?" The elder introduced him to their chief healer who agreed to make him her apprentice. He became a familiar sight in the village, old enough to be respected, but not too old to be useful. Each house hosted him in turn.

Autumn leaves carpeted the forest floor. Frost had appeared on the leaves and the lake had a thin layer of ice when Big Sister brought Tree Frog to the village healer. Saiyen-gu watched without speaking. His hearing would not have brought him her words, but he had learned to read lips. Sometimes, he heard thoughts. Big Sister did not see him. She told the healer she needed expert advice. "My daughter grows big with child, but she says no man touched her."

"That is not possible," said the healer. "Wait." She brought Tree Frog inside her wigwam to examine her. When they returned, the healer said, "I do not understand how this can be. The girl's maiden shield is unbroken, but a child grows within her. It is a marvel." Saiyen-gu shook his head thinking it was a marvel indeed.

Big Sister brought Tree Frog home to await the birth of her baby. Saiyen-gu continued to watch over the girl. He often brought them food and inquired after their well-being. Tree Frog talked about how glad she would be when her baby came. Big Sister said it had better be a girl if it knew what was good for it.

Tree Frog's son was born the second full moon after the longest night of the year. Big Sister hid her annoyance, but when her daughter slept, she carried the babe to a frozen pond. She set him down, broke open the ice and dropped him in muttering, "I will not have a boy in my house."

As soon as she was gone, Saiyen-gu reached in and lifted the half-dead infant from the frozen mud. The icy water had stopped its breath. "Creator, please," Saiyen-gu implored. "He is your son as much as mine and Tree Frog's. Don't let the water take his life. Make him breathe!" He blew warm air into the tiny mouth and the babe gasped. In a few moments, it breathed normally, but trembled with cold. "Thank you," said Saiyen-gu. He tucked the child under his coat and shirt next to his skin to warm it.

Tree Frog awoke in the night, realized her babe was gone and wept until she slept from exhaustion. In the morning, her son was with her again, snuggled and warm between her and her mother. Tree Frog laughed in delight and nursed him while her mother tried to figure out what had happened.

When Saiyen-gu came by in the morning, Tree Frog told him what had happened as well as she understood it. "He was gone. Mother said to forget about him, but when I woke up, he was back." The baby made loud sucking noises at her breast.

"Such an amazing child should have a name," Saiyen-gu suggested. Big Sister bristled like a porcupine, but Saiyen-gu ignored her. "You can no longer live alone. Go to the village. Tell the elders I want them to give you a home and they will do it."

"What is it to you, Old Man?" asked Big Sister suspiciously.

Saiyen-gu speared Big Sister with his eyes. "The Creator knows what you did. If you attempt to harm the child again, you will find yourself under the water." Big Sister sputtered and backed away as far as the wigwam wall would let her. He turned back to Tree Frog. "The Creator already told me your son's name. It is Deganawida."

The girl repeated the name. It meant thinker in Huron. "I like it," she said and held the babe to her breast.

Chapter 3

Jekonsaseh

If a traveler followed the Niagara River from Erie, around the Falls, and continued to Lake Ontario, he would find the current flowing northeast into a longer, wider river. It passes through many lands on its journey to the Ocean. If the traveler kept going, he would leave Turtle Island altogether. Turtle Island held all tribes and all lands. Only birds can leave it, but since there is nowhere else, they must fly back.

East of Ontario, the traveler would find five narrow lakes. Each could be crossed by canoe in less than a day. They were like the fingers of a hand. The large town of Tyo-den-he-deh sat at the north end of the easternmost finger lake. In it dwelled people of Onondaga Nation. A palisade of sharpened, outward leaning birch and elm saplings protected Tyo-den-he-deh's inhabitants like quills.

The town's zigzag entry allowed for better defense. Sentries secured the town day and night. Tododaho, their respected Bear Clan war chief, made sure of that. One could never be too sure of one's safety. The Longhouse Tribes sometimes made war one upon the next, but Tododaho kept Tyo-den-he-deh secure.

Each clan was ruled by a matron. Otter Clan's longhouse was home to fourteen families, seven apartments per side. Opposite sections shared a fire pit and seven smoke holes released plumes of smoke into the frosty air. The house was usually filled with activity and conversations, but one winter night eight-year-old Jekonsaseh sat cross-legged on the hide-covered floor alone. No one came to comfort her. She did not cry or behave like a child suddenly bereft of her mother.

That afternoon her uncles brought the body home. It had been found broken and frozen at the foot of Suicide Cliff. Jekonsaseh watched the ice melt from her mother's braided hair and clothing. Her eyes had been frozen open, but now, they appeared to cry blood tears. Her grandmother, the matron, had tried to lead her away, but she would not be moved. The child's face was expressionless. Her manner kept even the faith keepers, whose job it was, from offering words of comfort. Her grandmother announced that at daylight, the body would be wrapped and laid in the cemetery's winter house with the other winter dead until the ground could be opened.

War Chief Tododaho, Jekonsaseh's father, did not interfere. Family matters were for women. The embers had been pushed together and covered with ashes to keep them alive until morning when they would be fanned back to flame. The air in the narrow hall was warm and humid. Thick hide curtains kept out the cold, but young Jekonsaseh hugged her knees and rested her head on her crossed arms. "Mother," she said with a sigh. "Why did you go away?"

Jekonsaseh's father crouched on his bed-bench, knees drawn nearly to his chin, his mouth to one side like a sacred false-face. His brows shadowed his deep-set eyes. People said the girl resembled him. Jekonsaseh sensed his emotions which were usually masked to others. He was being thoughtful now, not sad. Why didn't he grieve for her mother? Softer emotions in men were scorned, but some were not embarrassed to weep at the loss of a loved one.

Jekonsaseh pushed to her feet, rubbed her arms and legs, and leaned over the corpse. "Answer me, Mother," she said softly. There was only the steady drip of melt water from the smoke holes. After a while, Jekonsaseh turned from the dead to her father. She felt his anger at the people of his wife's clan. Instead of consoling him on the loss of his wife, they blamed him. Jekonsaseh knew this.

When men married, they moved to their wife's longhouse to hunt for her and her family. Wives could divorce themselves from disagreeable husbands by putting their furs and weapons outside to show they were no longer wanted. Her mother had not done this, but sometimes, Jekonsaseh knew she wanted to. She also knew her mother was too afraid of her father to do so.

Father's black eyes gave pause to even the strongest chiefs. Some whispered they penetrated men's souls. Once, Jekonsaseh heard him say she should have been a boy. Since he belonged to Bear Clan, he had little to do with her. He was expected to mentor his own clan sons, his nephews, in hunting and war craft. Even though fathers did not have much to do with daughters, she knew he liked her. Sometimes she felt his attention and would spin too fast for his smile to vanish. He took pride in her abilities. She approached him and stared into those hooded, secretive eyes that others shied from. Her question was perhaps foolish, but she felt compelled to ask. "Why didn't you stop her?"

His voice rumbled. "Some things can't be done." She prepared to turn away, but he spoke again. "I tried to make her understand me, but she would not." He would not admit helplessness in anything before his wife's clan. Jekonsaseh understood this. Again she would have left him when he said, "Ask her what you want to know. I have tried, but she tells me to go away."

So he had been speaking to her mother's spirit from his bed bench. He could reach further than she, but she was young. She had to get closer and ask harder. Jekonsaseh felt her father's power around him like a cloak blown by the wind. It pushed her back. He made a decision. He looked to her for a moment, and gathered up his weapons, clothing and furs. "My wife is dead," he announced. "You don't want me here. I won't stay." With that, he strode to the entrance, pulled aside the door curtain, and walked into the twilight.

People huddled, discussing how this evil had befallen them. Never before in the memory of the elders had a healer taken her own life. No one looked toward the bereft girl. They pretended not to see her. She returned to contemplating her mother's body. The open mouth seemed misshapen. Some of her teeth had cracked in her fall. Dry blood covered her chin. Had she screamed? Had anyone heard? Before she jumped, why hadn't she spared a thought for her daughter, or did the angry words she hurled at her husband when she fled blot out all maternal feeling?

Resentment grew in the girl, nearly obscuring her grief. "Mother? You talked to Father. You told him to go away. Now talk to me. Why did you leave me?" Greenish fog lifted from the body, coalesced above it, and formed the shape of Jekonsaseh's mother. No one else seemed to see.

"Your father said it would disgrace him for me to put him aside. He threatened my sisters and mother. He means to change the Creator's

Law. He would make fathers heads of their families. I had to get away from him. I had no choice."

"You should have thought of me."

"You have my mother and your aunts. You are not alone."

"I am alone. None of them understand me. Look at them. They are afraid of me because we are talking."

Mother's ghost was quiet for some time, but Jekonsaseh waited in case she had more to say. She did. "Other children don't talk to ghosts. Your father understands you better than I ever did. He should have married Sweet Water, but she is Bear Clan like him so the faith keepers forbade it. He wants to change the custom so a man can marry who he likes. If Sweet Water married your father instead of Hiawatha, I would still be alive instead of where I am."

"But you wouldn't be my mother and I would be someone else." The ghost showed no interest in this. She began to fade away like wisps of smoke against the curved wall. "Don't go yet," the girl implored. "What will happen to me?"

The ghost re-formed. Jekonsaseh avoided looking at the corpse in favor of the more vivid ghost. It flowed up and over the wall and ceiling until Jekonsaseh backed away to see all of it. Sad eyes nearly filled her face. Her mouth was a dark hole. Her lips did not move when she spoke. "You are your father's girl, Jekonsaseh. Go live with him in Bear Longhouse. They'll accept you. His own mother is afraid of him. Maybe you can influence him to turn away from Younger Brother's influence. I could not."

Younger Brother was the Creator's younger twin, his opposite -- the opposing force of creation. He attempted to destroy the good his elder twin had created. Thorns were his work, and diluting birch and maple sap so it was not sweet until the water was boiled off. When meat rotted or pumpkins became moldy, it was Younger Brother's work. Elder Brother, the Creator, was born first. Younger Brother did not like being second. In his impatience; he pushed through Earth Mother's side, tore her open and killed her. His time was night. His places were wilderness. His desire was for chaos instead of harmony.

Jekonsaseh heard the story each winter since she was old enough to stay awake when storytellers entertained them on the long nights. Elder Brother buried Earth Mother. From her bones grew the Three Sisters -- Corn, Beans and Squash. Holy tobacco vines and leaves grew from her skull so people could burn fragrant smoke to speak to the Creator. It reminded him of his mother.

The girl protested. "I can't live in Father's clan. They are Bear. I have to stay in Otter Clan, with Grandmother and my aunts. It's the Law."

"Since your father is so anxious to change our Law, he can begin with you. Heal him of his wrong thoughts if you can." She faded into the moss against the wall until she was gone.

The girl spun at the intake of breath behind her. Her grandmother and aunts huddled close and stared at her fearfully. "What?" Grandmother's lips worked, but the girl heard only her terrified breath. "What is wrong?" she demanded, hands to hips.

The old woman found her voice. "To whom were you speaking?"

"To my mother, of course," the girl replied. "Didn't you hear her? She said to go live with my father, but that is not right. I'm an Otter Clan girl."

One of Jekonsaseh's aunts looked to the corpse, then to Jekonsaseh. She scrunched her nose as if the girl had been playing with skunks. "I don't want the witch girl here," she said. "She sees dead people and talks with them. Send her away!"

Grandmother seemed to pity her for a moment, but then her face lost all warmth. She looked at Jekonsaseh as she would a stranger. "If you have anything you want to keep, get it now. I'm taking you to Bear Longhouse. Let your father rear you."

The loss of her mother and her clan in one day might shatter one less strong, but Mother said she was meant to be her father's child. She would not show weakness as her father had not. "I was born to Otter Clan. I don't want to go. If you send me away, you anger Elder Brother and you will be sorry. He will hurt you."

People shuddered at the girl's calm voice. Jekonsaseh's aunt shrieked. "Jekonsaseh cursed us. Only a witch would speak so."

Grandmother said, "Bear Clan Mother must accept you. I won't have a witch child in my longhouse. Are you going to walk, or do we carry you?" It did not seem possible but Jekonsaseh met her gaze and the old woman lowered her eyes.

"I will walk," she said stiffly. Jekonsaseh gave a last, lingering look to her mother's corpse and to the extended family that should have comforted and cared for her. She pressed her lips together to keep them from trembling, and put her hide blanket over her shoulders as her father had.

With her hands holding her second dress, her leggings and extra moccasins, she walked ahead of the old woman into the snowy night. The two walked, not touching, to the eastern door curtain of the main Bear Clan Longhouse. Otter Clan Mother pulled it aside and gestured for the girl to go before her. Jekonsaseh had never visited Bear Longhouse. These children were not her clan-cousins. Nor were the adults her aunts and uncles. People watched the newcomers curiously, muttering behind their hands. Jekonsaseh looked for her father. He watched, but would not interfere. Still, she felt better knowing he was near.

Bear Clan Mother greeted them. "Welcome to my house, Otter Clan Mother," she said. "It is a sad thing for you to lose a daughter and for Jekonsaseh to lose her mother. Let me comfort you both in your grief. Will you come to my bed bench and accept a warm, sweet drink?"

"Thank you but no. Indeed, it is a sad thing to lose a daughter," Otter Clan Mother agreed. "This child has been speaking to her mother's ghost." She held her hand above her granddaughter, taking care not to touch her. "My daughter's spirit said Jekonsaseh should leave my longhouse and live here with her father. Therefore, at her request, I bring her to you. If you refuse to adopt her into Bear Clan, I shall give her to the forest for the wild things to deal with."

"A child does not live in her father's clan!" said a woman from one of the open bed benches.

"How could you disown your granddaughter? Why punish her?" asked another angrily. "She should remain in the clan she was born to."

Jekonsaseh's father came forward, his eyes unreadable in the dim light. He looked up and down the long room. Silence came over the house as if at his command. Bear Clan Mother faced her son. "It seems your dead wife's daughter has no home or clan unless I adopt her. You heard Otter Clan Mother's words." Jekonsaseh's grandmother said nothing. "The Law does not forbid a child to dwell with her father's clan, although it is unusual. If my son asks me to do so, I allow this child to live with us. I will adopt her into Bear Clan, but you, Tododaho, must take responsibility for her."

"I accept that, but can a man teach a girl to sew and prepare food? Will my clan cousins be her aunts and teach her?"

A woman stepped out of her family's section, five girls beside her. The older ones were nearly of marriageable age, but the youngest was Jekonsaseh's size. "I will teach her, Tododaho," the woman said. "I'm Sweet Water, your father's cousin. I will be your aunt and my husband Hiawatha will be your uncle. Is that acceptable, Cousin?"

"I would not burden you, Sweet Water," Father replied. Jekonsaseh had never heard him speak so tenderly to her mother. Mother's ghost said if Sweet Water had been allowed to marry father, it would have spared everyone grief. The woman held out her arms, inviting her. Jekonsaseh walked into them.

"It is no burden. She will be good friends with my girls."

Her husband spoke up warmly, saying, "My name is Hiawatha. You will be like a sister to my girls. Welcome to our family."

"She's mine!" Jekonsaseh's father said dangerously.

"Of course," Hiawatha agreed. "She will be my niece."

Tododaho's mouth lost its dangerous edge. "Good. It is settled." He turned to Otter Clan Mother. "I won't forget that you threw out my daughter."

Jekonsaseh's grandmother blinked rapidly as if ashes had flown into her eyes, but she thanked Bear Clan Mother politely. In a moment, she had ducked behind the door curtain and out of Jekonsaseh's life. A cold wind rippled down the long room scattering ashes and sparks, but the rising heat from five hearth fires chased the chill up and out the smoke holes.

Tododaho spoke again. "Thank you, Mother. Come to me, Jekonsaseh." He held out his large hand. Taking it in both of hers, she looked up to her tall, strong father. "My clan cousin Sweet Water and her daughters will teach you what you need to know. Would you like that?"

"Yes," she replied, and looked around at her new home, so much like the old one except for the unfamiliar faces. "Where will I sleep, Father?"

"In my section, next to me. I will show you." He led her to his bed bench, part of the bed bench that extended the length of the wall, separated from others by wall curtains. It contained his furs and weapons, his cup and spoon. She laid her extra clothing and furs next to his and felt for the night bowl under the bed. It was there. She would manage.

Her hair was torn and she had scratched her cheeks according to custom when she saw her dead mother. Her hair was unruly now. Father said, "I will comb your hair for you. You must look your best when you thank Bear Clan Mother properly for adopting you. Have you eaten?"

She had not. Sweet Water brought her a bowl of corn gruel and a cup of warm tea. Jekonsaseh sat protected and warmed by her father's acceptance. The light of his hearth fire reflected from his eyes. He might frighten others, but no one would harm her while she was in his care.

After she had eaten, he took the bowl and cup from her himself. "We will fix your hair now," he said. "I borrowed a comb." He opened her braids with his fingers, and cut out the worst of the knots with his flint blade. Next, he applied grease from a small bark jar to his hands and worked it through her thick hair before he used the comb. Mother had never combed Jekonsaseh's hair so gently. He left it hanging loose. She would braid it again in the morning.

She took the comb from his hand. It had been a caribou fawn's shoulder bone, carefully notched. "Let me comb yours now, Father."

Tododaho's eyes widened. "Comb my hair? No one has combed my hair since I was a boy." It stuck out in all directions. It was time someone did, the girl thought.

She could hardly imagine her imposing father as a small boy. "I'll be careful. I won't let the comb hurt you." She stood behind him and dipped her fingers into the grease. Her terrible day began to fade into the shadows as the powerful Tododaho lowered his head for her to comb the tangles from his hair.

Chapter 4

Starlight and a pale moon silvered great bunches of braids of husked corn that hung drying from the cross beams. Warmth from the banked fires rose to meet winter and condensation dripped from beams. Droplets fell and sizzled on the hot cook stones around the hearths. The corn husks swayed in the circulating air, crackling and clacking like the dry bones of unburied warriors. The sounds and sights of night had never frightened Jekonsaseh, but she'd never been away from Otter Longhouse and her mother. "Mama?" Tears fell at last.

She was startled at the comforting hand on her shoulder. "You are safe with me," whispered her father. He didn't call her strange. His clan was her family now. He rubbed her shoulders, neck and back. "Sleep." His deep voice filled her with strength and safety. At last she obeyed and relaxed.

Daylight filtered into the house. The mothers had fanned the banked embers back to life and were cooking breakfast. Good smells filled the room. Burning hickory wood, and the steamy smell of corn mush made her hungry, but she had a more pressing need. People were going in and out, pushing aside the door curtain. She looked to see which entrance was nearer when a girl approached her. "I'm your cousin Ogan-nis'tah. I'll show you where we go and then Mama will feed you. Our fathers went hunting."

Jekonsaseh pulled on her moccasins and robe to follow her new cousin into the white winter morning. "Do you have your eating bowl?" Ogan-nis'tah asked.

"No. I forgot to take it. I think they'll give it to me if I ask." She did not want to enter her old longhouse as a beggar.

"It isn't important. We can share mine for now and my father will make you a new one." Sweet Water gave the returning girls a smile as

29

sweet and inviting as her name. "We are happy to have you with us. You can always come to my hearth to eat or just to be with us. Would you like that?"

"I would." Could she really become part of this family with its agreeable people? They looked at her with frank curiosity. She looked back, meeting each with her probing gaze. Did they know she saw and heard ghosts? How long before they, too, called her a witch girl and cast her out?

Sweet Water ladled ground maize dumplings sweetened with maple syrup into Ogan-nis'tah's eating bowl. "This should be enough for you both. If not, there is more. I made extra for when the men come home."

Jekonsaseh thanked her new aunt and bit into a sticky dumpling. This was better than mush. As soon as they were done, her cousins wanted to show Jekonsaseh their snow-blanketed planting hills. They brought hide mats for sledding and were just leaving the longhouse when Hiawatha and Tododaho arrived. They had left their wet hunting jackets and moccasins on the covered porch. Jekonsaseh turned back, telling her cousins she would join them after she greeted her father.

Tododaho looked her over and nodded affectionately, both to her and Sweet Water who filled the men's bowls with the steaming dumplings. The men sat upon Hiawatha bed bench and stretched out their legs toward the hearth. "Jekonsaseh," said Father. "How do you like it here?"

"Good," she replied shortly. She licked her lips. "Very good."

"I agree." Father swallowed, making a sound of enjoyment. He had grown up in Bear Longhouse. "We were lucky. We have meat for later." He gave a grunt of satisfaction, set down the bowl and told Sweet Water the food was good.

Jekonsaseh had never heard him praise her mother's food. Whatever had been wrong between her parents, it had driven Mother to her death. Jekonsaseh did not care to dwell on that. Obviously Father had put it out of his mind so she would be wise to do the same. Her cousins were waiting for her on the porch.

Five days after the new moon of the month with the shortest days, Tyo-den-he-deh celebrated Midwinter Festival. The Maple Festival came next. In another month, the trees budded, the streams flowed again and spring birds returned.

Jekonsaseh helped her cousins prepare Bear Clan's corn hills for the seeding. Women used strong forked sticks to rake winter's composted soil into the earth. Rain and warmth combined to make the planting hills receptive. The faith-keepers watched for the oak leaves to become the size and shape of a fawn's ear to tell the women when it was time to plant the Three Sisters - maize, beans and squash. Only when Otter Clan women and girls passed by and her former cousins were pulled back from greeting her by their mothers, did Jekonsaseh recall she was an outcast.

After the first harvest, the Green Corn Ceremony, Tyo-den-he-deh's hunters left for a long hunt, coming home with plenty of meat to be smoked and dried for winter. The beans ripened in their pods, tassels waved on the maize and the pumpkins were turning yellow. It was about then that the deer vanished from Tyo-den-he-deh's hunting grounds. The last of them were seen migrating northwest.

Jekonsaseh entered Bear Longhouse to a discussion among the men. "We will fish until they come back," Hiawatha said. "We don't need to follow the herds into Cayuga land. They don't follow them here when they come to us."

"We are stronger than the Cayuga People. Why not expand our territory?" asked Tododaho as if it were a most reasonable question.

"There is no reason for strife. We can get along without big game for a few months. The deer will return as they always do." Girls did not give opinions when men discussed hunting, but Jekonsaseh, sitting silently with Ogan-nis'tah against the wall of her cousin's bed bench, agreed with her uncle.

"You don't want to leave Sweet Water's cooking," Tododaho jeered. The men laughed. Father had spoken in jest but there was something antagonistic behind the teasing. Tododaho pointed out his reasons to follow the herds. "Are we to exist on fish and dried beans? Warriors need red meat. Our young men must learn the skills of war so we can enlarge our territory. Once the Cayuga Tribe accepts our domination, we will be their elder brothers. All the longhouse Tribes must learn that Onondaga is to be feared and respected. With the Tribes united, we will conquer Huron Country. No one will be able to stop us." The nearest Huron village was on the western shore of Lake Ga-nun-ta-ah, north of the greater lakes.

"Why do we want to own others' land? Is ours not enough for us? Better make a new treaty with Cayuga so when the herds come back, they can hunt here. There is no reason for Tribes to quarrel," said Hiawatha.

Tododaho cleared his throat. "Lazy and cowardly men may fish and feed off the women's efforts. Those young men who are brave, pack for a trek and come with me for battle training."

Hiawatha must have felt the sting of Tododaho's challenge. Jekonsaseh knew her uncle was neither lazy nor cowardly. She wanted her father and her uncle to be friends and companions as before. Discord made her unhappy. It reminded her too much of the strife between her mother and father. Most of the younger men were more afraid of Tododaho's scorn than of meeting enemies in battle.

Father changed. During summer, he took to wearing green stripes across his nose and cheeks for camouflage. His followers copied his fashion and practiced stealth and aim. The leaves colored and fell and the air took a chill. The wars began. Under Tododaho's management, the Onondaga wrested hunting land from Cayuga territory, and made them accept Onondaga leadership. The women discussed this, but no one dared counter Tododaho leadership except Hiawatha. Even the matrons were intimidated.

By the following spring, Tododaho's reputation had grown. Hiawatha arguments for peace led to contemptuous words from her father's followers. Jekonsaseh felt torn. When Otter Clan Mother took sick and died, Tododaho kept Jekonsaseh back from the mourners. "She cast you from your birth clan and Otter Longhouse. Not one of your aunts fought for you. Do not console them in their mourning."

Tododaho turned her chin up to him. Her eyes did not have so far to travel to reach his. He gave her one of his rare smiles. "You should understand better than most why matrons must give up their authority. Otter Clan Mother took too much on herself when she cast you out. She is dead now for disrespecting me and what is mine. Clan matrons can continue to direct their daughters in the growing and preparing of food, but men must make decisions. When you are old enough, you will help me spread the new Law, my Law. The old women will need convincing."

Despite her misgivings, Jekonsaseh bowed her head, yielding to her father's authority. He pulled her into a quick embrace. "The matrons will obey me. Onondaga will rule the Tribes and I will rule them."

While Tododaho's influence increased, Uncle Hiawatha studied with the healers, older men who had given up their warrior status, and grandmothers who incorporated herbal healing with spiritual.

Jekonsaseh was in the planting hills looking for the last of the harvest before the frost withered the vines. A cool wind shivered through the dried leaves when Jekonsaseh realized Sweet Water stood a few hills away with her digging stick, pulling up the last of the sweet taproots.

Jekonsaseh would have closed the distance between them and spoken to her aunt, but danger pricked at her scalp. She made herself small and kept low behind a corn hill. Tododaho aid, "Hiawatha has become a healer," he said. "He no longer supplies this house with meat and has no interest in protecting you from our enemies."

"What enemies do you speak of? You make them when they did not exist before. Could my enemy be one who desires more than he needs and wishes to subdue others? Could he be one who tries to rule others and decide for them what is best? Could my enemy be one who speaks badly of my good husband?"

No one ever spoke to Jekonsaseh's father like this. Jekonsaseh wanted to close her senses to the danger in the air between Tododaho and her adoptive aunt, but she could not. She kept still as a fawn trying to blend in with the leaves, but she listened.

"I'm not your enemy," said her father, not angrily but persuasively. "Let Hiawatha keep to his medicines. Let him shake his turtle shell and blow ashes over the sick and injured, but put him away. Tell him to return to Snipe Clan. You need a strong and brave man to warm you at night and supply you with meat."

Sweet Water raised her lovely eyes to Tododaho's. Jekonsaseh felt their spirits clash and her hair stood on end as before a thunderstorm. "I have the bravest man in all of Tyo-den-he-dah for my husband. Only he will stand up to you."

Jekonsaseh pressed her trembling hands against the earth and prayed silently for her father to go away. Sweet Water's white aura pushed against the dark one surrounding her father. The dark withdrew and the danger was suddenly gone. Jekonsaseh looked up to see Tododaho striding away. She left her hiding place and came up to Sweet Water. "I heard it all. He won't hurt you," she said, hoping it was true.

The woman held the girl closely, but tears ran down her cheeks. "As long as he doesn't harm Hiawatha, we will not speak of this."

Sweet Water died during the maple festival when a dead oak branch fell on her head, crushing the life out of her. Hiawatha mourning was deep and long. Bear Clan did not require him to return to Snipe Clan since he was well loved by his daughters, but others walked softly and kept their eyes low when they walked by his family's section of the bed bench.

The more Hiawatha resisted Tododaho's plans and schemes, the more he suffered. Year after year, his daughters died until only Ogan-nis'tah remained. The girls cooked their meals and ate together, but after a while Jekonsaseh decided to cook for her father at Tododaho's fire. Because he no longer visited Hiawatha bed bench or fire pit, it was not seemly for her to cook and eat there.

Ogan-nis'tah and Jekonsaseh blossomed into maidenhood. Since they had no mothers to choose husbands for them and since all her sisters were dead, Ogan-nis'tah grew ever closer to her father. He held her hand when they walked together as if to protect her from what might happen. Although Hiawatha was neither old nor feeble, it seemed to Jekonsaseh sometimes that his mind wandered, as if he was with his beloved Sweet Water once more. He did not say so, but Jekonsaseh felt it was only because Ogan-nis'-tah needed him, that he did not go to Suicide Leap cliff as her mother had.

Tododaho made more alliances, forcing each war chief and elder to swear allegiance to him. His aura had grown so large and dark that Jekonsaseh no longer wished to sleep at his side, but she saw no way to move without giving offence. One day after her moon flow ended, Tododaho solved her problem. He told her he intended to marry her to an allied war chief to seal their alliance. She would live in a town several days' travel south of Tyo-den-he-dah.

"You will encourage the clan mothers to give up their authority to me and my Law. Women must learn to obey their husbands and fathers and in return, be protected by them. It is best. In the end, everyone will see the wisdom of it." Jekonsaseh could not speak. "Have you nothing to say?" he asked.

She tried to keep her dismay to herself. "Who will I marry, Father? What clan? What is his name?"

"Onoji of Otter Clan. He is a bold hunter and warrior, and loyal to me. He will treat you well and you will bear him sons to follow me."

34

She had come to her full height, tall for a maiden, the crest of her head reaching to the middle of his forehead. "But he is Otter like me."

"You are Bear Clan now."

She thought this was changing the Law too much. She hoped her timorous demeanor would deflect her father's anger. "The matrons have always decided who may marry into their clan."

"Jekonsaseh." She had to force herself not to pull away from the darkness that spread from the spirit that dwelled inside him. "If matrons always ruled correctly, there would be no reason to change, but they do not. "Otter Clan Mother would have given you to the forest. We changed the Law when you came to me. You must see that."

So it was her fault that her father decided to make the changes. Still, she did not have the inner strength to oppose him. "I understand now, Father."

Jekonsaseh stood passively while he stroked her hair as he had when she was a child. "There is one thing about the Hurons that I admire. Do you know what it is?" Her mouth was too dry to speak. "I see I must instruct you. Huron women obey their men. I will do what is best for the Tribes I conquer. To help me, you will explain to your new matrons that my Law will make us stronger and the children are more secure. It can be that way for all the Longhouse Tribes."

Jekonsaseh thought of Sweet Water and her older cousins, now bones in the cemetery, because Sweet Water rejected him. She could never be as brave as her aunt and uncle, to tell her father that his new Law flew in the Creator's face and that they would all be punished for it. "I will do as you wish, Father," Jekonsaseh said, seeing no choice.

"Onoji will make you a good husband."

It seemed prudent not to argue. "When must I leave?"

"When deep snow ends the fighting season, he will come here to get you and bring you south."

She had another two months, maybe three. If she hated Onoji, would her father's Law let her put him aside? Who could she appeal to if no one held more authority than her father? How soon before chill winds chased the fallen leaves into piles around the trees? How soon before winter closed the war trails and Father gave her to Onoji?

Chapter 5

The matrons lit the All Clans fire. Afterward, as Tododaho demanded, they left their accustomed benches to the war chiefs and went to sit at the edges of the council with their daughters. The warriors had returned, having bested more Cayuga towns. Tododaho had summoned them to decide where to attack next.

Jekonsaseh sat back with the women, watching their faces while the men made plans. No one dared protest her father's decisions. Those who opposed him died. Although none of the deaths had seemed purely natural, few dared even whisper of sorcery or Younger Brother.

Hiawatha place was with Snipe Clan. Otter, and Snipe war chiefs sat on the bench to one side of the sacred flame, Bear, Beaver and Wolf on the other. Tododaho laid out his plans. "Before winter closes the warpath, my trusted followers shall take our campaign to the north and the south. We have brought their chiefs here to learn to obey me. Over winter, they will apply my new Law. Next spring, we will go to Cayuga's northland and Seneca's eastern. When we have consolidated the Western Tribes, we shall go to Oneida. When we have subdued them, it will be time to challenge Ganeo-gaono, the best fighters of all, until now. In the end, we will win. In five years at the most, they will surrender to me. My Law will spread over all the nations of the Longhouse people. It will be time to subdue the Huron and make them submissive to us. We shall be the elder brothers to all the lands between the Great Lakes and the Eastern Algonquin. Our names and victories will live forever in our people's songs and ceremonies."

In the silence that followed this pronouncement, Hiawatha rose to speak. "It is true, Tododaho, that war is the business of men, but you have shut out the voices of our matrons, even within the town. Our old ways served us well for generations before we were born. The Creator

36

honors and respects women, as he did his mother and the Three Sisters. He won't approve of your changes and wars for control."

Tododaho glared but Hiawatha would not back down. "Let us hear what the matrons think about your Law and how it will destroy our families." He looked to the women but they shuddered, not wanting attention. It could make things worse.

"They are silent as you should be, Hiawatha," said Tododaho. "You are a healer now, Hiawatha. War is no longer your concern. I have brave men enough. Go sit with the women since you value them so highly." People muttered disapproval at the disrespect. Hiawatha was a respected healer and had some power too, but he was being foolhardy. He had lost too much already.

Hiawatha would not give in. Tododaho's followers moved away, leaving the two to face each other. Jekonsaseh and Ogan-nis'tah had been watching and listening with the women, but at this, they came closer. Crying bitterly over the death of her last sister had left Ogan-nis'ah's lungs weak. "What will your father do to mine?" she asked, squeezing her friend's hand.

It was whispered that her father could call on unnatural forces. One of Ogan-nis'tah's sisters died of a spider bite, another of a fall, another of a deadly mushroom that had looked innocent and the fourth from the scratch of a rabid squirrel. Jekonsaseh did not want to believe her father had a hand in the deaths. Hadn't he protected her when she was an outcast? Hadn't he offered words of comfort to Hiawatha and his daughters when Sweet Water died? The girls strained to listen.

Tododaho explained patiently. "The squirrel does not rule the bear; nor does the otter. Weaker tribes should be led by the stronger, as women must follow men. I will protect our honored clan matrons. I will hear their concerns in private, not at a war meeting." Some looked away uncomfortable at the blatant violation of their old way. He proceeded to say who would go with him, who with his captains, and where they would meet. "Are there questions?"

Only Hiawatha spoke. "Will you continue to make war on those who have done us no harm? You curse the rest of us by continuing to break the Creator's Law." His strong voice carried, reasonable and sorrowful. Jekonsaseh recalled what Sweet Water said when her father accosted her in the planting fields. Hiawatha was no coward. Only he was brave enough to stand up to her father. Secretly, she hoped he could succeed.

"I told you to sit, Cousin, but I will explain again. Once the Longhouse Tribes are mine, no outside nation will oppose us – not Huron, not Erie, not Algonquin. Our matrons ruled us when we were boys, but now we are men. I, not the elders or the matrons, will unite us and vanquish all opposition. The Younger Brother is my guide. He lends me his power." Tododaho admitted he had turned to dark powers. Whispers broke out, but ceased when the war chief spoke again. "The Creator has given in to him. Our old Law is dead. The Younger Brother's Law rules us now."

The murmuring resumed until Hiawatha lifted his voice. "The Younger Brother destroys what is good. Only a twisted mind desires strife and sickness when there might be peace and health. He distorts your view, Cousin Tododaho. How can you follow him? Didn't the Creator show his displeasure when the animals left? Next, the Three Sisters refuse to bless our crops. How will we survive then?"

Tododaho's hooded eyes regarded his rival. Hiawatha remaining friends tried to pull him out of harm's way. "Hiawatha is in mourning. Let him go to his last child," coaxed an elder. A bent grandmother took Hiawatha hand to lead him to Snipe Longhouse. "Be quiet. Haven't you suffered enough?" Hiawatha pulled out of her hands and returned to the Council circle.

"Get away from him, Father," Ogan-nis'tah shouted hoarsely, coughing at the strain on her lungs. "He will kill you."

"I am not a coward," he said. "How much evil will you do, Cousin, before you are satisfied? How many more will you sacrifice to your greed to control everyone? The Creator set matrons over the families. They gave us life. Instead of overpowering other Longhouse nations, let us reach out to them in friendship. Let us be a family of nations with an equal say in our Council meetings. Let us return to our Law where clan matrons rule families and men rule the forest. Consider what this Tribal war will cost us, warriors of Onondaga."

Several grumbled that such consideration would take too long. "We are ready to fight now," complained Wolf War Chief. "Men don't sit and *consider* for months like old women," said the Snipe war chief. The men laughed nervously.

Tododaho lifted a conciliatory hand. "Hiawatha," he said, "Cousin. You were like a brother to me once, and I loved you. We stand on opposite sides now but it is not necessary. I feel for your losses, but do not interfere with me. Go back to your herbs and medicines to heal our injured. Save yourself further grief."

Jekonsaseh kept her arm around Ogan-nis'tah's shoulder, lending her support for she seemed even weaker.

Hiawatha crossed his arms. "If you continue your aggression, we will lose more than we gain. To prove your power, you choose death over life, shadow over light. You have become a creature of darkness. People will remember you for the curse you brought upon our people with your Law. The Elder Brother will remember."

Jekonsaseh felt a huge shout building inside Tododaho. He kept it from emerging, saying instead, "My friends, shall we lose our pride? Shall our enemies tell how fierce the Onondaga once were, and laugh because we became old women at Hiawatha bidding? It is not I who would change men and make us feeble." A few men wavered, but clearly Tododaho had the most followers.

"Tododaho will kill my father," Ogan-nis'tah whispered frantically.

"No!" Jekonsaseh held tight to her to keep her from rushing toward Hiawatha. The other girl's skin was hot. "Your father must give in."

"Tododaho just called my father an old woman. If I were a man, I would kill your father myself." Jekonsaseh buried her face in her friend's neck. Afraid and ashamed, she said nothing. The emotions in the sacred circle shook her like thunder. She nearly felt the ground shake.

Hiawatha addressed the undecided. "If you continue to follow the Younger Brother, we will soon have no town, no food and no wives. There will be no more generations and all our land will be wilderness. There will be no more Tribes."

Tododaho appeared to grow taller with anger. "You preach weakness. The time for weakness is over." He crossed his muscled and scarred arms. "Strong men take the women they want."

Hiawatha held out his hands, fingers splayed as if to touch his listeners. "Would you be like the male otter that seizes the female with his teeth and takes her without her consent? Would you behave like animals instead of men?"

Tododaho brought down his hand sideways in a chopping motion. "Enough! I have already chosen Jekonsaseh's husband."

An older man near Hiawatha spoke in a voice made high with age. He had fought his last battle many years ago. His age gave him respect and people listened when he spoke. "That goes completely against custom."

Tododaho pointed to Jekonsaseh. "Don't you understand that I have changed the old customs? Jekonsaseh will marry whom I say, and her sons will call me grandfather. The matrons have had their time. It is over. Men rule the families now."

"You can't make that big a change," said another old healer. Tododaho looked for the speaker, but mortified at his temporary boldness, the man hid behind others.

Tododaho's deep voice carried. "Those who oppose me die, as you may have noticed. I offer you a last chance, Hiawatha. Lend me your strong voice. Help me convince others that I am right and we will be friends again." He extended his arms. "Join me, Cousin. Don't oppose me and lose your last child." He turned to the assembly. "Warriors of Tyo-den-he-deh! Will you follow me?"

Ogan-nis'tah walked resolutely toward her father. People parted for her. "My fever will not kill me, Tododaho," she said. "I'm not afraid of you." Warriors stepped back, abashed at the brave maiden. "The Creator wants us to live in peace." She drew attention as a flame draws moths. They waited to see what would happen.

"You are sick. Don't use up your strength," Hiawatha warned. "Go home."

Ogan-nis'tah turned to the war chiefs. Jekonsaseh would never have been so bold. "Brave warriors of Tyo-den-he-dah," she said. "Be brave like my father is brave and don't listen to a sorcerer."

Hiawatha pressed his cheek to his daughter's forehead saying, "You are not well. Jekonsaseh, take her home."

"Come," Jekonsaseh begged. "This is not for us to decide. Let us get you to bed." They walked to Bear Longhouse and stood under the porch overhang.

"I want to hear," Ogan-nis'tah said. "Then, I will rest."

Hiawatha strong voice reached them. "No one has questioned our courage. It is not too late to make peace with our neighbors and return to the old ways."

Tododaho's deeper voice filled Jekonsaseh with alarm. "You are brave, but foolish, my cousin. Go to your foolish girl and keep silent, for your words condemn her."

Hiawatha did not retreat. "Think for yourselves, my friends. Tododaho cannot kill me and he knows it. Leave him and go to your homes. Go to your wives and hold them close. Think of your children." Jekonsaseh had never seen anyone so brave, yet the men wavered, unable to decide for Hiawatha and reject their formidable war chief.

"Let the Creator and his Younger Brother decide," Hiawatha suggested. The Council waited in silence to hear how Hiawatha expected the two sky brothers to do this. "If the Younger Brother is dominant, let him send a serpent to us as a sign. If the Elder Brother desires peace, let him send an eagle to alight atop that pine." The tree stood just outside the palisade. The town had grown up in its shadow.

Tododaho held out his left hand to Hiawatha and their fingers touched. "I accept your contest. Ask first. If no eagle comes, it is my turn."

Eagle or serpent? Their future depended upon the outcome. People peered into the darkening sky and the gray clouds for an eagle and listened for its cry. "Let me lean on you," said Ogan-nis'tah. "I want to see the eagle."

"Better go inside. I will come in later and tell you. Please. It is not safe for you to stay here."

"I want to see it," Ogan-nis'tah repeated, but her voice was faint.

"Your father will be distracted with worry for you. I will go in, too."

"Not yet. When the eagle comes, I will go inside." The two leaned together, Jekonsaseh supporting her cousin.

Tododaho waited on the bench while Hiawatha made his plea. "Creator, hear me if you would show us your desire for us. Send your eagle to that pine tree to prove you still rule Turtle Island and we must keep your Law." Other birds were settling down for the night. The sun would descend to its resting place soon. If neither eagle nor serpent came, what would it mean? Jekonsaseh wondered if the Creator were busy somewhere else. What if he did not respond?

"How long shall we wait for your eagle, Hiawatha?" Tododaho asked. "No messenger eagle comes from heaven. Are you ready for me to call upon the serpent and the earthly powers?"

"Wait until the sun sets," Hiawatha said.

The light was fading in the dusky sky when a distant screech reached their ears. "The eagle!" Someone shouted. "It flies to the tree."

Tododaho jumped to his feet. "It can't be," he bellowed. "Men - get your bows and quivers," he commanded. "The Creator will not interfere with my war." He pointed to the houses. Obeying orders, men ran for their weapons. "You," he said, pointing to a young man who had not yet made up his mind. "If you won't get your own bow; get mine, and my quiver. Do it!"

The direct command impelled the man to obey. Among the many, his feet were only two, but in his rush, he held his arms straight, palms forward to make his way through the press. He hardly noticed the two maidens in the porch. Jekonsaseh fell sideways. She pulled herself to her feet and scampered out of the way, but Ogan-nis'tah fell back. Others, unseeing, tramped over her, pushing her down. Jekonsaseh screamed for them to stop, but they did not hear. "Get up!" she shouted, and tried to help her friend out of the way, but the warriors rushed forward, not seeing them. "Are you blind?" she shouted. "You crushed Ogan-nis'tah!"

Ogan-nis'tah's groans could hardly be heard above the tumult. Jekonsaseh shouted for help, but the damage had been done before she could grasp her friend under the arms and pull her away. She could not carry her, so she leaned her against the wall. How had the men not seen her or heard Jekonsaseh's warning shouts? Her friend's ribs had been crushed. Blood ran from her mouth and nose.

Tododaho received his bow and quiver from the young man and praised him. Swiftly, he nocked his arrow to his bowstring and released. The eagle had just spread its talons to perch on the highest bough. It dropped with Tododaho's arrow piercing its breast. Blood reddened its white breast feathers. Those who had hoped screamed in fear and shock. "He killed the Creator's messenger." Jekonsaseh heard, but she turned back to her cousin. Ogan-nis'tah tried to breathe, but the effort caused more pain. "My father killed more than you and the eagle today. Now many people will die."

"I'm glad I won't live to see it." Ogan-nis'tah's words did not leave her lips, but Jekonsaseh heard her inside her head. It was like speaking to a ghost.

"Uncle Hiawatha!" Jekonsaseh screamed. "Come! Ogan-nis'tah is dying." At last people stepped away from the mortally injured girl. Ogan-nis'tah's lids trembled as Hiawatha cradled her to him. Jekonsaseh heard what she was thinking. *You are my last sister, Jekonsaseh. Watch over my father. He has no one else now.* The light left his daughter's eyes.

Hiawatha took a few unsteady, confused steps, then swayed on his feet and crumbled. "The earth has lost laughter," he murmured, for her name meant Laughing Water. Jekonsaseh faced her father. If he had not done the deed himself, he was responsible. "You killed Ogan-nis'tah, no one else." Tododaho might have replied, but he was not looking toward her but at Hiawatha

The bereaved father walked erratically, hands before him like a blind man, until he faced his enemy. His fingers curled like the eagle's talons. Men and women rushed up to him to pull him back. Words of condolence died on their lips when they how he glared at his daughter's murderer. "Tododaho, you are the death-bringer. Your hair has become snakes. They hiss."

They were the last coherent words Jekonsaseh would hear Hiawatha say for many years. Tododaho pointed one finger to Hiawatha. No one dared interfere. "From this moment, all men are animals in your eyes. See their clans in them. For opposing me, I curse you to live alone in the wild parts of the forest. Take your weapons and leave the places of men."

Hiawatha shook his head as though to clear it. "No!" he shouted, stumbling forward to his knees. "Where did everyone go?" he cried as the images faded in and out. "I see and hear only beasts. Where have the people gone? Someone died. Who was it?" In his non-deliberate movements, his eyes fell on Jekonsaseh.

"Uncle, I'm Jekonsaseh," she said. "See me and know me!"

He looked at her without recognition. "What is this creature?" he asked, looking at her directly. "First it is a bear and then an otter. It changes back and forth. Whoever heard of such a thing? I won't kill you, strange creature. Until people return to the world, I shall live in the forest." He staggered to Bear Longhouse. No one tried to speak to him after Jekonsaseh's attempt. Hiawatha ran from Tyo-den-he-deh with his bow and quiver heavy with arrows. The forest path became dark. His silhouette was soon lost to sight, but his mournful voice came back to the people. "Where did all the people go? Where am I and who died?"

Chapter 6

Ogan-nis'tah's death and the loss of her beloved uncle were more than Jekonsaseh could bear. She would have recoiled into herself, but Father was mollifying his men and excusing them. "It was an accident the girl was trampled and that her father went mad. We must accept these things." She heard his words, but also his thoughts. *Hiawatha was in my way. His daughter believed in him so she had to die.* No one else heard, just as no one else saw Ogan-nis'tah in their way. "The tragedy pushed his mind beyond its limits. Elder Brother may heal him. It is beyond our power."

Jekonsaseh looked toward the crooked passage where Hiawatha had disappeared. Her father took her shoulder gently but firmly. She controlled her impulse to shake it off. "We will bury poor Ogan-nis'tah and mourn her," he said. "It is tragic, but these events shall not change my plans. After autumn's last battle, I will bring you to Onoji myself. When you are his wife, you will convince the matrons and their daughters that the new Law is best. You can also tell them what happens when people oppose me."

Pleading would show weakness and Father despised that. If he bothered to listen closely, he would have seen past her words just as she saw past his. The best she could do was say, "My heart is too full of sadness to think of this now, Father. May I help the burial society prepare Ogan-nis'tah's body?"

"Of course."

When the earth was ready, her father's forces were back on the war path. He left men for patrol and defense. Jekonsaseh thought as she washed and dressed the body that to her father, her loyalty was unquestioned, but she was like a favorite dog to petted and cared for as long as he could use her.

When the others left the grave, Jekonsaseh lingered. "He closed his warriors' eyes to you, didn't he?" she asked. A pale image of Ogan-nis'tah rose from the mound. Jekonsaseh saw the glow and felt the presence. She knew her friend heard her. "No one noticed us standing in the porch. Only the dead and the mad feel the unnaturalness of my father's powers. I am not dead, so I must be mad."

"Were my father and I mad or only foolish to speak against war?" The ghost grew more vivid. "You have a loving heart, Cousin. At times like this, that is enough to be considered mad. Do you know you share some of your father's abilities? Who else among us could see and speak with ghosts? I never could."

Jekonsaseh considered her cousins words and lowered her head. "I don't want to be like him. He arranged for me to marry his follower, Onoji, and to spread his new ways to the southern clan matrons. Tell me what to do, Ogan-nis'tah." Tears dripped down her cold cheeks, but she barely felt them. "He's too strong for me. Must I die to escape him, as my mother did?"

"No. Grow stronger so you can save the rest of us."

"It is too late to save you. I don't know how to save anyone. Who will teach me?"

Ogan-nis'tah looked down at her grave. "I don't like being dead, but there are advantages. I can ask the dead matrons' spirits. Visit me again tomorrow night. You'd better go home before you are missed."

Jekonsaseh was not sure the spirits could direct her to a teacher who could strengthen her *orenda*, but at least, she would escape her father. Death was still an option. She had lost her fear of it. A quick fall from a high place, a rush of wind, and the pain would end swiftly. She could join Ogan-nis'tah in the spirit world.

She behaved normally the next day, pounding corn to meal, fetching water and tinder, being pleasant to everyone. She swept her father's section and arranged everything neatly. That night late, she wrapped herself in her blanket, and filled her pouch with corn meal and a flask to carry water.

She waited until the patrol passed, took a last look back at the palisade about Tyo-den-he-day and entered the cemetery. Above her friend's mound, she crouched and touched the soft earth with her fingers. "I am here," she said. "Do you hear me? I decided to leave.

Come up so I can ask you where to run. I made up my mind. If I cannot escape, I will cast myself off a high place as my mother did."

She was hardly surprised when bits of luminescence rose from the new grave. The bits came together, a stronger image this night. Ogan-nis'tah appeared as herself before her illness and her death. "Don't die yet. My father needs you."

"Can I revoke curses? I see and hear ghosts only when they allow it. My father's *orenda* is stronger than mine, but I heard his thoughts. He wanted you and my uncle gone. The two of you were starting to make his men think again about following the Younger Brother. You were emboldening the matrons. I already tried to speak to your father. He saw me as an otter and then a bear, my birth clan and my adopted clan. He does not see people but animals."

"Try again."

Her friend's words hurt. "Why can't you find him with your spirit eyes and talk to him the way you're talking to me?"

"He's blind to me because of the curse. He came to my grave last night and wept, but he didn't see me. If you are mad like my father, he might see you. Help him!"

Jekonsaseh lifted her palms, tired of arguing. "I will try. Did you ask the dead matrons where I can find a teacher?"

"My great-grandmother's spirit said for you to go west to a river called Niagara between the two most eastern Great Lakes. The river tumbles over a cliff. Behind the Falls lives a wise man who is part spirit. His ghost wife knows of our trouble and recommends that he teach you."

"I will go and ask him. Tododaho will never use me; that I can promise you." She reached for Ogan-nis'tah, wanting to embrace her, but the dead and the living can't touch. Her hands went through the image. Ogan-nis'tah appeared pacified by her promise. The shape of her cousin dissipated and sank back into the earth. The burial ground was dark and silent again.

The night winds covered her footprints as Jekonsaseh ran, but she did not look back. Her thoughts outraced her feet. Father's men would not learn of her departure until she was long gone. The pale clouds and moon lit the trail gray against the black cliffs of the forest. She wore no moccasins. The soles of her feet were hardened with calluses. Until morning, she plodded though old pine needs and cedar mast. She found a rivulet sliding over rocks and bent to drink. She did not stop to cook, but took a mouthful of corn meal, softening it in her mouth until she could swallow it. When she was too tired to take another step, she stopped where she was and pulled a blanket of leaves over her.

At first light, she awoke and began again, keeping the rising sun behind her. She slept in trees, wrapped in her blanket. She foraged to supplement her cornmeal, digging roots with sharp stones and bitter acorns. Sometimes she found a forgotten ear of corn in a fallow field, but she resisted the fires of people. Towns and villages may have heard of her. When she could find nothing else, she overturned rocks and rotting logs for the grubs and beetles. She knew how animals felt, grateful for the occasional walnut or acorn she might find, running from lair to lair, hoping to avoid being eaten herself.

One day, she caught a fish with her fingers. It did not take much to fill her belly. Rain quenched her thirst between streams, leaving muddy streaks across her face, but nothing mattered as long as she made progress. She circled the northern tip of Lake Neah'ga and followed the trail to the next lake, Lake Do-Sho-weh. She wondered where her father's men were fighting. If they controlled these western villages and towns, its people might deliver her to him. She saw a town protected by a wooden palisade, and smelled food cooking over hearth fires. She might starve before she reached Niagara and its man spirit. Frost whitened the veins of fallen leaves. Soon winter would freeze the rivers and lakes and lay a thick blanket of snow upon the land. She was cold and hungry, but she picked a way around the town, and remained undiscovered.

Towns and villages came closer together. Warmth and food tempted her, but she would not give in. She was tempted to lie down and sleep. She didn't have the strength to climb a cliff, but it did not take energy to starve. If a cougar or fox smelled her, she might keep it alive for another day or two. Death began to look tempting as a warm bed after gathering firewood. She would make a bed for herself in the leaves, but until then, she would walk. She reached the bank of another lake. Clouds closed in overhead and wind piled the water into gray waves. She bent and drank, and feeling revived a little, looked out over the water. The sun broke out of the clouds and lit the silver maple bark of a small fishing canoe.

Jekonsaseh could have disappeared into the shadows, but curiosity drew her to the bank. She did not know what impelled her, but she stood in a sunbeam, savoring the warmth. The fisherman saw her and paddled closer, stopping a few feet out. Jekonsaseh stepped forward and met the man's eyes.

"You aren't from my village," he said. "What are you doing here? Are you lost?" She took a breath but her tongue forgot how to speak. It was a month since she used her voice. When she did not respond, the fisherman looked for her companions. Finding none, he asked, "Have you lost your family in the war?" Her voice was stuck in her throat and did not know how to come out. *Do you know the way to Niagara?* she thought, as if other people could hear thoughts.

"Are you simple or are you mad?" the man asked. When she did not reply, he beached his canoe. He said, "I will take you to my town and ask if anyone is looking for a lost girl." He reached for her, but she shied back, making thin animal sounds. It appeared he made his offer in kindness, but she would not enter a town. Someone there would know of her and return her to Tododaho. Why had she not run and hidden herself in the forest? She could not outrun a turtle. Her wild hair covered half her face.

The man spoke gently. "Don't be afraid. My wife will feed you." She was so cold and empty. It would be good to be warm. The man encouraged her to climb into his canoe. "It is not safe in the forest. Haven't you heard of the cannibal Hiawatha? He comes this way sometimes. They say he was once human, but now he ambushes humans and boils them for soup. Do you want to be his next meal?" He reached for her, but seeing her fear, did not touch her.

She thought of her cursed uncle and Ogan-nis'tah and her mother. She thought of her father's Law that began with her. Everything was her fault. She gasped for air. Sobs tore from her throat and tears dripped freely from her eyes. Jekonsaseh had never cried like this. She covered her face with her muddy hands, ashamed.

"You understand me," the man said. "You don't want to be cooked into soup. Come with me. You'll be safe." She did not shy this time, when he laid down his paddle and gripped her wrist. "Where do you live?"

"I can't say." Her voice was hoarse and foreign-sounding. If she died at Hiawatha hands, perhaps he would return to himself, see what he had done and end his life too. They could ascend the star path together to find his family and her mother. Together, they might influence the Creator to return order to the world.

The stranger began to tug her to his canoe. "No!" Jekonsaseh screamed, her eyes wild. "No town. No village!"

Startled, the man let go, but she had no strength left to run. "Insane girl, I won't harm you. The gentle mad are holy. It is said the guardian of Niagara was once like you. He lost his mind when his wife died. He lives in a cave behind the Great Falls. We Cayuga call him Hidden in Mist. He might be able to help you."

Jekonsaseh stopped struggling. Her voice was harsh with lack of use. "Hidden in Mist is the guardian? Can you take me to him?"

The man pointed to his canoe. "My family is waiting for me and my fish, but I can bring you to the other side of this lake. Are you hungry?" She nodded and climbed in. "I have fish, but it is raw." Her hide blanket was in rags. She pulled it tighter. The man tucked his blanket around her, too. He had brought it to ward off the morning chill, but she needed it more. He did not ask her name, but offered her one of the gutted fish from his net. She nodded her thanks and ripped into the pale flesh with her teeth. She peeled the skin back like a bear and bit off huge chunks, swallowing them nearly whole.

"Slowly," advised the man. "Eat too fast and it won't stay down." She cut her finger on a bone and licked away the blood. "More?" She bit into a second fish. Finally, she dropped the remains over the side and dipped her hands to wash and drink. She rubbed her face, cleaning off the mud, and rested her eyes, feeling the sun. The canoe passed harvested fields and the palisade of another town. "My home is there," he said, but he kept paddling.

Her Otter aunt and cousins had called her a witch. The man had called her insane. "Why are you helping me?" she asked.

"The Creator likes us to deal kindly with the mad."

She recalled that this was true. "Has the war reached you yet?"

"Yes, but we have escaped notice so far. Did you lose your family in the fighting?" He paused and the canoe glided to a stop. She feared she had begun to sound too rational. If he no longer thought she was insane, he might cease being kind.

"Yes. My mother and father, and all my sisters are dead. I ran."

"No one knows how this war will end. Tododaho and his warriors are cruel to leave a girl like you homeless. His men have made too many

49

angry ghosts with no one left to mourn for them." His sympathy made her eyes ache with tears.

"The man clicked his tongue and the canoe moved again to the stroke of his paddle. He banked at the western end of the lake and helped her out. "This is as far as I go. Keep the blanket. Follow the trail that begins between those oaks. It will take you north. In a few days, you will see the Niagara River dashing over rocks in the riverbed. Follow it downriver. No one will interfere with you. Hidden in Mist imposed his sacred peace over the Niagara. No one may fight there."

"I hope your family will be safe," she said. He set off and soon, his canoe vanished into the glittering surface of the lake.

She followed the path, sleeping once, until she came upon the river. Violent and troubled, it raced and tumbled on its way. She felt wild as the river, disconnected from her past, not knowing the future. She followed the narrow river until she neared the edge. Here was a wonder words could not describe. The river broadened and, on the surface, seemed to have ceased moving. Then it disappeared over the cliff. She could barely make out the bottom. Mist rose around her like white smoke.

No one was in sight, no man, no guardian. She called. If he was part spirit, he would hear, but there was only the roar and the mist that clung to her. The old matron's ghost must be wrong. She had traveled for nothing. Perhaps, if Hidden in Mist wished to save her, he would reach out from his cave behind the Falls and catch her as she plummeted. Either way, she would never have to face her father again.

She prepared to step out into the nothingness. "Wait!" a child's voice called. She looked around, but saw no one. She fortified herself again with thoughts of joining her cousins. She imagined falling, pummeled by cascades of beautiful white water until her soul flew free. She opened her eyes for final view. The sun escaped the clouds and touched the mist. She had never seen a rainbow except in the sky. The arc of colors split and became two arcs. It was too beautiful. She stared, unable to move.

"Wait!" the young voice repeated. She could see him now, a small boy running to her. His face was sun-darkened but his eyes were beautiful. His lips parted a little as he ran and she heard his labored breathing. He sighed with relief as he caught hold of her and tugged her away from the edge.

50

"You are not Hidden in Mist. Why do you stop me?"

"He is old and doesn't run so fast any more. You are not supposed to die yet. My mother's mother tried to drown me when I was born, but the guardian pulled me out. The Cayuga call him Hidden in Mist. The Huron call him Father Mist. Some call him Grandfather – *Hoc-sote'*. I call him Father, but don't tell. It is a secret."

"I don't tell, but why tell me?" asked Jekonsaseh, nearly too astonished a spirit guardian could have a son to remember her intention.

He kept her hands in his. "Be-because I trust you. No - nobody else knows who my father is, not even my mother." His hands were warm and strong, and comforted her. "His ghost wife told him you would come. He will – will be your teacher."

He did not speak her language, but the enchantment of the place made all things comprehensible. "What may I call you?" she asked, knowing some names were holy and must not be pronounced except at proper times.

"My name is not holy yet. It is Deganawida. It means Think-Thinker in Huron. Do you speak Huron?"

"No."

"You can learn. Come – come meet my father."

She followed him to a shadow in the granite wall. The mist opened to reveal a man sitting on a ledge and beckoning. His eyes were kind. His gray hair floated about his head like smoke. A reminder of the man he must once have been showed in his well-muscled legs and arms. Deganawida pushed her to him. She felt the guardian's spirit, his *orenda*, probe hers. It was strong, but gentle as he seemed to be. "My name is Saiyen-gu," he said. "Niagara has taken most of my hearing, but we can mind speak. You've done it before." He smiled. "Your *orenda* is strong too."

"But you know what I think and what I want." He nodded. "Can you teach me to do that too?"

"I think so. You are very worried about your father. You feel two ways about him, both good and bad. Your feelings fight within you and make you weak."

Jekonsaseh lowered her face to her hands. "He protected me when I was cast out, when I had no one else, but he means to give us to Younger Brother and cast down the matrons. That is wrong!" Her tears fell although she scrunched her eyes. Could a spirit man understand people? Then she remembered. The boy called him Father. "My father is Tododaho. He can hurt you if you help me."

"I know who you are. I have no fear of him. My son will heal your uncle in another few years. Be comforted." Jekonsaseh lifted her head. "You wonder how I know. My wife Red Wing is dead more than ten years, but she visits me. She says I shall be your teacher, and so I shall. But for now, eat and drink, and then sleep and heal. Come inside. A meal is waiting for you and a sleep roll. You come too, Son."

Chapter 7

Saiyen-gu's cave was not dark and dank as she expected, but cozy and welcoming. His hearth fire glowed, and good smells came from his cooking bowls. Cured hides covered the stone floor, soft against her feet. Crevices held shelves of storage baskets and bowls. Herbs for flavoring and healing dried in bunches on basswood cords. The guardian must be a healer. "This bed is mine," said Saiyen-gu, pointing to the bed platform. "There is yours. My son helped me fill it with balsam boughs. Your sleep will refresh you." She sat on her bed roll and breathed in the good smells. Its springiness would soften her rest.

"In the morning, Deganawida must return to his mother, but he wanted to meet you. Drink this and you will soon be warm." He ladled heated sassafras root tea into three cups and handed them out. It was delightful. In this company, with thoughts of acceptance and learning, morose thoughts faded quickly. Deganawida sipped his drink and gave her a bashful smile. She smiled back.

It didn't seem possible she could have been expected, but since she saw the rainbows, anything might happen. Saiyen-gu scooped fish stew into bowls, speaking while he spread them out for his guests. "Thank you, Hidden in Mist," she said.

"Call me Saiyen-gu. Thinker will be your little brother while you stay with me. I will teach you Huron speech and you will teach us Longhouse. Tell us while we eat, Jekonsaseh, what caused you to run away?"

She told them about Onoji and how her father removed the Clan Matron's control over the families. "He expected me to help him spread his Law after he married me to his ally. I won't belong to any man he chooses for me." She wondered if she was asking too much. Saiyen-gu was human once. His customs might be different.

"My wife Red Wing chose me," he said with a reminiscent smile. "I would have asked her father for her because that is how the Erie Tribe makes marriages, but she crawled into my sleeping roll before I could ask. She made me very happy. She was everything I could want in a wife." He glanced toward the Falls that curtained his cave. "And still is."

"Is she here now?"

"Yes. She is here."

Before Jekonsaseh slept, she thought of Sweet Water and Ogannis'tah and her mother. She thought of being able to help Hiawatha.

She awoke in semi-gloom. The fire had burned low. Deganawida was gone and Saiyen-gu was sitting on a hide mat, his back to the door curtain, legs crossed, and puffing on his pipe. The pine and resin-tinged smell in the air remained, but tobacco smoke teased her nose. It curled around the Saiyen-gu, hovering like a cloud before it was caught by a channel of air and escaped.

Her people sent prayers to the Creator with tobacco smoke, but Saiyen-gu inhaled it and blew it out again. Well, he was spirit and human together, so he had the right. His hair resembled the torrent outside, trails of white locks between the dark, and his eyes were like rainbows. He personified the Niagara River.

When she had washed outside on the ledge, she came back and sat cross-legged before him. "Are you rested?" he asked.

"Yes. How long did I sleep?"

"All day. It is dusk again."

She felt lighter now, nearly as if she could rise like the white tobacco smoke. Saiyen-gu pointed to a bowl of cooled cornmeal mush. She ate. "Why did the Creator let my father kill his eagle?" she asked.

"Your people had a choice. They weren't ready to resist your father. You will help make them ready."

Jekonsaseh tried not to tremble. "That means I will go back," she said, not trying to hide her fear. It was impossible to hide anything from her host.

"When you are ready, you will go back. After your time with me, you will be ready. In a few days, we will go to Huron Country. We will stay at Deganawida's village for a while. You will pretend you don't know him. I will call you Apprentice. No one shall know who you are."

He began their next day explaining the herbs he had drying in his cave. She knew them from her childhood. He pounded them into powder for infusions, lotions and teas and made signs with the cords that bound them in small packets. Next, he demonstrated how to bind injuries. Later, he showed her how to send holy tobacco forth to the Creator and other benevolent spirits. "Do as I do." His extra pipe stem was a narrow reed and the bowl, a hollowed-out corn cob. He filled the bowl with dried shredded tobacco and held a burning twig to it.

When the tobacco caught and glowed, he took a mouthful and exhaled smoke rings. Jekonsaseh did not find smoking pleasant at first, but she learned to show the pipe to the directions, east, west, north, and south, sky and earth. "Add a prayer."

Hearing him in her head soon became normal and was easier than trying to use her ears with the Falls roaring beside the cave. She thanked the Creator and Earth Mother for her life, her teacher and her little brother. She added a request, knowing Saiyen-gu heard it. "Please help me learn." She puffed again to punctuate her prayer.

The next day after breakfast, they explored the nearer regions of the lower lake. Back from the bank, an old fire had burned. The trees were lifeless, but colorful mushrooms grew among the stumps. They picked the last of the herbs before the snow killed them. Life grew out of death.

They gathered fallen bark shreds for absorbent bandaging. He began to teach her Huron while they foraged for starchy roots, walnut husks and acorns. Saiyen-gu checked his fish lines and showed Jekonsaseh how to make a smoke fire in a narrow tipi to dry the strips of salmon. While they smoked, they worked on their snow shoes. He gave her his extra mittens and boots, stuffed to fit her.

On the trail to Huron, they spotted a fat black bear some twenty yards away with thick coat of matted fur. Its backside waddled and swayed as it walked. Jekonsaseh stilled like a fawn, hoping the cold had made it too sluggish to attack them.

"Father Bear," said Saiyen-gu. "Greetings. Are you ready for your winter sleep?" The animal turned, sniffed, and rose to better see them. It was terrifyingly male, but when Saiyen-gu lifted his arm in greeting, the bear grunted, dropped and waddled off to vanish among the trees. "He has found a good place to wait out winter. Let us continue to ours."

Jekonsaseh was too astounded to speak for some moments. When she had thought it through, she asked, "Will I be able talk to animals?"

"I expect so. Pictures work best. I spoke words for your sake, but animals think in pictures."

As they walked, Jekonsaseh told Saiyen-gu an idea she had been mulling over to bring peace to the tribes. "What if all the warriors killed each other? No warriors – no wars. Would that be good?"

"Do you wish for this?"

"Women pull weeds from corn hills."

"When Tododaho attacks, if a town or village has no warriors, how will they defend themselves? If there are only women and children and the elderly, they will be overrun and forced to give in."

"I had not thought of that." He was kind enough and wise enough that she felt at ease to ask him anything. She had already learned so much. It would not be easy to leave his tutorship and protection.

They slept snug in a small lean-to, sharing their warmth. Before sleep, Saiyen-gu told Jekonsaseh how Deganawida came to be born. "That is between you and me, and him, of course." She marveled that the boy's mother did not know how she conceived and yet her son did.

"Tree Frog's mother never spoke of men except to say that we are all dangerous and should be avoided. The village boys taunt Thinker for having no father. Since Tree Frog and Mina – her name means Elder Sister - went back to live among people, Tree Frog lives less in dreams. She has a husband now who hunts for them. Mina must behave or go into exile again, alone. Thinker stammers, but try not to notice. His speech causes people to underestimate him. You will see for yourself what a bright child he is. You will soon meet his family."

"And that grandmother?"

"Yes, but remember. You know nothing. A child needs confidence. That is why he visits me and why I made you his sister. Do not speak much. You are my apprentice. That will be your only name."

They reached the lines of corn hills and finally the village, a clump of wigwams. Tall spruces, blue above the snow, closed them in. Saiyen-gu stopped and pushed back his hood. The children saw them first. He was a man away from Niagara. "Saiyen-gu! Who is the woman?"

He read their questions from their lips. "She is Apprentice and will stay with me while I teach her to be a healer. Tell your elders we request shelter."

Deganawida kept behind the bigger boys, but Jekonsaseh felt his greeting and returned it. *Brother!* She pictured them embracing, although in reality they did not draw closer. *Sister!* He sent her a mental picture of a dazzling smile.

56

They were welcomed in every house and invited to the councils when the elders discussed the intertribal war in the south. One, who had hunted in the south, repeated what he heard. "An Onondaga wizard called Tododaho changed Longhouse Law. His scalp grows snakes instead of hair." Jekonsaseh pressed her lips together.

She accompanied Saiyen-gu to the sick or injured, binding wounds and setting bones as he showed her. When hunters returned with frostbitten toes and fingers, she sat before them in the cozy wigwam to remove their moccasins and moose-hock socks while the ice melted from their eyebrows. She cupped her fingers around frozen toes and fingers and blew on them, warming them slowly. She dripped cold water against an injured hand and massaged the muscles gently to return its life-giving blood. The tip of a man's nose would remain black and unfeeling. There was only so much a healer could do. "Apprentice is a good healer already," said the patient.

When toddlers cried, Jekonsaseh gave them smoked-hardened salmon to chew to soothe their teething gums. Willow bark tea treated both fever and pain. When injuries were too severe and death might be delayed, Saiyen-gu taught her which mushrooms gave peaceful dreams and which painless death.

She learned more than healing. Most wigwams housed three generations, and sometimes aunts or uncles. They were not like entire clans, but people provided warmth. She studied the Hurons to understand them. The women did not rule, but they had much in common with Onondaga. They cared for each other.

During their second month, a young man approached her seeking a wife. Saiyen-gu made it clear Apprentice was not to leave him until her training was complete. Boys ran with their age mates, like the boys of Tyo-den-he-deh, to wrestle, practice nocking arrows to their bowstrings, hitting targets with spear or arrow, and scaring each other with war whoops. Thinker did not run with them. His stepfather taught him to hunt, but the boy hunted alone.

When the other boys called him fatherless, he said nothing, but Jekonsaseh felt his sadness. Jekonsaseh wished she could protect him. One day, she noticed a gang of boys interrupt her brother who was in quiet discussion with two girls. She crouched behind a thick, snow-covered clump of brambles by a thick oak. "Don't let them see me," she thought to the bushes and the tree.

The boys' leader said, "You play with girls. Do boys frighten you too much, Thinker? C-c-can you talk to girls without tripping over your tongue?" They laughed derisively. Deganawida turned away. The leader went on. "D-d-don't cry. Try to be b-b-b-brave." His companions laughed.

"Go away," shouted the oldest girl. "You're not half as smart as Thinker."

"Oh, is he smart? No one notices because he never says anything."

Refusing to let her defend him alone, Deganawida repeated, "Go away."

"Or what?" His foray into speech only made the boys laugh harder.

Jekonsaseh smoldered, wanting to punish the rude boy. As if in response, when the boy took a step, the oak tree's root tripped him. He slid forward on the icy ground, lost his balance, and fell headlong into the bramble bush. Thorns scraped his cheek open and tore his leggings. The girls covered their smiles. The boy got up, whistling. "It doesn't hurt," he said raggedly.

"Better have your mother sew up your cheek and your leggings," taunted a girl. The boy limped off, passing Jekonsaseh who stood up as if she had just arrived. She put on a serious mask, but inside she was glad. She had learned she could blend in with shadows and that sometimes Nature obeyed her wish. Deganawida's eyes met Jekonsaseh's for an instant before he returned to his friends, but he sent her the image of a smile.

Later, when Jekonsaseh and Saiyen-gu were alone, she told him. "Did I make it happen? I wanted to punish the boy and make him stop teasing."

"The tree's spirit agreed with you and lifted its root. You might have tried thinking peaceful thoughts instead of harmful ones. It is how I keep peace at Niagara." Her father cast curses. She didn't want to do that. She would practice using peaceful thoughts if they could achieve the same ends.

Tree Frog, Deganawida's mother, no longer lived in dreams. She and her husband welcomed Saiyen-gu and Apprentice to their wigwam. Mina, Thinker's grandmother, looked cross. Jekonsaseh hoped they were not depriving the family of needed food. She could imagine the grandmother trying to drown infant Thinker. Tree Frog's second son, about seven, sucked his thumb. Thinker's half sister filled bowls of food and cups of hot maple water since her mother was nursing a new baby girl. When everyone was served, she plopped onto the old woman's lap to receive a smile and a hug.

Tree Frog's husband said, "Saiyen-gu, you and Apprentice are welcome. You have looked in on my wife and her first child many times. It is a pity the boy can't speak properly. Can you do something about his stuttering and stammering?"

Saiyen-gu said, "Sadly, I have no medicine for that. If he does not run with the village boys, it is because he will find his own path." Thinker looked toward him, but quickly lowered his eyes to a spot on the floor between his bent knees.

"My wife's mother Mina dreamed if he lived, he will bring trouble to us. Perhaps she was right to try to drown him." Jekonsaseh masked her face again, but coughed to cover her gasp. "Somehow he was saved. At least, he is a decent hunter and sometimes brings game home. He is best at being silent."

The grandmother shrugged. "If he cares for his mother's people at all, he will go far away when he is big enough, and stay away."

Jekonsaseh heard Deganawida's thought. *I will do that. I'll come to you, Sister, in Longhouse Country.*

"Anyway," said Tree Frog, "I like him. Thinker is a good boy and good company." Deganawida lifted his eyes to her for a brief moment, but he remained silent. "I have more stew if you're still hungry. It's our honor to feed our guests."

"You are good hosts," Saiyen-gu said. "We are ready for sleep."

Jekonsaseh slept beside Deganawida. They spoke without words. *I will worry for you when we go.*

I can take care of myself. Deganawida pulled his blanket over them. By the banked coals' glow, Jekonsaseh saw only his form and his long dark hair. *All will be well. Wait and see.* She had wanted to comfort him, but he comforted her.

I love you, little brother, she sent silently.

I know. I love you, Sister. The early winter night closed in on the village in darkness and soon all in the house were asleep.

Chapter 8

Several Huron villages received them while Jekonsaseh trained to be a healer. Her *orenda* grew also, in its power. No one here knew she was Tododaho's daughter. Because she arrived as Saiyen-gu's apprentice, she was received with kindness.

At the end of a long day, she wrapped herself in her hide blanket. Sisters shared the wigwam with both husbands. A baby fussed. Its mother reached for it and tucked it to her breast. The other couple shared love across the way. Their gasps and sighs reminded her that she had reached womanhood alone and was likely to remain so. She must learn to be satisfied with her own company. Saiyen-gu had his ghost wife. Jekonsaseh could not hear their conversations, but when Red Wing visited, she knew and did not interrupt.

The war did not affect them directly, but the battles were a frequent topic of conversation among the Huron. Hunters carried home more tales they had picked up at chance meetings. War Chief Tododaho's name was no longer used. He was the Snake-haired, a wizard whose word was the new Law. Jekonsaseh wondered if her desertion had made him worse. Would he never be satisfied?

Two moons after the shortest day, the maple moon was full. It reflected brightly off the snow. The sap rose and the villagers went to their groves to harvest it. They boiled and stirred the sap in felled, hollow logs to condense it into sweet syrup. Besides flavoring, Saiyen-gu taught her if syrup was applied to a fresh wound, it did not fester.

The sun's path came further north each day. Snow melted and streams flowed again. First plants poked out of the earth, twigs budded and the robins returned. Saiyen-gu said it was time to go home.

They stopped beside a rushing stream to fill their pouches with young herbs and ferns. She broke off a group of knobbed onion stems and set them in her pack, keeping one to chew. When she knelt to fill their flasks, water bubbled around her fingers and tadpoles swam between them. Geese nested around the lakes, birds that had not been seen all winter flocked, and squirrels danced crazily in the trees.

The last village before they left Huron Country had been the first. It was Deganawida's. Thinker had grown. His dark eyes smiled them a silent welcome. His stammer always brought laughs. Jekonsaseh heard. *Five years until I'm a man. I will never come back.*

Don't forget to cure my Uncle Hiawatha, if you can.

Him first, Sister.

The new corn broke the surface of the village's corn hills. The squash leaves were small. Narrow bean stalks bunched around the corn, waiting to climb until they were higher. The villagers gathered under a wide sycamore to enjoy the warm breeze and talk before sleep. "Apprentice and I go home tomorrow," said Saiyen-gu. "We will make a ceremony for you first."

He asked for the children to prepare a fire but not light it. He struck the firestones himself. When it grew into flame, he filled his pipe, pulled out a flaming twig and lit his pipe. Like the Onondagas, Hurons did not inhale holy tobacco. They scattered it over fires to lift their prayers to heaven with the smoke.

Saiyen-gu said, "In thanks for your hospitality, we send up holy tobacco smoke to ask the Three Sisters to provide for you. Let the Creator send you a summer of peace and a good harvest." He exhaled smoke rings and invited Jekonsaseh to do the same. She thanked their hosts, but added her own silent words. *Send peace to my father.* The Huron thanked them with dried meat, maple sugar, and tobacco.

The sun winked a rainbow into existence to welcome them home to Niagara. Jekonsaseh entered their cave, sniffed and said, "I will tie back the curtain." She had grown used to speaking aloud. "A birch wood fire will sweeten the cave and then I'll make us something to eat."

Saiyen-gu had not been her only teacher. An old medicine woman taught her herbs and roots he would not know. They were used to ease menstrual pain or to strengthen the muscles of childbirth. She showed Jekonsaseh how to prepare the special tea. "You give it to the mother when the child fears to be born. The pushes become stronger. Also, when there is famine or war, it is not a good time to bring a baby into the world. Drink this early, and it pushes out the tadpole before it becomes a baby. You have come to us for three winters now and learned our speech. Tell me you understand what I say, Apprentice."

"I understand and I will remember."

One day after they had returned home, Saiyen-gu said, "Your *orenda* has grown within you." He looked at her with thoughts too deep to sound in her mind, but she knew he was already missing her. She had to keep her own people alive and hopeful. They agreed together not to use Deganawida's name, but to say a man would arrive from the north to bring peace to her war-torn people.

She prepared for her journey, wondering where she would go. Not home to her father's town in Onondaga. She might be a healer now, but she was not a warrior. She had sturdy moccasin boots and a coat with the fur on the inside. She would not be the ragged beggar who found her way to Niagara, but a medicine woman. She arranged with the children who visited for a fisherman from their village to bring her to the southern bank of Lake Huron.

On their last night, Jekonsaseh and Saiyen-gu sat on the ledge to watch the last rays of sunset color the few clouds reflect on the puddles like pink and orange flames. Early fireflies flitted around them like stars. Soon true stars filled the sky. "I see why you gaze at the sky," she said. "There are spirits in the air, more than I can count. Were there so many stars above your prairies?"

"Let me show you." He pictured high grass with few trees, and those bending and dipping into streams and rivers. He pictured prairie flowers in the grass, blue and pink, white and yellow. He pictured the herds of grazing antelope and buffalo, with their young, endless numbers of them. She saw sunsets and stars illuminating the grass with silver light. She saw the moon. It was the same one.

Saiyen-gu would never see his birth country again. She took his hand and raised it to her cheek. "Do you miss it?"

"I miss the prairies and being a father. Of all my children, only my last shared my dreams. His heart follows mine. His *orenda* is will be even stronger."

She had taught Deganawida her language, but he would never sway her people if he could not speak smoothly. "My people honor good speakers, but they will turn away from Thinker, as his own people do, if he stammers."

Saiyen-gu's expressive eyes glittered. "That is why he will cure your uncle first, to speak for him."

"If he can." Hiawatha had been a good speaker, but her father cursed him even before she ran away. His very existence must have changed him. Once he remembered the horror that had been done to him, and the atrocities he had committed, how could he be sane? The god-touched were treated kindly, but the cursed were another thing.

The dry fall of the settling embers was the only sound. The night was warm. The cave walls glowed slightly orange when Saiyen-gu asked, "Have you decided where you will go and how you will proceed?"

"I think so. I will feed and care for injured warriors after their battles. I will not ask their tribe but treat each man the same. I will impose peace on my home, wherever I erect it, as you do here. In thanks, I will request of those I help to bring me supplies. I will also tell them a man from the North will come to defeat the Snake Haired. A time must come when they will long for the old ways and peace."

"It is a good plan. I will miss you, Jekonsaseh. Come and lie beside me." He had never requested this, but she obeyed as always. He pulled her back against his chest and stroked her hair. "You won't be alone on your journey. Spirits and beasts will know you. Don't close your heart to humans either."

"I share my heart with you and Thinker," she reminded him.

"We share ours with you. Red Wing is your spirit grandmother now. She will tell me how you fare. Spirits travel on the wings of thought, but there may be a man who will touch your heart."

She took comfort in his nearness, doubting she would see him again after she went away. Her breath slowed and she slept. She dreamed of a battle. The warriors' pain and anger saddened and troubled her. With taunts and war whoops, they drove each other on to greater viciousness. She smelled sweat and blood, and more evil smells as bowels and bladders released in death.

Souls flew about her, pale as they ascended, their earthly emotions transmuted by death to wonder at their new estate and sadness for those left behind. The enemies looked up from their grisly work. Each man wore her father's face. Snakes writhed from their heads, tongues tasting the air for her scent. *He doesn't see you,* Saiyen-gu sent to her. *You are as the air and the trees to his eyes. He can't hurt you or punish you for running away. The Creator gives you this gift through me. Don't be afraid to use it.*

She relaxed and her sleep deepened. Saiyen-gu withdrew from her mind. It was time to let her go. She was like a young eagle, newly fledged, but ready to fly. Her people needed her far more than he did. He wondered how many summers would pass before he would see her again.

Jekonsaseh heard the fierce battle yells and shrieks near the narrow bank of a crooked river. She ducked low, trying to see without being seen. A nearly naked man with hideous war paint caught an arrow on his shield and rushed the defender with his tomahawk. In a moment, he had caved in his head with the heavy war club.

More arrows and more spears, used at close range, found their mark in hearts and throats. Men wrestled on bloody and slippery earth. War cries gave way to moans and screams as arrows and spears were pulled free. As the fighting moved downstream, impatient crows and buzzards left the trees before the bodies could be collected. They had waited long enough to enjoy their feast. Jekonsaseh wished she could block out her senses. Her father had caused this.

As the battle moved away, she thought if she could not stand to see, hear and smell the results of carnage, what was the point of her training? She walked through the field of battle, looking for the living. Some might be saved. Women and children crept up from the village to look for their men. "Who are you?" asked a wrinkled woman with white hair. She smelled of herbs.

"I have some healing skill. Let me help." Her offer was more important than her name and the healer did not press her for an answer. The old woman stopped and crouched beside a corpse. Blood poured from the dead man's mouth and his eyes stared at nothing. Flies had settled but flew off at their intrusion. "I'll carry him from the crows. See if you can find someone who might live." The old woman bent to the shattered shell of her child and gathered him in her arms.

Jekonsaseh dipped her flask in the stream several times. People asked her tribe and clan, but not her name. "Was your town destroyed? Did you lose your family?" She said yes, they were lost to her. "I have no one now."

"There are many like you."

She came upon a man with a shattered leg. "I will try to put the bones straight if you can bear it," she told the warrior. He nodded and gritted his teeth. She put a loose scrap of hide between his teeth, then moved the bones into place. She broke the twigs off a branch and used scraps from her pack to set his leg to heal straight. She had seen enough bones set badly.

"What is your Clan?" asked her patient. She told him. "You will sleep in our village tonight," he said. "My mother has food."

The day was closing, but a last knot of enemy fighters turned back. A tall man walked by some distance away. She was drawn to him, but she bent low. His hair was long, curved wands of matted hair. One of them moved, turning small black eyes on her. It tasted the air with its tongue. *Don't smell me*, she thought to the snake. *Don't see me*. She crouched lower. Her dream had come to life.

The woman beside her hissed low, "That is the Snake Haired, the wizard who follows the Younger Brother. Pray for an arrow to find him." Tododaho turned his head, sweeping the area with deep-set eyes. Jekonsaseh knew she should take this advice, but she could not manage to do so. *Do not see me, Jekonsaseh thought. I am the air and the trees.* Her father called to his warriors and they moved away.

Some of the survivors would never walk straight or set arrow to bow again. Eyes and hands were smashed, heads caved in by war clubs. The dead were lucky for they were beyond struggle. Jekonsaseh worked steadily and swiftly. The village had lost. Onondaga's war leaders informed them they now belonged to Younger Brother and his representative, Tododaho. "We will stay behind to explain our master's Law to you. If you vary from it, he will know." To her father's war captains, she was a village woman, bending over the sick.

Jekonsaseh helped bring the injured to their bed benches. She fed those who could use their arms. When the injured had been helped and fed, she called the clan matrons and their women to her. "I have been with Hidden in Mist," she said. They gave her their complete attention. "There will be an end to this war. A man from of the north is coming to vanquish the Snake Haired. The Snake Haired's power will end. The Peacemaker will lift the curse from Hiawatha the Cursed, to show the Tribes his power."

Her listeners took a better look at her. Several spoke at once. "Hidden in Mist said this? Who is this Man from the North? What does lifting the curse on the man-eater, the monster Hiawatha, have to do with us? Let him keep to the wilds, far from us and our children."

"Hiawatha was a good man. I knew him before he was driven mad." The looks cast her way became suspicious. "That is all I can tell you, but be prepared. I say this and my name is Jekonsaseh." She would do as she said, and aid all warriors after battles. She would not ask their Tribe or allegiance, but give them shelter, food and water, and tend to their injuries. Peace would dwell with her wherever she put up shelter.

"I dreamed of a woman like you," said a blind man. "Are you the Mother of Nations?" He had not lost his eyes in war, but cataracts veiled them.

"I am no one's mother," she replied, but if you dreamed this Mother of Nations would do these things, you may call me by that name.

"Let me touch her," he told his daughter. She led him to Jekonsaseh. He felt her face with his fingertips, her forehead, her nose and lips. He placed one hand over her heart. "I can feel her *orenda*," he said. "Young Mother of Nations, it is our honor to shelter you tonight as you will shelter our men."

"Jekonsaseh moved her fingers gently over the blind man's chest and face. "I will leave in the morning, but I will follow the battles. Tell warriors to look for me. The Good Mind is preparing the Peacemaker in a holy place." She touched the blind man's eyelids. "You will see him in your dreams. I cannot say when, but he will come to defeat our enemies. If you desire peace, be prepared to help him."

Chapter 9

Jekonsaseh's first two guests had injured each other earlier that same day, but they had already accepted drink and food from her when the Seneca warrior saw the Onondaga. They reached for their weapons. "In my house, there will be peace," she said sternly. Their tomahawks seemed suddenly too heavy to lift. "Sleep here tonight. Tomorrow, you can tell your clan mates when they come to my dwelling, they will find peace, food, water and protection. I accept food in payment, but also firewood and clean water, clothing and bandages."

"Our commander will have something to say about this," warned the Onondaga. "You may assist his followers, but not our enemies."

Jekonsaseh fixed them both with a mild gaze that nevertheless sent chills through them. "In my house, there are no enemies. Protecting the injured and hungry is a sacred trust. Come to me for protection and you will receive it. Look for me with thoughts to harm anyone and you will not find me."

Over the next years, many found her dwelling on the trail home, for she moved it according to the wars. They were treated and fed and sent home. People began to call her Mother of Nations because she treated each warrior with the same compassion. Families brought her food and water, splints and strips of leather for bandaging and binding on behalf of their men. When the war moved, she gathered her supplies, her barks, roots and herbs, tied the bundles to her travois, and moved with it.

She was scraping willow bark near a beaver pond when she heard a whimper above her in the tree. She tilted her head and peered into the branches. There was a child there, but not a human child. A half grown black bear clung to the trunk. It looked down pitifully and whimpered again. "Where is your mother?" she asked.

The cub continued to whine. Jekonsaseh looked into the cub's mind where she saw the picture of the mother bear slain and being dragged off hunters. Bear meat was a prize since so many of the herds had gone. What should she do about the cub? What could she do? She returned to the tree. The cub still clung to the branch, too fearful of humans to descend.

"Your mama can't come back," she said. She felt a kinship between them and exhaled sighed. Both of them had lost their mothers too soon. The bear's father was not about to rear it. "I'm of Bear Clan," she confided. "I can be your mother until you grow and can manage on your own. If you want to stay with me for a while, come down."

She sent a picture to the cub of them walking together. Could the cub receive her thought? It descended warily, watching the human's face and hands for danger. "Are you hungry?" Jekonsaseh asked. "I know where there is food." She pictured roots and berries, and acorns. The cub regarded her, sat to take thought, and then, extended a paw to scratch her hindquarters. It looked to her, lifting its nose as if to ask what to do next.

"I'll get my supplies and we'll go. Let us find us some roots and berries, and maybe a fish or two. If you decide to go your own way, I won't mind." She expected the bear to take her own path after a while, but it continued to follow her. "If you're going to stay with me, we'll have to find a place where hunters won't find you. I shall call you Lili." It meant little girl. The name would suit until the bear grew enough to leave her.

Lili filled herself with berries and tender shoots and drank at a stream. Jekonsaseh joined her and filled her flask, but when the bear pushed over a rock and ate her fill of grubs in her clawed forepaws, Jekonsaseh decided not to follow suit. She had done so once on her trek west. This time, she had beans and cornmeal in her pouch.

Jekonsaseh followed the stream eastward to see where it would take them. More streams fed into it, until the stream became a small river. By the third day, the river had grown too deep and wide to ford. This must be the Wide River. Small islands appeared in it, rocky and covered with trees. They stopped before one large enough to force the river to divide. The current became gentler with the lessening flow. At the furthest point of the island, the halves of the river rejoined in a splashing greeting and continued.

She walked back a little, looking for a good place to climb the granite island base when she spied a cove. "Let us stay there for a while," she said. "We'll find plenty of roots and berries, acorns and grubs. I can make lines and cordage so we can fish and trap birds. The trees are old. There will be windfall enough for my cook fires. I'll leave when the leaves begin to change. You'll be old enough to leave me then."

The bear watched her as it might watch its mother. She made a little raft with cords to lead it, then removed her dress and moccasins. She looked to Lili and descended into the water. The current was weak enough that she managed to land where she intended, at the cove so they would not have to climb up the island's lip. Lili paddled through the water, enjoying herself, and diving for fish.

Jekonsaseh dressed again and inspected the shore of her temporary home for foraging. Cattails and thick ferns swayed in the marshy bit of beach, and sassafras grew in thick clumps. She squeezed a leaf to savor its sweet scent. No one would see them through the thick foliage. She would find a place to set up her dwelling.

She explored their new home for a good place to set up her house. Bent and broken branches would do for the supports, scraps of bark and hide for the walls. It needed to be on a slight incline to drain away the water when it rained. When she was done, she found Lili lunching on reeds, sumac and young bark. Old oaks, elms and maples shadowed the center of the island. Her injured and hungry warriors would miss her, but she needed this time to restore herself. She set off again to gather windfall to make her fire to cook her first meal on the island.

Only a few days later, she was stretched out on the shelf to pull in her line. A fat salmon had caught itself on one of her lines. She was cleaning it when she heard an odd sound, something between a moan and a cry for help. A man! She tensed. Her island was between Longhouse and Algonquin country. Had there been fighting, she would have heard war whoops and seen birds circling. A helpless wail reached her ears. She moved back and peered through the leaves. "Man." she warned Lili. The black bear gave voice to her alarm. "I won't let him have you."

The harsh whisper came again. *He's afraid to call louder,* she thought. *He's afraid enemies are on the island.* Keeping behind trees, and stealthy as a doe mother with wolf scent on the air, Jekonsaseh watched the canoe float closer. The man was lying prone and attempting to paddle toward the bank with his hands.

"Is someone there? Help me," he said. He must have noticed her. If he had dropped his paddle, why not get into the water and tow his canoe in? The tie rope was still tied to the prow. Out of the current, the canoe floated more slowly. Jekonsaseh followed it, keeping in the shadows, but the man must have heard a twig snap under her foot. He rose to his knees and looked toward her.

His complexion was sun-brown, but of an odd hue. His face was neither Tribe nor Huron nor any Western people like Saiyen-gu's plainsmen. His braids were the color of autumn oak leaves. Tribal men had little facial hair until they grew old, and by then, it was white. She could not hold back a surprised gasp at his beard and mustache.

The canoe drifted to a pool where dead trees leaned over the water. A termite-ridden trunk had fallen in some years earlier. Clumps of moss clung down the dead branches that reached like claws to the slimy water. The pool might have been designed by the Younger Brother. The canoe rope snagged on a branch and stopped.

The man's eyes widened when he saw her plainly. He spoke, but she could not make out his words. He continued to eye her piteously. "Please help me. I can't swim," he said in proper Longhouse. His eyes were green like moss. Everything about him was foreign but his distress and need for help. Not bothering to lower her voice, she asked, "What is your tribe?" He did not reply. "What are you?"

"I'm a Greenlander. At least I was one. I don't have a tribe."

How could a man not have a tribe? She gestured. "The pool is shallow or the branches wouldn't show. Get out and walk to me."

Sharp ends poked up from the murky green water. He broke into a hesitant smile when his feet touched the muddy bottom. He stepped, slid on the algae and went down. He broke through the water coughing and dripping algae, and sucking in air. "A few more steps," she encouraged.

He was nearly to her when he took hold of the dead tree for balance. He winced and looked down. The jagged length of brownish pink root must have nicked him, she thought, until the root moved. The slim snake dropped into the water and disappeared. Blood trickled into the water and spread thinly over the surface. She had seen such water snakes. Any hesitation on her part would allow the venom to spread and work. Its bite was death.

She gripped his arms and dragged him onto her island. He fell, grabbing at his leg. "Bad snake," she informed him. His use of her language was limited and pain would make it worse.

"Yes." He was trying not to scream. She had to admire that. "Help me."

She yanked the leather tie from her hair and wrapped it around his lower leg above the bite. "Keep still!" She showed him her flint knife. "I have to cut you." She motioned what she had to do so the new pain would not take him by surprise.

He clenched his teeth. She made a shallow cross-slash above the puncture and bent over him to suck out the bad blood. She spit it aside and did it again. From the current carrying him to the swamp-like pool to the rotted tree branches and the snake, every sign pointed to the Younger Brother. Why would he trouble to try to kill a stranger unless he meant her not to meet him? Unless she saved him, she would never know. "I won't let you die," she said, as much to herself as to the stranger.

His leg still bled. She released the tourniquet and moved it higher to keep the remainder of the venom from his heart, and pressed her ear to his chest to listen. His heartbeat was rapid. Above the line of his leggings, even his legs were pale. Cautionary tales were told to children to keep them from entering the forest too young or alone. She recalled tales of stone men, child-eating monsters with hair of fire. The man's skin was pale, but soft, definitely not stone. His hair felt like hair with clinging algae.

He shivered. She left him to fill her flask with clear water. "Drink," she said when she returned. She held it to his lips." She used the rest to wash away the blood and got more water. When his wound was clean, she applied moss to draw out more of the venom, and loosened the tourniquet. She covered him. He would need warmth now. His face had paled even more and his breathing was rapid and shallow. "Who are you?" he asked faintly.

"Jekonsaseh, Bear Clan, Onondaga. Can you walk?" He tried, but his leg would not hold him. She gave him her arm and he leaned on her. "Who do I call you, man without a tribe?"

"Ole Halvardson." She wondered if it was a name or a title as her father was currently Snake Haired. "Will I live?" he asked.

"I don't know." He crumbled against a tree and his eyes closed.

He floated above his pain. On the inside of his eyelids, bright splashes of red and gold spun like wheels of light shot with sparks. Burning heat gave way to icy cold. A warm hand pressed his forehead. A clear, high voice penetrated his darkness, urging him to breathe, reminding him he was safe. It seemed he had traveled for so long, he had forgotten his destination. The ocean had heaved him up and cast him far from his homeland. Along the way, he had lost his father and his brother.

He floated back in time, seeing the fjords of Greenland, narrow elongations of the ocean that crept between cliffs like snakes. Cattle and goats grazed the lush grass. His people had been dairy farmers until the Sea Witch took it into her mind to expel them.

The District was in ruins. Even the two-storied, stone cathedral lay empty, where Christians, the majority of his people, begged their tortured god on their knees to intervene against the Sea Witch. No help came, only another enemy. The sun failed them and the people waited to die. The ship was full of Englishmen who expected to gather up whatever they could find of value. Instead, they met desperate resistance.

Families that lived on Greenland's west bank for generations sailed away. Some sailed east to an earlier homeland. Ole's family escaped in rowboats with the Inuit servants they had befriended. The refugees were accepted by the villages.

Ole Halvardson's fever dream showed him a time when the grass still grew high and the air was crisp. Like smoke in reverse, it pulled him down and inside his father's house. He saw himself kneeling beside his newly dead mother. The baby had died first and she bled to death. Father had drawn the blanket over her face. Ole yanked it away, releasing spills of his mother's bright red hair. Sweet, sick odors rose from the corpse. Her lips and lids were blue, and her face settled into the repose of death. He pressed his lips to the dead cheek.

"I lost my mother, too," said a woman's voice. The words were not Norse, but he understood them. "Your father wept. Mine did not."

Angrily, he retorted, "It didn't take him long to find another wife, a Skraeling. My brother hardly remembers our mother and the girl never knew her."

"What girl?"

"Ingrid. The Skraeling's daughter."

Saiyen-gu had taught her to enter distressed minds to soothe them, but her questions were making him worse. Heat rose from his skin. She saw a Tribe woman and a mixed-race girl with auburn hair. The father could be Ole in different clothing and older. Ole thrashed fitfully. "Get out," he cried.

"I am gone. Rest now," she commanded, and uneasily pulled her awareness away from his mind.

Warm wetness stroked his face and neck, like a sultry breeze off a summer lake. He felt protected as a cub in its den, sleeping safe within its mother's forepaws. The dreams ended and his sleep deepened. The rise and fall of his chest relieved Jekonsaseh when she returned. "Thank you for keeping watch, Lili," she said and gave the bear a fish. Lili held it close within her claws and peeled away the skin, gobbling down her treat before she shuffled away.

Jekonsaseh decided she would not move him yet. She made a fire and set the other fish by it to cook. That done, she sat beside her patient. Smooth as a soft breeze, she slipped back into his mind and saw his house. It had been built of stones. An old man with white hair, probably his grandfather, wore a long gray beard mixed with faded red. Outside the house, thickly-furred animals with horns grazed. "They are too small to be bison. You are not from Saiyen-gu's country," she said.

Her teacher never described people with red hair and white skin. Everyone knew the Great Turtle carried the world on her back. There must be other turtles on ocean and other worlds with different sorts of people and animals. Ole dreamed next of a craggy coast and choppy gray swells. Canoes with square sails tied to masts filled with wind skimmed the waves faster than a man could paddle. "Tell me what they are," she said.

"Rowboats. The seal hunt. My father went with them." Tears slid down his cheeks. Instead of giving him visions of peace, he was pulling her into his sadness. Young Ole climbed the hill behind his house. The grass smelled of clover and herbs. A stiff breeze dried salt tears on Ole's sun burnt cheeks. "You brought a Skraeling to take my mother's place? I hate you!" he had shouted at his father.

Jekonsaseh withdrew, alarmed and shamed and the damage she caused her patient. "You are safe now. Stop remembering bad things and sleep." Ole's hands unclenched. How had he come here, she wondered, and why?

Chapter 10

Ole Red Hair

Ole peered up the smoke hole, wondering whether the pink clouds presaged night or day. Birdsong and increasing light answered. He scratched his ankle and thigh, feeling the rough bandaging. The canoe he'd attempted to capture had captured him instead and brought him to an island. He'd wanted to surprise Ingrid and Runs Fast, their guide, with it, but when he'd scrambled in, his motion sent it back into the current. He searched for the missing paddle. The uncaring canoe had carried him back the way they had come, toward Algonquin country.

The Algonquin hated Norsemen. If Runs Fast had not gone back to rescue them, he would be dead and Ingrid a slave. He should have cried out, but Runs Fast warned them against shouting in the forest. Ingrid and he had learned a lot from their guide. Ole regretted wishing for a boat to hasten their journey. He had drifted farther and farther east, away from his sister and guide.

A drinking doe and her fawn lifted dripping faces and watched him float by. A curious lynx leapt onto a high branch and birds flew overhead from bank to bank, seeming to mock him. He had passed oaks, maples, sumacs and stands of crooked cattails. He could identify these trees now, in Runs Fast's tongue. Greenland had few trees, but stunted pines and willows near fresh water streams. One bent over and dipped slender branches into the river like fingers reaching for him. Near the island, he tried to steer the canoe with his hands. Perhaps, if the canoe brought him closer, he could walk or jump to land. Then, he saw the woman watching.

No doubt, he looked comical with his rump in the air, but she did not laugh. He sat back and begged her for help in Tribe language, hoping he had not drifted all the way back to Algonquin country. If so, she would take him for an enemy and call her men to slay him. At least Ingrid had protection. Runs Fast cared for her. He would get her to the safety of his community.

The canoe had entered a murky pool, snagged on something and stopped. In Tribal words, the woman told him to leave the canoe and walk to her. Holding the side, he climbed out of the canoe. His feet touched the muddy bottom, but he lost his footing. He righted himself and was nearly to land when the serpent had struck, dropped into the water and slithered away.

The woman pulled him in, showed him her knife, and said he would die unless she cut. Her blade stung, but her care seemed practiced and sure. Some venom must have entered his blood for he fell into old dreams. Green and blue lights curtained the night sky. The crumbling stone buildings were deserted. The ruined two-level cathedral stood caved in and empty. Like the carcass of a beached whale, it would leave its bones. Ole had promised to look after his half-sister. On a trade island with the dog she had saved, they met Runs Fast, a trader and guide. He had offered to guide them to his home.

The woman shook him and pointed to dangerous-looking clouds. The wind had turned brisk. It swept over the island and the river shivered. Thunder shook the ground. "A storm. We must leave the river. Come."

She handed him a branch with the twigs broken off to use for a crutch. He took it and rolled to his right, then levered himself onto his good leg and pushed up. He felt dizzy and disoriented. What was the woman's name?

"Jekonsaseh," she said. He was sure he had not spoken. Storm clouds blacked out the sky and wind rattled the trees. A flash of lightning lit the sky followed by a thunderclap and fat raindrops. It would be harder to walk in mud. "We go to my house," she said. "Safe from Heno, Thunder Spirit."

The small house was low and round, hides tied over the frame. Charged air lifted the hairs on Ole's arms and legs. They crossed a narrow drainage ditch, already streaming, and ducked inside. Jekonsaseh pointed to a platform of fir boughs covered with hides. He sank onto the fragrant mattress.

She stirred the banked embers to wake up her fire and fed tinder it. Rain dripped from the smoke hole into a baked clay bowl. She poured the rain water into the bowl she had keeping warm on her hearth stone and sprinkled cattail root and herbs into it. While the vegetables cooked, she laid her fish over her hearth stones. He had to admire how quick and efficiently she worked.

While they ate, she crossed her ankles and indicated his beard and red hair. "Are there others like you?"

"Just my sister, Ingrid. She and my friend will not know where to find me. Are you alone on this island? Where is your village?"

"No village. Only me and Lili, my bear." He gave her the disbelieving stare her Otter grandmother and aunts directed at her when she spoke to her mother's ghost. "Lili watched over you when I went for provisions," she said resentfully. She rose in one easy motion and ducked out into the dark under the dripping trees.

Witches kept familiar beasts. Ole recalled an Inuit tale about a woman who adopted a bear after her son died. She called it by her son's name, but it was still a bear. It grew up and ate her. He concluded that he must leave this island and its witch as soon as possible. If he followed the Wide River west, he might find Ingrid and Runs Fast, but how was he to get off the island? With his red beard and pale skin, he must look inhuman. He was lucky the woman had helped him.

With his crutch, he ducked outside. The storm had intensified the smells of river, plants and the woods. Worms slithered on leaves, having left their flooded underground homes. The sun glittered on the river and a rainbow hung over it. Jekonsaseh should be glad to see the last of him. He had experienced supernatural beings in his journey, from the Inuit god, Sea Woman, to their Angakkoq priest who sent his spirit to visit her. If Jekonsaseh was a witch, at least she meant him well. After a night's rest, he should be recovered enough to try to find his friends. He would thank Jekonsaseh, rescue his canoe and go, but this time he would make an oar out of his crutch to be sure to go in the right direction. He returned to the shelter and fell asleep

Ole did not feel the furs shift when Jekonsaseh burrowed under them with him and snuggled close against his back. She caressed his cheeks and neck, his shoulders, torso and legs. "Be at peace," she murmured. His aura altered from the orange of confusion and agitation to the blue-green of healing and calm.

But you suffer, too. Jekonsaseh wondered who said that, Saiyen-gu or Red Wing, or was she speaking to herself? For more than five years, she had fed and cared for warriors in need. If her little brother did not come soon, he might as well not come at all. The herds were mostly gone. Hunters went farther and farther into the forest because the crops suffered. She had retreated to this island. Lili was her excuse, but she had promised to be there for wounded warriors.

She slipped into her own memories of her mother's desertion, of the Otter grandmother who exiled her. Her father had defended her. Now she had to hope her adopted brother could defeat him. One of them might die. She buried her face in her mantle to cover her sobs.

Ole found himself stirred to wakefulness by her whimpers. His eyes, still creased with sleep, opened. "Jekonsaseh! What? Why?" She was in his bed, weeping softly. Her shoulders trembled. "Why are you here?"

"Did my father send you to me to disturb my peace?" she asked.

"No one sent me. I was trying to go the other way."

Jekonsaseh turned over and leaned up to see him. They were nearly touching, but both held back, wary. "Your mother left you when you were small, like mine left me."

"How do you know that? I never meant to come to you. I should not be here. Let me go." He had intruded on her solitude. His presence was a torment to her. She did not want him here, but he was still weak. He fingered her cape, made of many small pelts stitched together like the patchwork quilt his grandmother made for him long ago and far away. "What kind of hide is this?" he asked, as if it mattered.

"Squirrel. A warrior's wife gave it to me in return for healing her husband. You confuse me, Ole Halvardson. You make me remember too much. You make me sad."

"I do not wish to make you sad. I should go. Which way is my canoe?"

"I will bring you to it when you are strong, maybe tomorrow." She turned her back on him, but made no move to get out from under his blanket. He felt her warmth. It was a pleasant thing to be warm. He wanted to touch her, but he turned away and shut his eyes, willing himself to rest and heal.

In the morning, she told him to stand and try to walk outside the shelter. He levered himself up with his crutch, ducked outside and took a few steps. His dizziness returned. "Not yet. Go inside and lie down so I can clean your wound."

The swelling had gone down, but his uncovered raw skin was pink. She washed it gently with cool water and patted it dry. "Eat and rest and try again later." Her voice was flat, like a healer, but not one who had shared her warmth under the blanket. "Even if my father did not send you, I want you gone."

"I will be glad to go."

They were agreed on that, but her voice changed when she asked, "Who taught you your magic?"

"Taught me my what?"

She put it in other words. "To use your *orenda* like that." He had forced her from his soothing his troubled mind and into her own worst memories. She felt his fear. "How can you be afraid of me? You must be a sorcerer. Stop making me remember Hiawatha and Ogan-nis'tah and my father, and the day my mother died. I can't do anything for them." She trembled.

He did not know who or what she was talking about. He made no conscious decision to do so, but she was like a lost child. He could not help wanting to hold her. She cried against his chest, smelling from the forest and hickory smoke. He brushed his fingers through her hair and spread his fingers against her scalp.

It was how Saiyen-gu had held her the last night she slept beside him behind Niagara. She stiffened suddenly, in realization. Her beloved teacher must have sent him to her, but Ole didn't know. When she tried to touch him, he backed away as far as he could on the bed platform.

Ole misinterpreted her reaction. He had never been with a woman like this. She could not want what he wanted. "I am afraid I will do something you do not want."

Her face contorted with fury. "Don't do this to me," she cried. "You make me want to be near you and you back away." Not until she scratched him, did he take her hands and hold them to her sides. He barely felt the sting, overwhelmed as he was by her outburst. She collapsed back, not touching him. He let go of her wrists.

"I did not mean to do that," she said, troubled by the blood on his cheek. "You are safer away from me. I'll help you find your sister and your friend tomorrow."

He wished he could speak her language with greater skill. He wanted to explain that although he had no intention of harming her, he had never been so tempted.

She traced the blood on his cheek. "I will clean it. Be still."

Instead of rising and wetting a scrap of hide, she leaned close and licked the blood away. Her tongue and touch as she cleaned his cheek brought delightful tingles to his skin and to other places. He reminded himself Jekonsaseh was a witch who lived with a bear, but she was also the protector of injured warriors. In the turmoil and bleakness of his life, he had never before found the time to know a woman. Each day of his life had been a fight for survival. Anger had sustained him since his mother's death. He knew no soft emotions. He wanted what his body craved, but how could he give in and take what he wanted without harming or angering this strange woman?

He touched his lips to hers. He had never kissed before. It seemed a new thing to her, too. He traced her lips with his tongue, inviting her participation. She responded, as unsure as he, where they were going. Warmth spread pleasurably from her lips and her hands. No one had ever touched him there, or like that.

"Is it new to you to be with a woman?" she asked.

"It is. Do you want to stop?" She pulled him closer. He discarded his breech-clout. She dispensed with her dress and reached for him. They discovered what was needed and learned together until there was no space between them. He drew in small breaths. She made a sound. He stopped, for no one had told him what to expect. "Did I hurt you?"

"It is nothing."

Ole's breath quickened. Bolts of pleasure so intense shot through him. He felt like a cloud tingling with lightning. He was the sky and she was earth. When release came, he shuddered and cried out. For a time, it seemed he floated, and that some part of their souls would never be separated again. She licked his lips, light touches now, to remember how his mouth tasted. When she moved back, the dim light showed the curve of her body like two hills. He pushed her hair back from her face so he could see her eyes.

Back to himself, he questioned his situation. He needed to find his sister and friend. Jekonsaseh watched him thoughtfully, curiously. "Do you still want me to go?" he asked, wondering if anything essential had changed between them.

"It would be best. I have work to do. While you rest, I will see if I can find signs of your friends. You want to find them, yes?"

"Of course I do." Their passion had been like the summer storm, brilliant and deafening, but gone. Jekonsaseh slipped on her dress, covered Ole with her squirrel pelt mantle and ducked out of the wigwam.

Chapter 11

Unable to sleep, Ole inspected the mantle. It was a work of art, red pelts next to brown and gray in a geometric design. Stitches zigzagged between the seams. Jekonsaseh would not make something like this. Her house was sturdy and cozy, but nothing about it could be considered artful. She was unlike other women. After such intimacy, a Greenlander woman would not be in a hurry to send him away. She'd expect marriage. Was this world so very different, or was it only Jekonsaseh?

His father's wife came from this world. She had been brave and resourceful and protected her children with her life, but she was nothing like this island witch who kept a bear for company. She had made him no promise, nor had she asked for one. So why did he feel betrayed?

He found his steel knife under her bedding. She said she meant to return it, but her cool manner after their intimacy twisted painfully. He considered being quit of his debt honorably by leaving it for her, except that he needed it. He slipped the thong over his head and tucked the knife in its sheath inside his shirt. Finally, he pulled on his moccasins and, leaning on his crutch, ducked out of the shelter.

A deer fly buzzed near his ear. Surprising himself, he dropped his crutch and caught it. Jekonsaseh was nowhere in sight. Ole made up his mind to go while the light held and set off into the forest to find his canoe.

Jekonsaseh walked some distance before she looked back. Her house was just visible between the trees if one knew where to look. She dabbed at her eyes and cheeks and licked salty tears from the side of her hand. If the stranger guessed how much he had affected her, he would think her weak. No one had held and comforted her since she had left Saiyen-gu in Niagara.

She sniffed at the air and listened. Hearing nothing, she whistled for Lili. The bear ambled over, swung her muzzle a few times, sniffed to pinpoint Jekonsaseh, and let out a questioning grunt. "Here I am." She held out a hand for Lili to smell. The bear stuck out her curled tongue to wet her nose, tasted the air and exposed her fangs.

"That is Ole you smell. He will go away soon and leave us in peace." The bear grunted again, doubtful. "When you find your first mate, you'll understand. We need males sometimes, but it is best to have them depart quickly or they kill your cubs."

Lili stood on her back legs and growled. She sniffed again, closer to Jekonsaseh's hair. When the woman's smell covered Ole's, the bear relaxed. Sitting, she was nearly as tall as the human. "That's right, Lili. You know me." The bear's odor was strong, making Jekonsaseh wonder what she had been rolling in. "Come. Swim with me," she invited. She looked over her shoulder, encouraging the bear to follow. "Ole said he was on the south bank when he found the canoe."

They came to a sandy cove where the riverbank descended gradually into the river. After Ole's mishap, she checked to be sure the branches were free of snakes. She hung her dress over a low branch, and entered the water. She paddled a few strokes and whistled her 'come to me' whistle. Lili jumped off the bank with a splash. They had swum together before. This time, the bear surged ahead. Jekonsaseh wanted her well able to fend for herself before she sent her away.

Jekonsaseh made sure no one was in sight before she left the water, brushed off the drops and wrung out her hair. She walked upstream, taking in every detail. When she stopped, Lili bent to snack on watercress and pull up roots. She chewed slowly, looking westward and sniffing out a certain bush, one of her favorites.

"Raspberries. Good." Jekonsaseh copied Lili, eating cress, and raspberries. The bear set to ripping off the red globes. Jekonsaseh regretted leaving her gathering pouch behind, but she had more to do. She was looking for something in particular. There were many broken branches, but no sign of humans. Lili returned to her side, sniffing the air. If Ole's friends had made a fire, there would be the soapy smell of damp ashes and fat near where Ole found the abandoned canoe.

She heightened her senses, aware of every animal that left scat or nibbled a fern along the shore. "Were men here, Lili?" she asked but she doubted the bear would remember that particular smell. "Was there a campfire?"

Lili sniffed again and set off. While they searched, the shadows shifted from west to east. Bars of late sunlight fell through the trees. Lili came to the remains of a campfire and waited for Jekonsaseh to join her. "Good girl! Now, the river bank."

She found several heavy indentations in the sandy gravel below the scarp. Two heel prints were smaller and lighter. They might belong to Ole's sister, or a boy might be hunting with a man. The canoe might have been theirs. Cord was caught around a white birch, slivers of curled shell tied on at intervals. "Ole's line," she whispered, as if speaking louder would remove her clue. What was left of the indentations disappeared at the water's edge.

Searching for further signs, Jekonsaseh brushed against a small plant with deep green, saw-tooth leaves. She reached for the woman's root plant and worried the plant out of the earth, root and all. It made medicine to help a laboring woman. The Huron women taught her there when it is not right to begin a new life. She had been so intent on getting Ole where he belonged, she nearly forgot. She knew what might result from what they had done, but her life had no room for obligations.

Dried, pounded and seeped was best, but there was no time. This soon, the leaves should be enough. She had just closed her mouth around a few of them when Lili reached in front of her to pull up more of the plant. Jekonsaseh was Lili's example, as its mother should have been. If Lili found woman's root leaves good to eat, it might work on her as it worked on humans. The bear would never conceive! She spit out the leaves. "Bad!" she said aloud. "Bad. Drop it."

Lili dropped the plant, and spit out what she had begun to eat. Jekonsaseh continued to spit and make sounds of displeasure until there was none left in her mouth. She wiped the remainder off her lips and kicked dead leaves over what she had spit out.

She lifted her eyes to the clouds. "You know I have no time for a baby. There is war. I must get back my warriors." For the second time in one day, tears gathered in her eyes. "Come on, Lili. Keep close." The bear grunted and followed her.

The recent rain had eroded most human prints, but she found new ones in the mud. Ole's sister and guide probably came this way looking for him before they gave up and turned back. That would have been four days ago. Where were they now?

Lili growled a warning, sniffed the air and showed her fangs. "What is it?" she whispered, crouching low. The yearling bear could protect Jekonsaseh against cougars and wolves, but when men were about, no one was safe. There was a flash of movement. Lili rose up and issued a roar. A scampering of feet crashed through the low growth. Would the next moment bring arrows?

Reaching out with her *orenda*, she heard the frightened pounding of two human hearts. She whistled for Lili to get down. She made too great a target. The bear dropped, but the humans had already seen it. "Who is there?" she demanded. "Come out where I can see you."

"I tell you the bear talks," said a youthful voice. Trees hid them from each other. "Bears only talk except in stories," said a second boy. "I don't care what Uncle says; we shouldn't have come so far downriver. Remember Hiawatha who eats human flesh? There are monsters in the forest. No canoe is worth being eaten."

Jekonsaseh heard her uncle's name with sadness, but took a relieved breath. "Lay down your bows," she ordered. The boys did as she said, still whispering about talking bears. She could not keep them fooled once they saw the bear and her together. "What are you doing in my forest?" she asked, speaking low.

One of the boys rose for a better look. She saw him, but he did not see her because his attention was fast on Lili. "We are brothers. I'm the elder. Our uncle let us take his canoe fishing, but we were not careful. It turned over and spilled us out. We got it upright again, but it moved away. See? All we have left is the paddle." He pulled it from the quiver on his shoulder to show her. "Uncle said we were not to come home without it. We've been searching three days and we're nearly to Algonquin County. We don't dare go further and we don't know what to do. Have you seen a canoe?"

"What a fool you are," said the younger brother. "Do you think a bear knows what a canoe is, or cares about our problems?"

"It's not a real bear, I tell you. It's a woman's spirit inside a bear. We better not make it angry."

Jekonsaseh tugged Lili behind her. Then, she stood and met the boys' gaze. Their eyes opened wide. It seemed the bear had become a naked woman. "I will help you find your canoe if you do me a favor," she said. "I will tell you about the favor later. Do you accept?"

They leaned in to confer. Jekonsaseh had learned to read lips long ago, with Hidden in Mist. It had helped before she mastered mind listening. "If we don't, she'll kill us," said the taller boy.

"But what could a bear woman want for a favor?" said the younger. "Maybe she wants a mate and she'll turn one of us into a bear. Maybe we should run and take our chances." Jekonsaseh suppressed a smile.

"She'd catch us and kill us both. Let's see what she asks for." The taller boy spoke. "Since we don't dare go home without the canoe, we accept your terms, as long as you don't come too close. I'm Beaver Tooth. My brother is Fisher."

Jekonsaseh signaled Lili to stay put and approached the boys. "My name is Jekonsaseh. I have been helping a wounded man and I require your help."

Fisher found his voice first. "Are you the same Jekonsaseh people call Mother of Nations?"

"I am. Since you know of me, you know no harm will come to you if you do as I direct. I will show you to your canoe and you will use it to help my warrior find his home." She turned from the boys. "We are going now, Lili."

The youths blinked as they realized the truth. The beast had not become the woman; there were two of them. In their fear, they had become like gullible children. Even for a childhood story, this was remarkable. The Mother of Nations kept a bear for her companion. Beaver Tooth said, "We will do as you say."

"Pick up your bows then, and walk before us." She pointed the way. "I'll walk behind." She did so, keeping one hand on Lili's shaggy scruff. As they walked, Jekonsaseh asked, "Where do you live? Also, what is the war news?"

Beaver Tooth turned back to Jekonsaseh and the bear. "We live in the town of Doteoga at the south elbow of Wide River. Two of the clans are at war in Oneida, but fewer went this year. The matrons are worried we might not have enough hunters by winter. Our father died last year and our uncle can no longer draw a bow."

"You belong to Tribe Ganeo-gaono. Don't you want become warriors?"

"We are training. If the fighting comes east, we'll fight," Fisher replied.

"I can't find fault with that," Jekonsaseh admitted. If nothing prevented it, the war would spread east. "What about you, Beaver Tooth? What do you think about Tododaho's war?"

"I don't like it. If it goes on much longer, no one will be left. No more Onondaga. No more Ganeo-gaono. The animals headed north of the lakes, away from Longhouse Tribes. If the river doesn't provide fish, it will be the end of us."

"I hear the Three Sisters are angry and the corn suffers," Jekonsaseh said.

"That is true." She could see the brothers had reached the same conclusion she had.

Beaver Tooth said, "If it is not impolite, Mother of Nations, what is your tribe?" They had begun walking again.

She turned back. "Onondaga."

Their faces fell. "Then you are our enemy."

"I am no warrior's enemy," she said. "I ask treat all injured men the same. Listen." They halted. "Have either of you seen or heard of a man and woman traveling west? The man is of your tribe, but he has been away. The woman is mixed breed with light skin and sunset hair. My warrior is her brother. They became separated when a canoe with no paddle drifted past him. It carried him to me."

Fisher touched his brother's arm. "We know nothing about these travelers but where is the canoe?"

"You will see." She planned to bring them to her house first to check on Ole and then lead them to the stagnant pool where she last saw the canoe. They could take Ole to Doteoga if they could release it from the roots and into the river. They must also avoid snakes. Ole would be glad to find his sister and their friend and she could go back to helping the wounded and preparing the people for Deganawida.

She looked at Lili who was nearly grown. It was time to send her away to begin her solitary life, as bears must until they mated and produced cubs. Jekonsaseh's respite was about to end. She could no longer live on an island with a bear.

Deganawida was still young. He would have sixteen summers, she guessed, but he would be judged man enough to set out on his own. It was pointless to speculate on his arrival and how he would begin his undertaking. Once Ole was safe, the foreigner would no longer be her concern. She would ride with the boys and Ole to Doteoga and tell them to expect the Peacemaker who would come to end their war.

"Stop here," she directed. "This is where we will swim to my island. You will meet my warrior and, tomorrow, I'll bring you to your uncle's canoe."

Chapter 12

Fisher and Beaver Tooth held their quivers and arrows dry, paddling to her island with one arm. They climbed onto the island were drying their arms and legs when Lili shook herself and they had to start over. Jekonsaseh squeezed out her hair as best she could and dried herself. She dressed and told Lili to find food. The bear set off to forage for herself. Jekonsaseh told Beaver Tooth and Fisher to wait while she informed Ole that they had visitors.

"I'm back," she said, crawling in. A shaft of dusty sunlight slanted into the deserted interior. She left the house and crouched to look for his footprints. There were several, but they were swallowed in the brush.

"Beaver Tooth, Fisher!" The boys came up to her. "My warrior has gone out. His name is Ole Halvardon." They repeated the foreign name. "I know it does not sound like a name, but he comes from a distant country on the other side of the ocean." The boys attempted to not look incredulous. Mother of Nations was not known for joking. "When you meet him, you will find he is as odd as his name. He was bound for Doteoga before your canoe carried him to my Island and its rope snagged. When he climbed out, a snake bit him. He is mostly healed now."

"What is his tribe?" asked Fisher.

"Greenlander. He says he can't go home. He wants to join his sister and friend. He might be trying to free your canoe now. Follow me."

"He can't have it. It's our uncle's!" said Beaver Tooth angrily.

A roar erupted from the bushes at Beaver Tooth's exclamation. Lili rose to her hind legs and searched for the danger to her mother. She turned in their direction, showing fangs. "Lili. I am safe. Get down. Go find Ole." Calmed, the yearling sniffed the air. Satisfied she did not need to kill the new humans, she padded off.

Ole had been unable to find the murky pool. The trees were too thick. The river seemed to be carrying the island as it had carried his canoe. His leg ached, he had been up too long and it was still weak. He had been a fool to try to leave the island without telling Jekonsaseh goodbye. Where was she now? He should go back to her shelter, if he could find it again. She had made it clear she was obligated to help him, but he should leave as soon as he could manage. She did not really want him.

He turned swiftly at the crackle of a trod leaf, nearly lost his balance and grabbed a branch to keep from falling. It scratched his arm. He shut his mouth on the sting. A black bear came into view. He hoped it was Lili because if it was another, he had only his knife against claws, teeth and muscle. The animal turned to Jekonsaseh and grunted. "Good Lili. You found him. Thank you. Go finish your supper. Lili lumbered away and in another moment, had disappeared into the woods.

Ole felt like a disobedient child. He would not be dead in moments, but he had now to face his savior's displeasure. He wondered briefly if he'd have preferred an unknown bear. Jekonsaseh's squirrel cape reminded him of their passion. Their closeness must have been a fleeting weakness on her part, for only a few moments later, she reminded him that he must go. He would be wise to do so. There was little doubt that she had bewitched him.

He braced himself for sharp words when he noticed the boys. One was about fourteen; the other a few years younger. They whispered and pointed. It would be too much if Jekonsaseh rebuked him now. It seemed she would not, but the reproach in her eyes said enough. "Are you recovered, since you left my protection?" she asked.

"I'm well enough," he replied, gruffly.

"Are you well enough to protect yourself from a bear who is not Lili?" She was within her rights to speak to him like this. Embarrassment suffused his cheeks.

"No," he replied, "but I have taken too much of your time. I hoped to free my canoe and find my sister and friend."

"It is not your canoe," growled Beaver Tooth. "It is ours." Jekonsaseh beckoned them forward. Ole's cheeks flushed. Jekonsaseh had humiliated him again, and he just discovered that he was a thief.

It seemed pointless to argue, but he said, "The canoe was empty when I found it. Jekonsaseh, let me go. I regret my mistakes."

She beckoned the boys. They approached cautiously, not knowing what to expect from the pale stranger who fingered the knife hanging above his shirt. Beaver Tooth touched the hilt of his. The stranger was built more strongly, but he was recovering from snake bite. "You are on my land," Jekonsaseh said sharply. "I forbid fighting." Ole and the brothers dropped their hands.

"These are Beaver Tooth and Fisher, men of Ganeo-gaono Tribe. This is Ole Halvardson of Greenlander Tribe."

"Ole Halvardson," Beaver Tooth repeated, struggling with the name. "The canoe belongs to our uncle." He drew himself up and tried to look older, but his voice cracked a bit. "He sent us after it."

"We will help them retrieve it," Jekonsaseh said. "For our help, they will take us to Dotegoa. These young men will give their uncle his canoe. Ole will find his friends and I will learn about the war. We will try for the canoe in the morning when the day is new. The reflections are wrong now to see the snakes."

They agreed to her plan and the imposed truce. "How did your boat get away from you?" Ole asked them.

Beaver Tooth replied. "It was my fault. I overbalanced pulling in my net and it rolled. We fell out. The side was too slick and we could not hold on. All we have left is the paddle."

"A paddle and canoe should be together," said Ole.

Pale lashes and brows like caterpillars framed his eyes. Hair grew on his lower face. His skin was too pale and mottled, yet if one did not look, he spoke like a man. Beaver Tooth asked, "Where do Greenlanders live?"

"Nowhere now. I am the last of us." He was quite serious. "What will you do if we can't release the canoe?"

"Go home without it, but Uncle will treat us like children." Ole nodded. A boy wants to be a man.

Jekonsaseh led, but looked back to see how they were getting on. Ole took the opportunity to say, "Mother of Nations. I did not mean to anger you. I thought you wanted me to go."

Her mouth softened. "I do, once you are well." For a moment, she resembled the woman who had held him in the night and let him feel her sorrow and worry. He would not misunderstand her again. Jekonsaseh lived by her own rules.

They returned to the shelter. Jekonsaseh laid out a stone circle before it and built up a fire. She poured water into her stew pot and left it to come to a simmer. "I'm going to check my lines and traps," she said. "Ole, rest. Men, you can begin making your rope while there is still light."

Fisher and Beaver Tooth found a basswood tree and cut out the soft strands of inner bark. They brought it back to work on it. Ole pulled out his knife to remove more mast from the bark. "Your blade is loose in its hilt," said Beaver Tooth. "If you'd like, we'll bind it." Ole handed it over.

Once they wrapped the shaft connection to the blade, it felt firmer in his grip. He slipped back over his head.

"What sort of knife is that?" asked Fisher. "I never saw such a stone."

"The grip is ivory. The blade is Spanish steel." His knife had caused envy and trouble before. He hoped it would not do so again.

Jekonsaseh returned and got busy. While the fish baked on the hearth stones, she sprinkled corn meal into the water. She had also taken a pair of wood rats from her traps. She cleaned these and skewered them to roast.

They ate as dusk descended. The brothers kept up a light conversation until they were ready to wash away the grease. Jekonsaseh pointed out a good place for them to build a lean-to while she smothered the fire. Ole wondered if he ought to sleep beside the boys, when Jekonsaseh said his name. She must want to speak with him privately.

In the small shelter, it was impossible not to breathe in the scent of her skin, pine wood, smoke and sweat. Her healing herbs clung to the air and her mantle. "You are not like Longhouse men," Jekonsaseh said. "Your *orenda* feels different."

"I don't know the word," he admitted. From context, it seemed *orenda* meant a mystic kind of power. It did not equate to anything in Norse.

Moonlight through the leaves patterned her face as she regarded him solemnly. "It makes you who you are. It lives behind your eyes, but it sees things that you can't. When an *orenda* is strong, it can protect you or make things happen."

He shook his head. Christian priests spoke of souls, but they were foreign to him as well. He preferred his grandfather's gods, Odin and Thor and the rest. They were sensible. Besides, he had no time for mystic powers. "What do you mean?"

"You are eager to leave my care. Other men prefer to stay longer."

"You wanted me to go. When I can, I will bring you a gift for healing me, like the warrior's wife sent you the cape." She did not reply. She might want his knife. Everyone did. He fingered it, thinking he did not like to part with it. The knife was the only thing he had of value, and his only weapon. He needed it. "My father gave it to me to protect my sister. Please do not ask for it."

Her voice came from the dark. "Did I say I want your knife?"

"Then, what do you want?" He returned his knife to its place.

"I want to know why the river brought you to me and why the snake tried to kill you. Someone did not want us to meet."

He took a breath and blew it out. He agreed there was something suspicious about the canoe and the snake. "I would like to know that too." He leaned back and crossed his arms. When he lowered his hands, she took one and pulled him to her. She accused him of being different when she was as different as night and day.

"You have to go," she said. He thought he heard regret, but her words were a new acquisition, gained during a year in Runs Fast's company. He could not be sure of a speaker's nuances. Her breath warmed his cheek. She was like a lodestone, drawing him to her. He pressed his lips to her neck.

She clung to him and her tears wet his cheek. He wanted to protect her from sorrow and loss, but any words he used would be presumptuous. Rather than speak, he used his hands and body and lips to express his feelings. Their souls were connected. Although neither knew it, they could not feel complete when they were apart. Before long, they were looking for better ways to satisfy their mutual longing. Passion carried them back to that realm of delight Ole had not imagined until last night, and had not expected to experience again.

Chapter 13

They had turned from each other. In sleep, Jekonsaseh's back pressed warmly against his. It might have been the hoot of an owl that pushed him over the edge of consciousness, or a full bladder. Ole eased out from between the furs and the mantle and took up his crutch. He needed to assure himself that there had been no threat.

The boys still slept in the lean-to. The trees were still black against the lower forest growth. He reached the ledge and looked over the river. It was a liquid path reflecting the ribbon of stars above it. Frogs and crickets chirped to each other. There was no smell of dawn, but the constellations showed it was past midnight.

Ole breathed in the muggy odors of night, forest and river. A sultry breeze trembled through the delicate birch leaves and the supple willow branches that trailed into the creek. It rattled the cattails and make ripples dance on the water. A bat swooped nearby. Ole emptied his bladder, retied his breech clout and stood quiet, listening to the sounds of the night and watching the river. A fish arced through the water, white bubbles following. A bullfrog croaked and leapt away. Moonlight flashed from the pale underside of a silent owl wing. He wondered if it was after the frog and if the frog escaped.

He walked along the bank. Something felt wrong and communicated itself to him. Perhaps it was his *orenda,* warning him of something out of place. He attempted to focus. It was not a reflection of the moon on the river, but the yellow glow of fire. This was a no man's land, a section between the Tribes and the Algonquin. Neither side crossed it without purpose, yet someone had. What did it mean?

Ole returned to Jekonsaseh's shelter, touched her shoulder gently and spoke her name. She turned, a smile beginning, when he said, "I saw fire across the river."

The smile disappeared. She sat up and her eyes creased. She rubbed the sleep out of them. "Fire? The forest is burning?"

"Not the forest. A campfire near the south bank."

Jekonsaseh rose smoothly, unashamed of her nakedness, like a graceful animal or a spirit of nature. She pulled on her dress. "Show me." If the boys heard or saw them pass their lean-to, they ignored it. The Mother of Nations and her warrior's business was none of theirs.

Ole had learned to walk as silently as his teacher, Runs Fast. Jekonsaseh caught his wrist. "We don't know if they are Ganeo-gaono or Algonquin. Perhaps they are spies, or perhaps the boys' uncle sent someone to find his nephews. Try for the canoe at first light. You know the way now. Look for the notched maple opposite the pool on the bank. I will visit the camp and learn if they are a danger to us. We may want to leave quickly."

"Can you speak Algonquin?"

"I lived in Huron villages. They are as close to Algonquin as Longhouse Tribes are to one another. I'll learn why they are here, but they won't see me."

The hairs on Ole's arms stood. Perhaps Longhouse people accepted witches and he was the odd one. In any case, he had already fallen victim to her spell. "Be careful."

"Of course. Wear your cap and tuck in your braids. The strangers may decide to come to my island. I will be uneasy until you and the boys have regained the canoe and we are away. Watch for me."

"Can't you prevent them from coming here?"

Her eyes narrowed. *What do you think I'm capable of?* Had he heard her voice or imagined it? Aloud, she said, "Get the canoe out of the pool and hide it out of sight. Then wait for me." She made barely a sound when she walked off. Soon the darkness under the trees hid her from sight. Ole heard a small splash.

He returned to the house, crept inside and crawled between the furs. Resting his head on his interlaced fingers, he looked up. The sky was graying to dawn and the stars winking out as Ole gave in to sleep.

Jekonsaseh approached the solitary man. Hunters and warriors seldom traveled alone. The sleeper moved restlessly. He might be Algonquin sent to spy on and report the number of Doteoga's defenders.

Early in the war, Algonquin raiders had attacked the town. Its warriors had just returned after an early snow and repelled them. A girl in a tree saw the war party and sent her companions home to warn the defenders. The attack was thwarted but the girl had been caught.

Jekonsaseh kept very still. *Red Wing*, she thought. *Hidden in Mist said you watch me. Please deepen the stranger's sleep so I can ask his intentions.* She seldom asked Red Wing for favors, but she had men she needed to protect. Ghosts were strongest at night when they could visit dreamers.

The man rolled onto his back. His open vest exposed his throat and chest. His right hand gripped his knife, but it slipped to the ground as his anxiety lessened and he sank into peaceful slumber. Jekonsaseh thanked Red Wing's ghost and crept nearer. "Why are you here?" she asked in Longhouse. She hoped she had guessed right and that he was Ganeo-gaono. If not, she would try again in Algonquin.

"I seek someone."

Jekonsaseh released her breath and willed the man to think a summer wind whispered through the leaves. She was the spirit of the forest. "Friend or enemy?"

"Friend."

"You are to harm no one," Jekonsaseh warned. "Above all, if you see a yearling bear, you are not to harm her. She is under my protection." It was not a question so the man made no reply. She asked, "How did you come here?"

"On the river. I don't want trouble. I brought trail food so I need not hunt. I didn't know the forest could speak. Don't harm me."

The man's friend must be important for him to risk himself. "If you do no harm, you will be safe. If you don't find your friend, what will you do?"

"Go home without him. His sister and I will grieve. He was a good friend."

Jekonsaseh's heart pounded so hard, she feared the man would hear it. "Don't give up your search," she whispered, backing away. "You will find him."

"Ole Halvardson. Wake up." Beaver Tooth had stuck his head into the wigwam. Ole turned. Behind the boy, pink clouds were visible.

"Why are you still sleeping? Mother of Nations said we should start early. Where is she?"

"I saw a campfire on the mainland during the night. She went to see who was there. She said to keep hidden in case Algonquin are in the borderland. If we get the canoe, we must bring it here and wait for her." His efforts the day before had tired him, but if all went well, he would ride in the canoe to his friend's town.

Beaver Tooth showed him their thick cord. "We worked late. I'll loop one end to my arrow shaft and aim for a rib in the hull. If it holds, we can pull it back without getting into the water."

That was better than Ole's original plan to bind a vine to a rock and throw it, hoping it would hold while he pulled the canoe to land. "Let's go."

They reached the murky pool. Ole could see how he had missed it the day before. The opening between the trees was narrow and the water was shadowy. Enough light entered to see that the canoe had not moved. Beaver Tooth's first arrow fell wide. He hauled it back, having to maneuver the fletching through the moss-slicked branches. The second arrow arced high, but entered and stuck. Beaver Tooth gave a tentative tug and the line went taut. "I did it," he whispered.

"Is one enough, or will we want two?" Ole asked.

"We don't have enough cord for another," Fisher said.

Beaver Tooth pulled, but the boat did not move. "Try from here," Ole suggested, moving to another angle. This time, the boat gave a little. It moved closer to the bank before the cord snagged.

Fisher looked up and down the tree. "It's the bow rope, not our cord. I don't see any snakes. Maybe I can get close enough to untangle it from the roots or cut it free." He straddled the trunk and shimmied toward its end until he came to something slippery and toppled in. Ole stretched out to try to pull him back, but he could not reach. He feared to touch the water. There was too much underneath that he could not see.

Fisher found footing on the rotted part of the trunk under the water. It would not have held Ole's weight. "I'm all right, but I lost my knife. I can't see it."

"Take mine." Ole held it out before he had time to change his mind. His offer might lose him his steel knife, but it was all he could think to do.

Fisher balanced, holding the branch with one hand and took the knife. He drew it through the roots and grabbed the cord. Water weeds made the canoe rope too slippery to untangle. Beaver Tooth held his cord taut so Fisher would not cut it by accident. The knife went through the rope and the canoe moved.

"I have it now," said Beaver Tooth hauled it to the bank. The canoe was nearly to his hand when a stray river wave yanked it away. The loop pulled free of the arrow shaft and the canoe slipped into the current. "No! Not after all our work!"

Beaver Tooth ran to keep it in sight. Fisher handed Ole's knife back to him, curled his basswood cord around his arm and sprinted after his brother.

Ole swore in Norse. If he were home, he would think Loki, the trickster god, was doing this. Who in this world wished him harm? He was incapable of running but he walked after the boys, still mumbling. "Of all the bad luck!"

"What is luck?" Concentrating on the boys and the canoe, he hadn't heard Jekonsaseh come up.

"We had the canoe, but it jumped out of our hands. Luck is when good or bad things happen that we can't plan for. This was bad luck. Maybe an angry god or spirit did it." He wasn't sure if he explained it right, but she nodded. If he didn't know the words, she could pull the concept out of his head. They kept to the bank, watching to see if the brothers could catch the canoe before it traveled too far.

Jekonsaseh said, "Someone doesn't want to you in Longhouse country, probably the same someone who told the snake to bite you."

"A bad spirit? Why would it want to harm me? No one knows me but my sister and Runs Fast."

Brambles seemed to jump into their path. A brown snake slithered over Ole's foot, but was gone before he could react. "Thorns and snakes," Jekonsaseh said softly. "The Younger Brother is doing this."

They reached the eastern point of the island. Sunlight sparkled off the wavelets. The canoe floated toward them. The brothers jumped in ahead of it and swam strongly to intercept it.

While they waited, Jekonsaseh said, "I found the fire and a single man next to it, asleep." Ole watched her nervously. "Look! Beaver Tooth nearly has it." The older brother reached with one hand to grab the bow rope when a second canoe came between theirs and the island.

Ole was already limping forward. "The man has a canoe. What does he want with another one? Beaver Tooth won't be able to fight him from the water."

"That canoe is ours," Beaver Tooth bellowed. The man shouted something back, but the river breeze carried his voice away. The man's hair hung lank and loose. Because he did not wear a scalp-lock, Ole guessed the newcomer was Algonquin. The stranger did not see Fisher seize the boat from the other side and tug it. The man lifted his paddle as if to strike the swimmer.

"He's going to kill Beaver Tooth." Ole lifted his hand as if to stop the man in mid- strike. "Jekonsaseh. Say something. Make him stop."

"Do you think I can speak to the man from here, and that he will obey?"

"Try," he said. "Save the boys."

She lifted one hand as Ole had. "Reach the paddle to the boy and help him climb in," she said quietly. "When you have him safe in your canoe, get the other boy and bring both boats to me."

Ole watched in astonishment as the man did as she said. He did not attack but reached the paddle to Beaver Tooth who seized it. The man's face was lowered to help the boy. Ole stared in wonder. "I wouldn't have believed it."

Beaver Tooth pointed to Fisher and the man paddled to him, towing the second canoe. Fisher climbed in and retrieved his paddle from his shoulder sling. Both canoes drew alongside the island ledge and stopped. "Did you make him do that?" Ole asked, trying to understand what he had just seen.

She turned to him, clearly puzzled. "Make him do what?"

"He was going to strike Beaver Tooth, but instead, he helped him."

"Why would he harm the boy? They are from the same town. Notice the shape of the canoes and the designs? They are of the same clan."

Ole only saw canoes with markings he did not understand. "But the man must be Algonquin. A Ganeo-gaono warrior would shave his hair into a scalp lock. Runs Fast said so. If the canoe is Longhouse, the man must have stolen the canoe."

"I don't think so. He did not seem like a thief when I found him sleeping last night and questioned him. He said he is looking for a lost friend."

Fisher and the man tied their canoe ropes to leaning trees. Beaver Tooth's long hair dripped as he directed the man toward them. The man turned and pulled in a sharp breath as his attention settled on Jekonsaseh. "It must truly be the Mother of Nations, as you said."

Beaver Tooth said, "It is. You can't tell yet because of shadows and his cap, but the man with her is from another world. His hair is red as the pelt of a summer fox. He was snake bit and would have died, but Mother of Nations healed him." The man's dark eyes slid from Jekonsaseh to Ole. His mouth opened and he nearly dropped his paddle.

Ole let go of his crutch in surprise and reached for his offered arm. "Runs Fast! My friend!"

Chapter 14

Runs Fast

Runs Fast climbed up and took Ole into a fierce embrace. "I thought I'd never find you, until the forest spirit said I would. "Do you know how you worried us? You might have left a sign, Brother," he complained. Fisher and Beaver Tooth stared at the two men. *Brother*? One was human colored; the other wore red fox fur on head, cheeks and chin. "Why did you leave us?"

"I didn't mean to. I found a canoe and climbed on. It had no paddle, and it carried me here. You, yourself, taught me not to cry out in the forest." He finally disentangled himself from his friend.

"So this is my fault? I've been searching for days. Ingrid sent me."

"Is she safe?"

"Did you think I would leave her alone for three days?" Runs Fast replied with his old show of audacity that hid his warm heart. "She is with her grandmother in Wolf Longhouse."

"Her grandmother? You can't mean that!"

By now, everyone was staring. Runs Fast was enjoying the attention, but Ole was determined to find out what he had missed. "Dreamer knew the names of her mother's uncle and favorite cousin. Some thought I coached her, but I reminded them that I hardly knew my own cousins; I had been away so long." He looked pointedly to Beaver Tooth and Fisher. "When I left, Beaver Tooth was just running and Fisher was barely out of his cradleboard. She couldn't tell them her mother's name so Wolf Clan Mother did not know what to think."

"You said Ingrid is with her grandmother. How did Ingrid prove it if she didn't know the name?"

"She told them her mother's story; how she saw the Algonquin from a walnut tree and sent the other children back to warn the town. She said her mother had to climb down so she couldn't get home fast enough."

Ole had heard that story many times. He was glad Ingrid thought to mention it. "But what about you? You didn't think they would take you back."

"Dreamer told them how I bravely rescued you both from the Algonquin. My mother decided to take me back, but I barely caught my breath before Dreamer sent me back to the river to find you." He made a long-suffering face. "Of course I would have come anyway. I couldn't let them catch you again."

Runs Fast had taken to calling Ingrid Dreamer as the Inuit had. During their travels, her visions had guided them several times. "When we get home this time, I want to sleep for two days, maybe three."

Ole noticed the boys and Jekonsaseh were watching. He made the introductions. "This is my friend and guide, Runs Fast. He led us from a Naskapi trade island in the ocean to his home along the Wide River. We were living with the Inuit, but Ingrid hoped to find her mother's people."

Runs Fast turned to Jekonsaseh. "Mother of Nations, my cousins say you wish to come with us to Doteoga."

"It is time for me to leave this island and learn how the war is going. The injured and hungry will look for me and not find me. I will come with you, but I will not stay long after I tell your people to expect the Peacemaker. It is time for me to tell Lili to go. She's big enough to defend herself now."

"Lili?" Runs Fast asked.

"Her bear," said Ole with a smile because he knew something his friend did not. Jekonsaseh and Ole led them to her house where she suggested the men strike a fire and the boys check her fish lines and traps on the north side of the island. "I must send her far away. I can't keep her safe now."

The boys returned with trout from Jekonsaseh's lines and a hare from one of her traps. They prepared them for cooking and laid them on the firestones. "Don't let them burn, Ole" Beaver Tooth said. "Help us make a bigger lean-to, Runs Fast. You will sleep with us. Ole and Mother of Nations won't want us in the house."

"What!" Ole lowered his eyes.

Runs Fast followed the brothers into the shadowed trees leaving Ole to keep their meal from burning. Jekonsaseh returned downcast. It must have been difficult to send the bear away from her.

After supper, the last of the day faded and the stars took their places. Ole peeled a green twig with his knife for a toothpick. They sat by the fire. It was too soon to sleep. Jekonsaseh asked, "Runs Fast, how long ago did you and Dreamer arrive in Doteoga?"

Runs Fast bent his knees comfortably and crossed his ankles. He counted off the days. "Four days ago. Wolf Clan Mother welcomed Dreamer and will adopt her into Wolf Clan. The next day, I borrowed a canoe to search for Ole. The storm destroyed our tracks, but I found the remains of our last campfire." He smiled at that bit of clever tracking. "This island is between Ganeo-gaono and Algonquin land. I don't care for war." He ran his fingers through his loose hair. "This is better than being alone." He indicated the company around the fire.

"Why do you call Ole's sister Dreamer?" Fisher asked.

"The Eskimo gave her that name because she dreams with open eyes. On Trader Island, she looked over the south ocean and saw an eagle flying. It must have been a spirit eagle because I saw nothing. That is how Dreamer knew she and Ole must come to my country and why I guided them. While we traveled, she saw another vision, a picture belt of purple and white wampum. She made a small loom. Each evening when we camped, she wove. She enlarged the belt with shells on yarn of twisted dog hair. Dreamer sometimes talks with her mother's ghost."

"I think Dreamer and I will understand each other," said Jekonsaseh. Ole faced her and she nodded. "You understand, Runs Fast. How did you find my island."

"We thought Algonquin seized him at first, but I reasoned. If they had, why did they leave us behind? There was no splash or sound of a fight. Dreamer's dog Boy would have barked if strange men came near our camp, but he slept. Ole would not have entered the water because he could not swim. I sat down where he vanished and invited the forest spirits to help me think."

"Did they?" Jekonsaseh asked.

"It seemed so. How could Ole have gone so quietly? By canoe. Why didn't he paddle back to us? There was no paddle. My guess was the current had him so I followed the current. Was I right, Brother?"

"You were."

Runs Fast rubbed the side of his nose. "To follow the current, I did not paddle, but allowed my canoe to drift where the current took it until the sun grew low. That is where I camped. While my food cooked, I walked along the bank and saw the island with a canoe caught in a creek. The sun has to be right. I nearly missed it. It was getting dark so returned to my fire, but I was sure if the canoe was there, Ole must be near it."

He indicated the boys. "In the morning I set out for the island and found the canoe had been set free. I followed and you know the rest."

"Thank you for your excellent story. We must rise early so let us sleep now," said Jekonsaseh. "Ole Halvardson, will you come with me?"

Ole did not understand her intentions. Perhaps she had questions for him she would not ask before the others. They had been intimate, but her mind was foreign to him. Was she, like Odin's daughters, the Valkyries, meant to gather warrior's spirits? Jekonsaseh knew nothing of Norse gods and goddesses, but she was a rule unto herself. On the other hand, he was alive.

Runs Fast looked after them, but Beaver Tooth tugged his arm and turned him to their lean-to. "They have been that way since we found them. They will not want to see us before morning."

In Jekonsaseh's dwelling, Ole lowered himself to his fur bed. She had lit no fire inside. The smoke hole allowed the clear light of a full moon. It highlighted Jekonsaseh's cheeks and lips, leaving her eyes in shadow. Tomorrow, they would arrive at the boys' town. Jekonsaseh made the rules in her house, but he suspected their association would change shortly. In any case, he was no longer the wounded and helpless warrior she had rescued. Her curiosity about him would be settled and she would leave him.

He thought over their last two nights, and felt a surge of renewed desire. How many had loved the mysterious Mother of Nations? How many had she loved? He had no more claim to her than they. He should not think of it. He dared not move, so he turned to the wall. "Are you awake?" she asked softly. She was Jekonsaseh again, not only Mother of Nations, healer and protector of both bears and wounded men.

He turned over. "I am awake. I remember that I owe you a gift. I have nothing yet, but I'll find a way to pay you for healing me."

She turned to her side. "When you find your sister and friend, I will try to learn why you were sent to me. In that, I will be compensated."

The warmth of her body reached out to him and her breath quickened. She didn't need to see his arousal, yet she remained on her own bed. "Will you come to me again before we part?"

He crept to her and settled beside her. She lifted one of his hands and stroked his fingers. He leaned half over her and pressed her lips with his, very lightly. She deepened their kiss. Because it was unlikely to occur again, he tried to press each touch and every feeling into his memory where he could treasure it. Satisfied, they fell asleep, holding each other.

In the morning, she built up the fire and simmered the last of Runs Fast's corn meal for their breakfast. "Shall we help you take down your house?" Fisher asked. Jekonsaseh accepted the offer.

"Lili returned during the night. She can't follow us to the dwellings of men. I must send her away again."

The yearling had not understood that she had been told to go. Lili waited behind some trees, jealously watching the humans who had taken her protector's attention from her. Mother bears did not explain. They growled and bit until the young one understood that it and its mother were no longer a family. Jekonsaseh's problem was that she was human and not a bear. "You can't be with me now. You can't come where I am going."

She walked away from Lili and pictured the bear swimming to land on the north side of the island. She made her voice cold. "Our time together is over. Leave. Don't come back." She made a long, throwing motion. "Go far away and find your mate." Lili ambled away slowly, but stopped and looked back. Jekonsaseh's voice was gruff. "Do as I say. Go!"

The bear turned away a last time. Soon, there came a loud splash and smaller ones as Lili plunged into the water and swam to the northern bank. Jekonsaseh returned to the men, wiping her eyes. There was no sign of her house and her bundles were loaded into the canoe. "I am ready. Let us go to Doteoga."

They carried the canoes to the river and climbed in. Ole said nothing when Jekonsaseh climbed into the boys' canoe. He had the last three nights to remember.

Runs Fast steadied his canoe for Ole to climb in. He seated himself awkwardly, his stiff right leg stretched out in front of him. Runs Fast climbed into the stern and settled above the thwart. "There's a second paddle in the bow," he said. "Use it."

They had to work against the current. They paddled without speaking for some time. There was something different about their relationship now, a tension that had not been there before. Ole had been with Mother of Nations and Runs Fast had been with Ole's sister. Ole spoke first. "You and Ingrid – she has come to care for you. Have you asked her to be your wife?" He was still his sister's protector.

"I asked and she agreed. Now we must get permission from our clan mothers. If they agree, I will move into Wolf Longhouse and begin a family. What about you and Mother of Nations?"

Ole shook his head. "I don't think Mother of Nations has time for a family. She can't belong to one man while there is war. She has to help warriors, all of them, until the Peacemaker comes. She will do that and go from town to village preparing people to receive him. We said goodbye last night."

They came to a break in the river at a slim island, smaller than the last one. They could not see the other canoe. Runs Fast said, "Pull up your paddle and I will steer." He maneuvered them around the island until they spotted Fisher and Beaver Tooth again, with Jekonsaseh. "Now, let's catch up. We'll sleep in Doteoga tonight."

They dipped and pulled, Runs Fast setting the pace and the rhythm. He pointed out their previous campsite, but they did not stop. The sun rounded its zenith and began its descent. They banked to eat, resting their arms. Ole was grateful to be with his friend, to hear his optimistic chatter that made light of his worries.

Runs Fast said that with Jekonsaseh in their party, the town should not refuse them entry. Ole was not so sure. "Stop." They set the flat of the canoe blades into the stream to halt the canoe. "There it is. Doteoga." Corn hills stretched far. Spots of yellow squash with wide green leaves grew low against the stalks. Bean vines climbed the corn stalks. Above the planting field stood the town, protected by a palisade of sharpened saplings that leaned outward like spears.

The sight might have put Ole off had he been alone, but he was not. Ingrid would be inside with her people, people who would see him as what he was, an outsider. He had come here to protect Ingrid, to help her find a home. Now that she had, what was to become of him?

He prepared himself for stares and questions. They carried the canoes towards the town and waited to be challenged.

"We aren't the only visitors today," Runs Fast said and pointed to a party of war canoes decorated with clan designs leaning against the wall. One canoe was smaller and stood alone. It was pure white. Jekonsaseh caught her breath and nearly stumbled. She spread her arms to catch her balance.

"What?" Ole asked in alarm.

"He said he would come on a cloud over water. He must be here."

Before she could say more, two guards approached. Their heads were shaved on the sides. The rest of their hair stood up, thickened with paint and mud. "Halt," they said. "Set down your canoes." The party from the island did as they were ordered. The guards looked them over and soon recognized the boys.

They did not take a closer look at Jekonsaseh, but Ole's striking differences brought the usual question. He had heard it in Algonquin and now he heard it in Longhouse. "You with the red hair. What are you?"

"A man from a far country," he replied.

"He is our friend," said Beaver Tooth. "We found our uncle's canoe. See?" He tilted it toward the guard.

Runs Fast said, "You know me. I'm Runs Fast from Bear Clan. I came here with Dreamer. Mother of Nations is with us too."

The guards took a better look. "Welcome to Doteoga, Mother of Nations," said one. "We will escort all of you in, but you must wait your turn to speak. Important visitors arrived this morning."

"Wait," said Runs Fast, taking the man's arm. "Who has come?"

"A young Huron arrived this morning in a cloud-white canoe with the cursed Onondaga Mohawk, Hiawatha." Mohawk meant man-eater. "Have no fear. The Huron has lifted his curse. He is no longer a danger."

Jekonsaseh's fingers clenched. She opened them and brought them up to her eyes. When she lowered them, Ole saw she had been crying.

"We could not stay to listen, but the elders invited them in and the matrons lit the All Clans council fire. The young Huron must be someone important. Come inside and see for yourselves."

Chapter 15

Deganawida

Young mothers and children stood farthest from the Council. They turned to scrutinize the newest arrivals. Those few who saw nudged their friends and more turned. They rubbed their eyes as if Ole's pale complexion, freckles, fire-red braids and short orange beard were a trick of the bright sun. The patrol kept close for a time to be sure the outlander presented no danger.

Ole leaned on his crutch. After a while, even his presence was overridden by the events at the sacred All Clans fire. The women turned back to the Council although some of the children kept their attention on Ole. The town guards told the group to stay where they were for the time being. "When the speakers are done, the matrons and elders may wish to question you."

Ingrid was here somewhere, but since Ole's vision forward was blocked, he looked to the nearest of the longhouses. He had seen and slept in wigwams sizeable enough to hold three generations. The longhouse roofs were curved. In the center, they were tall enough for a man to stand and not brush the ceiling. According to Runs Fast, they held up to seven families on each side. Shingles of bark and hide overlaid the tied scaffolding. They reminded Ole of gigantic, legless caterpillars.

The children, bored because they could not see and hear the council, began to come closer. One girl, bolder than the rest, ran forward and patted the red-orange hair on his legs. He wore only his breechclout and open shirt. He leaned down and gave the child a good look at his hair, beard and green eyes. "Bad manners," he said in Longhouse.

She squealed and backed away. "He talks," she shouted to her friends. The others continued to stare. "He talks like a human," said one child. "He's a bear," said another. "Bears don't talk." "He's a stone monster with fire for hair." "No. He isn't hot."

Runs Fast pointed towards the All Clans fire, and gestured the children to silence with a threatening slice of his hand. A sudden tumult rippled through the crowd. It had to do with them, for even the adults turned belatedly to the newcomers. They drew apart giving Ole a clear view to the Council. It also gave them a clear view of him. "What now?" he muttered.

Runs Fast said, "They want to talk to you. "Don't worry. Dreamer is here." He pointed to her. "She'll keep you safe." Ole located Ingrid by her auburn hair, but why was she with the clan matrons? An elder made directly for Ole. He could not retreat. These people scorned cowardice. Runs Fast had been exiled for it.

"Come with me," said man. "You come too, Runs Fast."

Gruff barking and the pounding of heavy paws cut through the crowd. A flash of shaggy black and white bounded up to Ole. It was Ingrid's huge mix breed dog, Boy. His tail waved hard enough to knock down children. Ole dropped his crutch and opened his arms. "Boy! Good Boy." The dog balanced on his hind legs, forepaws on Ole's shoulders and licked his face. He was nearly as big as Lili, Ole thought. He looked back. Jekonsaseh remained by the wall. Ole rubbed Boy's massive head. "I'm glad to see you too." He buried his face in the familiar fur. "Down with you now." The dog obeyed. Ole bent to retrieve his crutch.

"That is Ole, my brother, Grandmother!" He was close enough to hear her now. "Runs Fast, you found him! I knew you would. Come to us, both of you." Boy's enthusiastic greeting left dull claw marks in Ole's arms and his cheeks were wet from the dog's tongue.

"Dreamer summoned us. Move," Runs Fast urged. A backward glance showed Ole Jekonsaseh, arms folded, continued to hang back.

"Come here and g-greet your sister," said a long-haired young man in accented and stammering Longhouse.

Runs Fast gave Ole a small shove and followed, holding Boy by his ruff.

Ingrid's auburn braids hung down her shoulders. "My brother is hurt, Grandmother. May I go to him?"

"He can walk, Dream Weaver. Come here, Red Hair," said Wolf Clan Mother.

She was a small woman, quite wrinkled, but her posture and tone were commanding. Ole stopped a few strides before the bench. Ingrid's mouth formed a circle as she said his name.

An older man with slate gray, loose hair smiled in a friendly way to Ole. The younger man beside him seemed the leader despite the culture's respect for age. His intelligent eyes appraised Ole.

Not knowing the appropriate response, Ole looked to the old woman who rested a bony hand on Ingrid's knee. "He has come most of the way. Now, go to him."

Ingrid jumped from the bench, stopping a pace away. Ole had never been demonstrative, but he had defended his sister all her life. He touched her cheek lightly, as if making sure she was real. "Grandmother, may he stay here?"

He had not expected to get to that so quickly, but it appeared Ingrid was as concerned for him as he for her. "For your sake, Granddaughter, he will be my guest for now," the old woman replied. She spoke for her words to carry. "This is Dream Weaver's brother, Red Hair. He is my guest and under my protection."

"Thank you," said Ingrid. She spoke hurriedly in Norse. Runs Fast made frantic signals to her to speak in Longhouse words, but she was too breathless to stop. "We thought you must have drowned and your body floated away. Even Boy lost your scent. Why did you leave us?"

"I only meant to check our fish lines, but a canoe floated near. I thought it would help us, but when I climbed in, there was no paddle and it carried me away. The canoe belongs to these brothers." He pointed to Fisher and Beaver Tooth.

"Why didn't you call for help?"

"Runs Fast said never to shout in the forest."

Runs Fast heard his name among the jumble of foreign words. "Speak as I taught you. You are being rude."

It seemed their discussion must be public. Ole repeated as well as he could. "I found a canoe with no paddle. It brought me to an island. A snake bit my leg. Jekonsaseh, Mother of Nations saved me. There she is." He pointed to her.

"Mother of Nations!" Hundreds repeated her name in awe and reverence, but the two esteemed visitors in the Council seemed most startled.

The younger man lifted his arms. "Jekonsaseh!"

She moved at last, running to them. The crowd opened. Jekonsaseh and the older man met halfway and embraced. "Uncle!" she cried. "You are well." Hiawatha escorted her to the younger man who stood. They looked to each other in wonder before they came together and returned to the Council.

Hiawatha explained. "Esteemed matrons and elders -- Jekonsaseh lived with Hidden in Mist, the guardian of Niagara. She met Deganawida there. He promised her to remove my curse before he began his mission. He has done so and here we are."

Jekonsaseh grew tearful again. "The end of the war has begun." People repeated her words, some with puzzlement, but others with hope that it was true.

"You believed in me from the start, Sister" he said, smiling into her eyes. "I heard people call you Mother of Nations and suspected it was you. Permit me to tell them who you are."

"We know who she is," said a warrior. "Everyone knows Mother of Nations," said another. "She cares for and feeds every warrior who asks her for help, no matter what his nation. What more is there to know?"

"Tell them," she said.

Deganawida spoke to Hiawatha who translated in a carrying voice. "People of Doteoga, the Peacemaker prefers that I speak for him for he has not learned your words well. He wants you to know that Jekonsaseh, Mother of Nations, who has cared for many of you, is Tododaho's daughter."

A woman called upon the Creator to shield them from evil. A faith keeper fingered the many amulets that hung on his necklace and flung tobacco shreds on the fire to avert evil.

"The daughter of the Snake Haired has come inside our walls to help him destroy us," someone shouted. "She fooled us. The evil one himself spawned her."

Wolf Clan Mother rose so the people could see her and lifted both arms for decorum. The people took some time to obey but finally quieted. Now, Ole comprehended Jekonsaseh's reluctance to enter a town or village. They had thrown her heritage in her face a moment after they praised her.

Someone shouted, "The cause of our trouble sends his daughter to us. Should the daughter live after what her father has done?"

The three clan matrons stood together, and the people quieted again. "Let our honored visitors speak," said Turtle Clan Mother. The people obeyed but did not bother to hide their distrust and revulsion.

Hiawatha reminded them of Jekonsaseh's kindness. "Hasn't she fed and cared for you," he asked the warriors. He did not wait for a response. "Did she ask you to name your tribe before she helped you?" The warriors admitted that she had not.

An elder said, "She nurtured every man returning from battle in need. Let her continue to be known as Mother of Nations."

"Don't judge her by Tododaho," said Hiawatha. "I have lived under his curse for ten years." There were shouts and screams, but the man's gentle bearing did not alter. Again, the clan mothers signed for silence. Hiawatha continued. "I stand before you with the Peacemaker who was sent here by the Creator. He healed me. As young as he is, he is meant to overcome Tododaho and unite the Tribes."

A faith keeper in his bark robe made an incredulous face. "Are you or aren't you the very Hiawatha who terrorized the tribes, perhaps as much as the Snake Haired?"

"I was that man," he admitted. It did not seem possible. "Deganawida has brought a cure for all of us. Accept him and your children's children will recount how you defeated our enemy together."

Deganawida said he wished to speak in Longhouse. In halting words, he said, "If you vote to follow me, we will begin the Great Peace in this place. I ask for a few brave men of each clan to join me. Jekonsaseh, my heart sister, and Hiawatha, my heart brother, will show you great things." He held out his hands as if to touch everyone. "We will see peace before the end of next summer."

Jekonsaseh faced the doubtful crowd. "Before the war began, my uncle asked the Elder Brother to send us an eagle if he desired peace. My father asked the Younger Twin to send a serpent if we were to go to war. An eagle came. My father ordered his warriors to bring his bow and quiver. In their rush to obey, they trampled my friend, Hiawatha's daughter. My father killed the eagle. Because of this great evil, the serpent came and entered my father. It whispers in his ear. He wanted my help, but I ran away to Niagara and Hidden in Mist. I meant to throw myself over the edge, but he saved me."

She had a natural story-telling ability. Someone brought her a cup of water. She drank and continued. "Hidden in Mist said when the boy became a man, he would cure Hiawatha and bring peace to the Tribes. Both of them stand here before you. Hiawatha is cured." She waited for her words to be repeated until everyone heard. "As my uncle did on that terrible day, I ask the Creator for a sign of his approval. If Doteoga's warriors vote for peace, let an eagle fly over us and come to rest on a tall tree."

The faith keeper said, "What good are signs? While we speak in council and listen to promises, our men fight and die in the west. Do you think one man can end the bloodshed, Mother of Nations?"

"No, but many can, with the right leader."

"A Huron?"

Hiawatha lifted his voice. "He is has no tribe for he has left the people he was born to. He is the man from the North. Is Doteoga ready to see the end of war?"

Many said they were, but there were dissenters. "Are we to go without revenge for our losses?" The speaker was not alone.

Hiawatha responded smoothly. "If this war goes on, you will lose the freedom of the clans. A tyrant will rule you with fear instead of your matrons with a mother's care for your welfare. Serpents and spiders will dwell in burned-out longhouses. The Three Sisters will no longer support us and crows will eat our flesh." Even the children went silent at the cruel picture his words painted.

"What do the Red-Hairs have to do with us? Why do they sit in our Council?" someone asked.

Hiawatha said, "The Peacemaker is Huron. Our Confederation may harm his own people, yet he came at the Creator's bidding. His *orenda* was strong enough to lift the curse that bound me. He will explain what the Red Hairs have to do with us."

Deganawida took Ingrid's left hand and Ole's right, and raised both to form a bridge of their arms, with him as center. He spoke Huron and Hiawatha translated. "Here are sister and a brother. They share a father - not a mother, yet they are family. Our Five Tribes are like a hand with five fingers. We, too, are related. Decide if you prefer my vision to Tododaho's. Where he rules, women have no say in their own families. Send me away or follow me. Warriors of Doteoga, it is your right, to vote. Choose if you will have war or peace."

Many discussions filled the air at once. Jekonsaseh came to stand beside Ole. Dream Weaver had been receiving visions since her mother died. Now she saw an aura around each of them. Ole's was orange, like his hair and temperament. Jekonsaseh's was green like a serene lake. At the edges, both colors touched like sunset over the lake. Runs Fast spoke in her ear. "What do you see, Dreamer?"

"Sunset over a lake. Jekonsaseh and Ole. I hope the people decide to follow the Peacemaker. I don't want to raise our children in war."

"Our children?" he asked.

"Don't you want children?"

Runs Fast had shown unexpected courage when he risked himself to rescue them. He took her hand and she leaned her head on his shoulder. She knew his mind.

Bear war chief said, "If we are attacked, we will defend ourselves. A vote for peace does not deny that." Deganawida agreed that this was true. "Answer me this, Peacemaker. Do you expect our warriors who are at war not to accept our decision?"

They conferred. "As soon as it is possible to do," said Hiawatha. The late sun touched the top branches of the trees outside the palisade. "Vote. The Creator must know we are serious if we expect his blessing."

Each war chief called his men forward. A faith keeper tallied the votes by making charcoal lines on birch bark. When the voting ended, he gave them the totals. "Wolf Clan votes to follow Deganawida. We vote for peace."

"Bear Clan votes for peace."

"Turtle Clan votes for peace."

"Three clans and three votes, all for peace," said Turtle Clan's matron. "We will keep our Law and follow the Peacemaker. Does the Elder Brother welcome our vote?"

The beat of wings was heard and a golden bird flew toward them. It screeched as it circled over the town. The children shouted. The eagle glided over the western stockade wall and perched on the topmost branch of a tall spruce. The tree swayed under its weight. The gold of the sun rested for a moment on the golden head.

Jekonsaseh took her brother's hand. "It's a good beginning."

He lifted shining eyes to the tree and returned the pressure of her fingers. "It won't be easy. In the end, I may die, but today is a good day."

Chapter 16

People lit torches from the All Clans fire to relight the fire pits in the houses. They set torches outside to illuminate the dancing. The matrons led their women in a celebratory dance. Hiawatha positioned a borrowed water drum in the crook of his left arm. With a wrapped drum stick, he tapped out a lively rhythm. Players on a deer bone flute and reed pipes gave a melody while two bark-robed faith-keepers shook their turtle shell rattles. The women wove between the houses, stamping and chanting for the Peacemaker's success.

"They call him Peacemaker already, before he has done anything," Runs Fast remarked without much fervor. "Of course, it would be good if he succeeded," he added, seeing Ole and Ingrid's offended expressions.

Ingrid wanted to dance with her new clan sisters, but she was reluctant to leave Runs Fast and Ole. "Don't you think he can do it? The Creator sent an eagle."

"Yes, but the eagle flew off. Peace doesn't come because a bird lands on a tree and flies away. If the Creator could impose peace himself, he would have done it. Opponents have to make peace, and both sides need to agree on terms. How is that going to happen? Who will convince the Snake Haired to give up? You know me, Dreamer. I'll believe it when it happens. If you can believe it now, go ahead and dance with your clan sisters." She gave him an exasperated stare and walked off. "I've noticed even good marriages aren't always peaceful," Runs Fast said.

Ole looked after his sister. "I suppose you are right. Tell me why only the women are dancing? Do they have more faith in the Peacemaker's promises than the men?"

Runs Fast lifted his palms. "Most of these men want to believe in him, but not all. How long can men go without war? It's in their nature to fight. Women can hope the sides will come together, but no one can impose peace on the Tribes. Let us talk about something else. Dreamer and I intend to marry. To prove I can provide for her, I must hunt tomorrow. The herds have fled, although we found a few remaining in Algonquin Country. I don't intend to go so far, but perhaps north along the Wide River, I may find game. I'd ask you to come with me, but you can't run yet. We want you at the meal though, since Dreamer has to cook it."

"We've hunted and Ingrid cooked since we began together," Ole reminded him. He supposed he should be calling his sister Dreamer as Runs Fast did, or more properly Dream Weaver, but getting used to new names took time. There was so much to learn and remember. "When I was a boy in Greenland, and even when I was a young man when we lived with the Inuit, the father gave the daughter to a man of his choosing."

"Women manage these things here. The Snake Haired is trying to change the customs, but my tribe won't have any of it. We like things the way they are, most of the time, anyway. My mother is matron of Bear. Since Dreamer's mother is dead, Wolf Clan Mother will stand in for her. Both of them will attend our wedding feast."

Ole scratched absently at his nearly healed wound. "You will be my brother-in-law. Is there a word in Longhouse for a wife's brother?"

"Wife's brother. You just said it. I have to prepare for my hunt. Will you be all right if I leave you?"

"Go." Ole waved him off. Since that morning, he had forced his strength. His position on the canoe had been hard to maintain. Since they arrived, he had been standing. He sat heavily down on one of the benches by the All Clans fire which had mostly burned out. He looked above the embers to one of the longhouses. Five men entered it together. These men had spoken against peace at the Council.

Across from him, Jekonsaseh leaned against Hiawatha and held Deganawida's arm. The three radiated contentment. Curiosity about Ole had brought Jekonsaseh to the two men she loved. She had forgotten him as easily as she forgot Lili. What was he to make of her desire during the last three nights? Perhaps that is the way things were done here, but he did not like it. He recalled the sound of her heart and the smoky fragrance of her hair. He began to nod off when a man shook his shoulder. "These benches are for the elders and clan matrons. You live in Wolf Longhouse, Red Hair. Go to bed."

115

The man wore bark robes, faith keeper ceremonial garb. The music had stopped and there were fewer people about. "Sorry," Ole mumbled and got up to go. He paused to steady himself against a tree. When he began again, he had forgotten which way he was going. The faith keeper had walked off, but a wrinkled old woman approached him.

"I am Wolf Clan Mother, your sister's grandmother," she said, seeing he could not place her in the dark. She took his hand. "Come with me, Red Hair. I'll bring you to my longhouse where you may sleep."

Above the doorway, a light bark shingle showed the outline of a wolf. He could just make out the thick black lines. "Dream Weaver drew it," she said. "Come inside." She parted the hanging. Bed benches lined both sides of the long room. They were separated by hides. Lines of smoke lifted wraithlike to them from the fire pits.

"This is my section," she said, and stopped. "You will sleep here. Dream Weaver and I will come to bed soon." She showed him the clay-lined night basket tucked below the bed bench. Her leather dress slapped against her legs as she walked away.

To sleep without fear was a luxury. He crept against the curved wall, leaving room for his sister and her grandmother, and shut his eyes. Now that he was free to sleep, he could not. His mind was too crowded. Thoughts rattled around in his head and bumped into each other. Where was Jekonsaseh? The matrons had no authority over her. Did she ever really care for him? Finally, even his thoughts became tired and he fell into exhausted sleep.

Before dawn, Wolf Clan Mother reached out and nudged her granddaughter. "What?" the girl asked sleepily.

Ole moaned and twisted under his blanket. "Your brother - feel his face. He might be sick."

She did. He was cold, not warm, but at her touch, he pulled away, gasping. "Ole! Wake up," she said sharply.

"Red Thor! Where am I?" he exclaimed in Norse. He tried to sit, bumped his head, and reclined again. "Ingrid?"

"You are in Wolf Longhouse with me and my grandmother. We are safe." She cupped his cheek with her warm hand. "What were you dreaming?"

He covered her hand and breathed deeply the smells of a crowded house and sleeping people. He rubbed his eyes and stretched to release the tension between his shoulders. "I dreamed I was in a different place. Jekonsaseh was still a girl."

"Speak Longhouse," Ingrid said. He translated, speaking softly.

Wolf Clan Mother learned over him. "Perhaps your *orenda* went to the past. What else did you see there?"

"Hiawatha's hair was black. There was another man. People were afraid of him."

The old woman covered his lips with her palm. "If you saw Jekonsaseh's father, it is better not to speak of him. What else did your dream show you?"

"I saw a young woman die and I saw the man who made people afraid kill an eagle. No one reprimanded him."

Wolf Clan Mother looked at him suspiciously. "Dream Weaver, you did not tell me your brother saw visions."

"He never did, Grandmother."

They were more interested in his abilities than what he dreamed. He should not have told them. "It must be something Jekonsaseh said to me. I was thinking about it and dreamed it. I'm sorry I woke you."

Ingrid's grandmother said, "Dreams can be dreams or something more. For now, you should go back to sleep."

Dawn awoke the birds and birds awoke the people. A humid breeze found its way down the smoke holes and into the house. Someone hooked the door curtain to let out the smoke. The sun broke through and lit the long room. People awoke for the first day of the Green Corn Festival.

Mothers ordered their men and children outside to wash while they cooked breakfast. "Come with me," said Dream Weaver. "Let's go down to the river. If you're going to live here, it's time people saw you by daylight."

They threaded past the palisade and the planting field. Ole looked up and down the river. Children with dripping hair from their dip stopped chasing each other to stare at him. A boy on early crow patrol between the corn mounds climbed down from his platform to stare in disbelief. Two youths came up to them. Ole introduced Beaver Tooth and Fisher to his sister.

"Come with us, Ole," said Beaver Tooth. "With your sister's consent, we'll take you to the men's cove to wash."

It improved Ole's mood to see his friends from the island. Fisher told him what he wanted to know as they walked. "Your newness will wear off when people get to know you. They have more important things to talk about. The girls are swarming around Jekonsaseh, asking how it is that she has no matron she must obey. They envy her. If you want to know, she slept beside her uncle and brother in Bear's guesthouse."

Ole admitted to himself he did have some concern about that. Beaver Tooth added, "Runs Fast left on his hunt before dawn."

"You two don't miss much."

They grinned. Fisher said, "As long as we have you, we thought we would teach you how to swim so you won't be captured the next time an empty canoe floats by." At home in Greenland, no one thought of swimming. The fjords were frigid and the ocean was fearsome.

"I'd rather not."

"You must learn. We'll show you." They walked further and beckoned him to follow. Trusting they knew what they were doing, he took several steps more. The night-chilled water lapped around his legs up to his knees.

"Good. Now watch me and copy what I do." Beaver Tooth passed the playing boys and walked in deeper. Then, he slipped all the way under. Ole dared not move. Beaver Tooth emerged several canoe lengths away and seemed to stand in the water. Surely his feet would not touch the bottom so far out.

"You can learn to do what he does. It can save your life. Look, he is coming back," said Fisher.

Beaver Tooth swam on top of the water this time, reaching forward with one arm and then the next, and lifting his head to breathe every few strokes. "Were you watching? You're going to do it, too." He shook his long hair, spraying Ole with cold water. "Now look at this." He floated on his back. "You are a canoe and your hands are paddles. Watch my hands." He demonstrated, moving them gracefully just under the water and gliding smoothly away. Then, he flipped over and swam back. "Now you do it. I'll catch you if you get in trouble."

Ole tried to push off, but panicked and went under when his feet no longer touched the muddy bottom. He churned his arms until his head broke the surface, spitting out water and gasping. Fisher was beside him in an instant, holding him and telling him to breathe. They pulled him to shallow water.

"Don't feel bad. We'll try again later," Fisher assured him. "I never knew a man who couldn't swim."

"That was enough," Ole said firmly.

They walked back cross the corn field and into the town. The brothers pointed him to Wolf Longhouse and went to get their own breakfasts in Bear. Ingrid waved Ole over and handed him a bowl and a wooden spoon. "Grandmother offered to adopt you into Wolf clan, if you want," she said.

"I have to say yes," he said. The attempt at swimming left him hungry. He licked the corn gruel off his spoon and dipped it for more. "I promised Father to protect you. You don't need a protector now, but I can't go back to the Inuit."

"True. Your hair is wet."

"Beaver Tooth and Fisher tried to teach me to swim." She waited for the rest of the story. "I will need more lessons." He wondered if he would see Jekonsaseh before she left with her friends, but Ingrid was speaking of her marriage.

"Runs Fast will move into Wolf Longhouse. Grandmother will give us our own section for our home. It will be small for now, until our family grows."

"You are really happy here?" She nodded. "Then, I'm glad for you. Do you know when the Peace leaders will go?"

She studied his expression. "Does she mean that much to you?" When he did not reply, she said, "Probably after the festival. Come with me to the All Clans fire to hear the announcements. You should know it is customary to give a gift for your adoption and name." He followed her thoughtfully, knowing what he must give. He had nothing else.

The matrons spoke in turns. At hers, Wolf Clan Mother summoned Ole and Ingrid to her and had them face the crowd. "Here is Dream Weaver. She crossed the frozen ocean on a toboggan pulled by dogs. Since Runs Fast erased the stain of cowardice that forced him into exile by guiding and defending them, Bear Clan Mother accepted him back. She and I agreed to his marriage with Dream Weaver, daughter of my daughter Gahrastah. I adopt Red Hair as my grandson."

He drew out his knife in its sheath and cord from under his shirt and slipped the cord over his head to free it. He walked to Wolf Clan Mother on her bench and offered it to her, hilt first. "This was my father's and my grandfather's." She picked it up and pulled it out of its sheath. The steel was gray and the hilt had been reinforced with cords. "Unwrap the cord and you will see carvings in the whale tooth hilt. The carvings say my name in the words of my people."

Wolf Clan Mother did so. She fingered the marks and then lifted the knife. "This is a man's weapon, not a woman's. Take it back and use it on my behalf, remembering that it is mine." Surprised but glad, he took it back and rewound the cord. Now that it formally belonged to Wolf Clan Mother and not him, he was less worried someone would challenge him for it or steal it.

Bear Clan Mother had Runs Fast stand. "Here is Runs Fast, my son. He guided and protected Dream Weaver and Red Hair through enemy land. He taught them our speech. When Red Hair became lost, Runs Fast tracked him and brought him home. He also brought Mother of Nations to us. He has hunted and brought home meat for his wedding meal. Dream Weaver will cook it with new beans, corn and squash, in honor of the festival. My son will move to Wolf Longhouse."

After the matrons, Hiawatha received permission to make announcements. He said that he, Deganawida and Jekonsaseh planned to go west in the morning. "We request two volunteers from each clan. One may be a youth in need of training. While you decide, see what Dream Weaver has made for our Peacemaker."

Deganawida stretched out the wampum belt Ingrid wove over his head. The belt used water-smooth purple and white quahog shells threaded to picture a stylized fir tree with an eagle at the top, purple on a white background. "This is the Peace Tree."

The speeches went on. Ole sat among his Wolf brothers who were exclaiming over his knife, but his thoughts were on Jekonsaseh. Witch or not, her departure would leave him bereft. Dream Weaver and Runs Fast had each other now. What would he do with the rest of his life? Someone touched his elbow. "Red Hair."

Ole looked up. "Yes?"

"I am your Uncle Burned Lip and your war chief. Come with me. I must learn your skills and how to best use them."

Red Hair followed him and some of his new brothers to the shadow of Wolf Long House. Burned Lip introduced him to the others. Each name said something about its owner, as Red Hair said something about him - Big Hand, Wounded Shoulder, Bird Catcher and more. He could not remember all the names.

Burned Lip said. "Although we voted for peace, living here, near Algonquin land, we will always have enemies. We must try the strength of your arm."

Ole won a contest of strength against Bird Catcher, a man his size, lying down, arm against arm. Bird Catcher helped him to his feet with a friendly smile.

They got to their feet to find that Deganawida, Hiawatha and Jekonsaseh had been watching. "With your permission, War Chief Burned Lip," said Hiawatha, "Wolf Clan Mother said Red Hair might be of use to our Peace party. Will you allow us to test him?"

"If Red Hair can help the Peacemaker, I won't stand in his way."

They brought him to the guest lodge. The three sat on hides on the bed benches. Hiawatha spoke, but Ole could not make out his words. Jekonsaseh's features blurred until they became those of her childhood self. A groan escaped him. His nightmare returned. Once more, the evil one killed the eagle. A girl died. Madness possessed the younger Hiawatha. He smelled the coppery scent of blood. "Stop it!" He covered his eyes to block out the vision.

Hiawatha and Deganawida helped him to a hide and had him sit down. "What is wrong, Red Hair?" Jekonsaseh asked.

Jekonsaseh touched his wrists, but he yanked them away. "Don't touch me," he cried. His eyes moved wildly.

"What do you see?" she insisted.

He made his mouth work. "Hiawatha's daughter crushed. The tall man's hair becomes snakes." He buried his face in his hands and his voice trembled. "It is horrible. Why did you make me a witch like you to see such things?"

Jekonsaseh moved away from Red Hair and reached for her uncle, but she turned to Deganawida. "How is Red Hair seeing this?" she asked.

Deganawida knelt and touched Red Hair's cheeks and then his chin to hold his face steady. He gazed into Ole's eyes and laid both hands on Ole's shoulders. "Red Hair, you are with us and we will help you." His touch was calming. Ole felt safe. "You asked what Jekonsaseh did to you. We will search for answers together. Let me be your teacher. Will you come with us, hunt and defend us, and be one of my followers?"

The pressure of impending madness retreated. Since his mother died, Ole had not believed in much of anything. Now, he wanted nothing more than to be in the presence of this young man who could cure madness and lift curses. "If my clan mother and war chief allow, I will go with you and be your follower."

Chapter 17

"Let us begin." Deganawida's voice was confident and without impediment. Ole wondered if the stammering was meant to deceive his listeners, to keep them off guard. He decided not to question, but to listen. Deganawida said, "You have grieved long enough for what you have lost. It is time to put the past where it belongs."

"I know my own past. What did Jekonsaseh do to me that I saw her past?"

"That is what we will try to learn," Hiawatha said. "What did you do to Red Hair, niece?" He believed Ole that something had been done to him. "You have not been with him since you came here."

Jekonsaseh seemed to gaze inward. "It was on the island. I had gone there to protect a bear cub and let her grow a little. Her mother was dead and she was too young to care for herself." Hiawatha lifted his head. "Yes. You know." Ole felt left behind. They knew each other well.

"Then Red Hair came. A snake bit him. I tried to heal him." Ole listened quietly. "His memories were making him worse. I only wanted to help." Hiawatha moved behind her. With his fingertips, he massaged her shoulders and neck. She took a breath and blew it out. "I entered his dreams to learn what disturbed him. His world is so different. What I could not understand, I asked. I should have withdrawn, but when his mother died, I remembered my mother." She clutched Hiawatha hand.

Anger filled Ole at her invasion of his privacy. He felt sick. His mind had been invaded once before, by a northern sorcerer. Would he never be done with witches?

She was speaking again. "I remembered Sweet Water and Ogannis'tah, and all my cousins. I remembered my father. I was too weak to separate our minds." She met Ole's eyes briefly and sorrowfully. "That is why he sees that terrible day. It is my fault." She covered her face.

Deganawida's soft voice filled the small room. "You did not intend this, Jekonsaseh, but you opened old wounds for both of you. You and Red Hair became one in unhappiness. You opened a channel between you."

"I don't want this," Ole moaned.

Hiawatha said, "It has happened. Red Hair, we understand this is strange to you, but it does not have to change anything. You can learn to control your mind and block out the thoughts and memories of others. Would you like to use your power to protect yourself? We can help if you come with us."

They did not hurry him, but they were leaving in the morning. "I wanted to help my sister find a home. I did that. This is a strange country to me, full of forces I don't understand. When Jekonsaseh leaves, our channel will break, won't it?"

"Possibly," said Deganawida. "Think and tell us what you decide later. Your sister and Runs Fast are waiting for you. Go to them."

Outside, Ole thought the spirits of this wooded land had used him like a game piece. They had moved him where they wanted him to be with invisible fingers, first to Jekonsaseh's island, to Doteoga with Jekonsaseh so she could find her uncle and brother again. If the strange gods of this country had a use for him, could he escape by turning his back on those who offered to help him? As Hiawatha said, he had a marriage feast to attend. He could forget about gods and spirits for a while. He sniffed and detected roasting meat. Food did not require thinking. Here was something he could understand.

Both Bear and Wolf matrons were with his sister and Runs Fast. Dream Weaver welcomed him with baskets piled with boiled corn, bowls of succotash and succulent turkey. She dipped up crushed berry tea and poured it into a mug for him. His morning had increased his appetite. "You're a good cook, sister," he said around a mouthful of corn. She accepted his enjoyment of her food.

After the meal, Runs Fast thanked his wife and company and said he'd be back shortly. "Where is he going?" Ole asked.

"To get his clothing, furs and weapons," said Wolf Clan Mother. "He will live here now." The meal had sealed their marriage. Runs Fast returned laden with bundles, his sleeping furs over his shoulders.

"Good luck living with my sister," said Ole.

"My luck was in finding her. I think I'll manage the rest. My wife and I would like to be alone now, if you don't mind." He made a small movement as though to push them away.

Ole left Wolf Longhouse with the matrons who bade him enjoy the last day of the festival They took their accustomed benches. Ole found a hide mat and stretched out his legs. He tried to pay attention to the chanting and the discussions, but the words came too fast for him to follow.

Parts of his conversation in the guest house came back. He decided to take a walk through the corn hills to the river. Children scampered among the green stalks, hiding and finding, rolling wooden balls. Others escaped the tedium of the speeches and splashed in the river. Ole sat against a tree to watch them and lose himself in their freedom.

He watched carefully, trying to learn by observing. There was more than one method to move through water. Some boys swam on their sides like crabs. Others kicked like frogs. One pushed the water behind him, one arm at a time. He moved his hands like fins and his feet like a fish with two tails. If children found swimming so effortless, he should be able to do it, too.

He hung his breechclout over a branch along with his knife on its cord. Before he entered the river, he made a small prayer to his own spirits. Odin, father of the other gods, had traded one of his eyes for wisdom. Ole depended upon Red Thor for war luck, but Odin was the god to approach when one needed advice.

Ole kept close to the bank at first, copying the boys. The water no longer felt cold. He remembered Beaver Tooth's instructions, pictured himself as a canoe, bent his knees and pushed off from the bottom. He moved! Next, he tried the leaf posture on his back. After a while, he turned over again to see where he was. Moss and algae tinted the water green. Silvery fish darted out of his way.

He watched the fluffy clouds floating in the sky. He felt peaceful and sleepy. Almost imperceptibly, he floated out of the cove and into the wider river. Leaves and twigs floated with him. Had he wished, he could break free from the current and go home. He had the power to direct himself. After a while, he turned over and looked to the bank. There was no sign of the cornfields or the boys.

Flies buzzed around his head. He ducked to escape them and began to swim back the way he had come. Between the close trees, he noticed a smaller cove. He propelled himself toward it, thinking to emerge and find the river path. A split sycamore, one side dead, the other thick with leaves, leaned over the stream creating moving shadows on the water. He was reminded of the murky pool that had caught his canoe. That water was still, inviting insects. This pool was different, even more dangerous.

Twigs and leaves whirled around a vortex. Even as he propelled himself away from it, he saw driftwood and fish being pulled down in ever descending circles. He had heard of such things in the ocean, whirlpools massive enough to swallow ships. This one was enough to swallow a tree or a canoe, or him! He pulled hard.

He had been reckless to come here alone. He had not moved his legs like this since before the island. For the first time, he wondered if he would return at all. He pushed the water behind him, almost in a panic, until he saw the fishing canoes. Finally, he dragged himself into shallow water where he could stand. His breath came fast and ragged as he sucked in air. His heart pounded loudly. So glad to have made it to land, he realized he'd forgotten to watch for snakes. Then, amid splashes and excited barks, Dream Weaver's dog swam up to him.

Ole held onto Boy's thick ruff and waded to dry land where he collapsed amid a stand of cattails, panting. "Thank you, Boy," he said. His sore leg pulsed with indignation, and his arms felt weak. He barely had strength to rub them. He collapsed on the bank, laid back his head and closed his eyes.

That is where his sister and Runs Fast found him. "Ole," she said harshly. "We've been looking and looking for you, just like before. Where did you go?"

Still panting, he looked up. "Like before, I did something stupid. I was teaching myself to swim."

"You were swimming?" Runs Fast asked skeptically.

"I think that is what you call it. Did you know a monster lives underwater in a cove that way." He pointed downriver. "It nearly got me."

Dream Weaver looked to her husband in alarm. Runs Fast said, "I know about it. It lives there. Will you never learn not to go wandering off alone? Find your clothing and let us get you warm again."

They entered Wolf Longhouse. The curtain had been tied back to enjoy the long, lazy sunset. The food was cold, but the women had been keeping the sassafras root tea in a pot over the hearthstones. Dream

Weaver brought him a cup and covered his legs with his hide blanket. Wolf Clan Mother heard Ole's story. "Yes. Unless you are in a hurry to feed the monster, don't go there again. What about your talk with the Peacemaker? Did you agree to go with him and be one of his men?" Of course she would know.

"They speak of things I do not understand," he said.

"Most of us don't. You can still defend the Peacemaker's followers against the tyrant and his Onondaga warriors."

Ole touched his knife. "I can try."

"So you are going to leave us already," said Runs Fast. "I thought you would." Now that he was safe, the couple had other things to do.

Ole pulled his blanket over his head. He had not slept long when the door curtain was pulled back. The hearth fires shot up sparks in the sudden draft and seemed to roar. He sat up and rubbed his eyes, trying to make out what happened. Several men entered at once and stood together, defiant. Wolf warriors rose to their feet, hands reaching for clubs and spears. Ole drew his knife.

"Come outside, Wolf Clan," shouted the newcomers' leader.

"What are you doing here, Turtle Claw?" challenged Burned Lip, the grip of his heavy war club in his right hand, its strap around his wrist.

"We have a new challenge for the Huron, a better test than his trained eagle. We refuse to end the war until we have shattered our enemies. Come outside and see if your Peacemaker will survive."

It seemed to Ole that in her anger, Wolf Clan Mother grew taller. Her women stood by her, but Burned Lip whispered something in her ear. "Go then," she said. "But if he kills the Peacemaker, no woman of Doteoga will feed him again."

"That's a threat she can keep," Runs Fast explained as they walked. Turtle Claw and his companions stopped at the All Clans plaza. The longhouses had emptied, mothers carrying babes on their backs to hear the challenge.

Deganawida stood alone, guards with torches around him. Turtle Claw's men held Jekonsaseh and Hiawatha back. Ole had not seen the clouds piling up, being asleep. Lightning flashed over the river and thunder rumbled.

Chapter 18

With their hide mantles settled over their shoulders, the three clan matrons stood side by side, projecting a wall of authority. Within the houses, they were unquestioned, but war remained the domain of men. They could only advise. Hardly a sound issued from the crowd. No one objected as Ole shouldered closer to see.

"What is this about, Turtle Claw?" demanded Turtle Clan Mother harshly. "The men voted to follow the prophet."

"Not all of us." He crooked his thumb at Deganawida. "The Hurons are no friends to the Tribes, and this one has barely left the cradleboard. He must prove himself to us before we will follow him."

"The eagle came," shouted a woman vehemently.

"Women are quick to believe what they want. Why would the Creator send a Huron youth who has never been to war to the Tribes to lead proven warriors? You have never fought in a war, have you, Peacemaker?" He snarled the title.

"No."

Remembering his promise to defend the Peacemaker, Ole advanced on Turtle Claw, his knife half-drawn. Deganawida spoke in his mind. *Do not interfere, Red Hair. I must prove myself alone.* Ole moved back.

A Bear war chief said, "The Peacemaker's coming has been foretold. He promised to lead us to victory and to overthrow the sorcerer. Have you and your friends thought this through, Turtle Claw?"

That man glared at him. "You and those who voted for peace have not thought. Your Peacemaker is nothing but talk. He can't even do that for himself, but needs the cursed Hiawatha to talk for him. I do not speak against Mother of Nations. Everyone honors her, but the truth is that she hates her father. She would follow anyone who promised peace. Women don't understand honor. How can we hold up our heads if we beg our enemies for peace? While I can hold a war club, Ganeo-gaono Tribe will not be dishonored."

His words were echoed around them, mumbled and repeated. Someone spoke sharply. "Are you calling us cowards?"

Turtle Claw rounded on him. "Either we destroy the Snake Haired or he will rule us. Shall we lay down our clubs and beg him for mercy? There is no peace without victory and no honor either."

The other man might have spoken again, but Hiawatha stopped him. "Deganawida said Tododaho will not rule you." Turtle Claw stepped toward him. The torches cast his shadow menacingly on the Peacemaker.

"Those are fine words, but I don't want to hear from the cursed one. I don't believe him and I don't believe you, Hiawatha. Huron, if the Snake Haired is not destroyed, we are beaten and he will rule us. As bad as that would be, at least he is not Huron!" Turtle Claw spat on the ground. "We Ganeo-gaono are proud, and the proud do not surrender." Behind him, his friends lifted their voices in support. Disagreement had been subdued. When it was quiet again, Turtle Claw turned to Deganawida. "Speak for yourself, Man of the North, if you can."

"Do you think I am a threat?" he asked calmly.

"Not directly," Turtle Claw responded. "Tell me. If the five tribes unite, what will that do to your country?"

"That is not for me to say. I must do what I was called upon to do."

"What sort of man gives no thought to his birth tribe? You say the Creator sent you to unite the Tribes. Prove it, Huron."

"De-demand of me what you will. I will do as you say until you are sat-satisfied." Jekonsaseh stepped closer to him, her jaw tight, her body held stiffly. As he had done with Ole, Deganawida must have sent her a message, for she stepped back. This was his challenge and his alone.

"If the Creator wishes, he can protect you from death. Is that true?" Turtle Claw spoke loudly for all to hear.

"He has work for me. I believe he will protect me," said Deganawida.

"My challenge involves no weapon made by man. I will not touch you, nor will any man among us. There is a certain monster under the river known to us. It swallows anyone or anything that ventures near it. We challenge you to test your life against the river monster."

Ole gaped, remembering his near escape. Had he not seen it in time, it would have swallowed him. Deganawida appeared neither frightened nor angry, only determined. "If I sur-survive your test, will you believe in me and follow me?"

"I will." His companions repeated the promise.

"Then, be-before these witnesses, I say to you, if the Creator does not protect me from the monster, I am ready to die and you will not see me again."

Ole could only hope the whirlpool demon slept. If it did not, he did not give much for Deganawida's chances. Whirlpools in the northern ocean had swallowed whole umiyaks with families aboard. Their bones were never found. The sea hunters gave water monsters great respect. This forest world had gods Ole did not know, but he could not deny wind and water, storm and creation. It was all around. A man who could send thought and lift curses was not without protection. Since Ole had left his own gods far behind, he whispered a simple prayer to the Creator that Deganawida would survive. Billowing thunderclouds lit internally over the Wide River. They glowed and grew dull again, and rumbles followed, another reason to keep far from water.

A flash lit the sky and the thunder shook the ground. The boys ran ahead so as not to miss anything. They walked through a drizzle fine as mist. Waves lapped the bank. Periodically, lightning turned the river from a harsh gray with froth-topped waves running before the wind to a frightening white.

"He has to survive," said Dream Weaver. "I saw his Tree of Peace in a vision. It has to come true. He can't die here."

Runs Fast took her arm. "He's human, Dreamer. Humans die."

The wind blew harder. Lighting forked down to the water and a thunderclap followed that seemed to split the earth. "The Creator is angry that we allow this," Wolf Clan Mother shouted to her people. Many voices agreed. The dogs whined again, cowering at the power manifested by wind, river and sky.

Turtle Claw stopped by the split, half dead sycamore. Lightning had struck it once and might do it again. It leaned perilously over the river. Its white roots had half left the ground. Ole pointed out the bubbling water to his companions. It tumbled and swirled, reflecting the light within the clouds back to them. "It almost got me this morning. It might be angry I escaped."

"The monster is awake now for sure," said Runs Fast. "Even under water, how can it sleep through this noise?" He motioned to the clouds and the flashes. "Since you failed to feed it, it probably wants another victim. If the Peacemaker survives Turtle Claw's contest, maybe I'll follow him myself."

The matrons protested, claiming it could not be a fair test. Entering the river during a lightning storm was hazardous enough without entering the whirlpool's domain. Turtle Claw would not withdraw his challenge and Deganawida stood ready.

The boys ran ahead to assure themselves a good view. A father reminded them that that last summer, his son and a cousin dared to swim too near the cove to master their fear and prove their courage. Their fathers found their mangled and half-eaten bodies downstream, a few days later. Whether the whirlpool monster ate them when it killed them or the birds did so afterwards could not be determined.

Turtle Claw ordered Deganawida to climb the dead half of the tree. He did so without hesitation, stopping when he reached the highest branch that would hold him. The tree creaked and bent lower until its top branches skimmed the water. "The bank is crumbling," someone shouted.

A boy called out, "Look out!" Turtle Claw and his friends were pushing against the damaged truck with their combined weight.

"They're trying to kill the Peacemaker," shouted one of the girls

"It isn't a fair trial," Dream Weaver said.

Runs Fast stroked her back. Ole heard him say, "He must want to die. What a fool!" Ole could not take his eyes away. The sky flashed white and the wind wailed over the river, crackling the dead leaves. The river rose over the lower branches, breaking them off. A continuous roar of thunder pounded their ears. The tree shuddered. In fact, the entire forest seemed to shriek in outrage. With a crack and a groan, the tree gave way and splashed into the river.

Deganawida clung to the branch like a bear as it tumbled into the churning white water. Fisher and Beaver Tooth, with other boys, moved up for a better look at the floating, spinning tree. Their parents called them back. "The tree missed the whirlpool, but the Peacemaker isn't in it, anymore," Fisher called out as they returned.

Beaver Tooth kept watch. "He's in the water. He's not trying to swim away. It's dragging him down. The monster is swallowing him!"

Ole ran forward to see, not believing Beaver Tooth's report. He took a deep breath as if he could breathe for the peace leader. By the time he breathed again, there was nothing left to see. No one moved. The dogs set up a howling to match the wind. The whirlpool, sated, slowed and ceased to spin. Finally, the uprooted sycamore trunk was seen caught in the current and hurrying downriver.

Deganawida was gone. The town children ran down the bank looking for him until their mothers called them back, reminding them the Wide River flowed into Algonquin Country. What did they think the Algonquin would do to them?

They turned back, complaining, "He isn't coming out." "It's over." "He must be dead." Lightning struck a nearby tree. Thunder sounded. Mothers urged their children to hurry home before Heno, wind spirit, struck one of them with a lightning stick.

"He can't be dead," Jekonsaseh said nearly too softly to hear, but Ole heard her and shared her anguish. Hiawatha helped support her and urged her to come away from the river. "We will wait for him at home."

The subdued crowd returned along the bank and crossed the corn hills. The stalks, relieved of their first ears for the Green Corn Ceremony, were bowed and broken by the wind. Some had been felled completely by the rain that followed the last long thunderclap. Six Pebbles, Turtle Claw's nephew, walked with his uncle. Crooked Arm, Fisher and Beaver Tooth's uncle, walked with them, one arm on each their shoulders. He tried to console them for losing out on their adventure. They had been looking forward to joining the peace party.

Ole heard Crooked Arm say the war would not cease after all, but at least they would win honor before they died in battle. He would train them despite his poorly healed left arm. In spring, he would lead them west to fight with their Bear cousins against Tododaho's forces.

Dream Weaver walked with Runs Fast and Boy, and Ole. No one hurried despite the rain. Ole looked back before he entered the now forlorn town. Inside, women hugged each other for consolation. Even men spoke sadly of their disenchantment. Their hopes to bring an end to the years of privation and death had come to nothing. The Peacemaker had met his end. The war would continue.

Ole entered Wolf Clan House, found his bed bench and stretched out on his bed and tried to blot out the sounds of disappointment. With closed eyes, he saw more clearly. He didn't know if he slept and entered a dream, or if he saw a vision. It seemed to him that he saw through the longhouse walls and the palisade surrounding the town. His vision brought him back across the planting field to the trees on the riverbank, and back to the abode of the whirlpool monster.

He knew he was home safe in bed so did not concern himself with his safety. His formless dream body flew over the churning, fast-flowing river and descended into the whirlpool. He felt neither cold nor wet. Light came from somewhere. There was a sinkhole below the cove that dropped into a limestone cavern. The undercurrent tossed and pulled anything that entered the vortex. The sinkhole was underwater, but Ole's dream body did not need to breathe.

He saw when Deganawida was sucked down and into the cavern and heard a voice. It was not Deganawida's, but another's, deeper and older. The voice said, *When you were born, when your grandmother tried to drown you, I begged the Creator to spare you. I begged him to never allow water to harm you. Not only the pond, but each river and stream gave the Creator its word. It is not your time to die, Thinker. Wide River, give him back to the land safely. He has work left to do.*

Ole realized then it must be a vision he should keep to himself. No one would believe it. Perhaps Hiawatha would, but Ole would not tell Jekonsaseh. If it was true, she would find out soon enough. If it was only his hope turned into a dream, hearing it from him would be worthless. Water could not gather itself into a giant hand. Neither, in reality, could the river's hand lift the unconscious Deganawida to the surface and set him gently on the bank near the town.

Ole's vision brought him back to the muddy field, to the palisade wall and through it. He passed the three matrons standing under the dripping eaves of Bear Longhouse. His spirit heard Wolf Clan Mother say, "I hoped the Creator would make a miracle that would convince everyone. I believed in him."

"If I knew what Turtle Claw planned, I would have stopped his breath before I took him to my breast," said Turtle Clan Mother. "Now our sons and grandsons will die in battle for there will be no peace. Before many more turns of seasons, we will be gone from the earth and forgotten. The ghosts of our men can brag of honor, but no one will be left to hear them."

"Don't blame yourself," Bear Clan mother told the Turtle matron. "The Snake Haired once had a mother. She should have stopped his breath."

Turtle Clan Mother's white hair dripped and blew around her head from the rain and wind. "I don't deserve your comfort. My son ended the Peacemaker's mission. What he was going to do for us will remain undone. We might as well go to bed." They parted and entered their houses. The rain came down harder, although the lightning and thunder moved westward. It seemed that the sky wept at the people's lost hopes. In spirit form, Ole let the rain run down his face. He could blame the rain for his wet cheeks, should another disembodied spirit see him. He entered the silent longhouse. People had talked themselves out and had no more to say. The Younger Twin had won.

By daybreak, the rain clouds had fled west. They were just an outline of gray, leaving a clean blue sky over the town. Puddles filled the spaces between the houses and water dripped from roofs and trees.

A boy left his house to make water. On his way home, he noticed smoke rising out of the guest house smoke-hole. Without respect for the rules concerning guests and privacy, he ran to it and pulled back the curtain. What he saw caused him to shout loud enough to awaken the town. "Deganawida is back at the guest lodge. He is at the hearth like he was never dead, and cooking breakfast!"

Chapter 19

Hiawatha tied back the door curtain so people could see Deganawida for themselves, not only alive but in good health. Children sloshed through puddles to witness the miracle and the adults crowded after them. No one dared to enter the guest lodge. Deganawida smiled at the children's delighted screams and waved. Hiawatha greeted their visitors. "Good morning," he said. "We invite the clan matrons and our volunteers to come inside."

Seeing him hesitate, Scout took Ole's shoulder. "Nephew, he told us to come in." Ole stepped into the small room with his uncle, but kept back. Glad as he was to see Deganawida alive, he distrusted miracles. As Wolf Clan's newest member, they would not expect him to speak. At least, he could observe. He would like to make sense of what he had seen, if that was possible.

Jekonsaseh's strained eyes and mouth gave evidence. She had thought Deganawida dead too. Their minds did not have to touch to know she had not expected to see him alive again. She had been shattered last night and was as amazed as everyone that he was back. She met Ole's eyes briefly before she looked to the others. She must regret as much as he, that she had opened a channel between their inner selves. Memories of their nights on the island threatened his awareness of the present.

Deganawida was giving his volunteers instructions when a shadow filled the doorway. Turtle Claw stood there, a few feet away from him. Ole fingered the grip of his knife. Scout motioned him to wait. Hiawatha invited the Turtle warrior to come in. The others parted to open a path for him.

Turtle Claw stopped a pace away from Deganawida and knelt with lowered head in complete and humble submission. "Forgive me," he said, lifting his head. "You are who you claim to be. I will follow you and bear witness of my challenge and your survival of it to the farthest tribe on the last beach on Turtle Island, if you allow me to join your company."

Turtle Clan Mother sniffed when the Peacemaker lifted Turtle Claw to his feet and took his hands. The Huron stammered, "We won't go to the end of the world, only through Tribal land, but I would be pleased to have you join us. Be my witness. Who could be better than you?"

Ole watched their exchange with worry. It seemed the warrior's tight throat relaxed and he breathed easier. Turtle Claw did not ask how Deganawida survived, but the question remained. Deganawida said though Hiawatha, "I did not plan how to escape the river monster. I recall nothing but the cold water, but somehow, I am here. Turtle Claw and his nephew Six Pebbles have joined us and your companions are convinced the vote went the right way. You will help me establish peace among the Tribes. When all Five agree to my terms, I will go."

He paused for them to take this in. "The festival has ended. Eat breakfast with your families. Prepare your gear and have your women prepare your trail food. We will begin our journey this morning."

The volunteers carried the long war canoes overhead. Dream Weaver touched Ole's bare chin and cheeks. "You shaved again," she said, smiling up. "You look much more Ganeo-gaono now."

"Not enough to fool anyone who looks closely. I still wonder how this is going to work. I suppose I will find out. Fisher and Beaver Tooth are coming, too, with their Uncle Crooked Arm." She knew they were the boys who claimed the canoe. "I will keep my hair under my cap. I don't want to take attention from our leaders." He hugged Dream Weaver and Runs Fast, then lifted his pack and took his place with his Uncle Scout in the file to get into his assigned canoe.

Crooked Arm, Fisher and Beaver Tooth followed. Turtle Claw and Six Pebbles entered the last canoe. Their women handed down their packs. The two canoes pushed off after the slim white canoe that held Hiawatha, Deganawida and Jekonsaseh. The men dipped their paddles and they set off.

When the white canoe put in near a town or village, people hurried to see and hear this rumored 'Man from the North' Mother of Nations promised would come to them. Some of the women spoke about how youthful he looked to be a prophet. Warriors and boys appeared perplexed at this, but the women were shaken. When they were told Hiawatha accompanied him and would speak for him, alarm broke out.

In his beautiful, carrying voice, Hiawatha explained how his curse had been lifted by the young Huron. Reactions varied from shock and alarm to hope, but every assembly invited them to come inside and tell their story. The Peacemaker exhibited the wampum belts and explained what they meant. More belts would follow as women copied the designs and sent them to each community that voted for peace.

From Doteoga, the most northeastern town on the Wide River, they zigzagged to the most southern Ganeo-gaono town, Skahnektati, where two rivers joined. Chieftains and clan matrons ran their fingers over the two wampum belts, the Peace Tree and the united tribes. Hiawatha translated Deganawida's stammering Huron into lofty Longhouse speech. When people asked to hear the prophet speak for himself, they were less impressed. Good speakers had always been honored by the Tribes. "You're not one of us," said an elder. "Why should we believe you?"

Turtle Claw spoke up. "No human saved him from the water monster. We all saw him dragged down by the whirlpool. The next morning, he was seen back in the guesthouse with Hiawatha and Mother of Nations, making their breakfast. He gains nothing by helping us. In fact, his people may suffer, but the Creator sent him to us. He promised Mother of Nations and the matrons he will return our old Law and defeat the Snake Haired. I believe in him."

The people discussed this. Besides Jekonsaseh, faith keepers and chiefs had dreamed of his arrival, if not exactly how he would look or speak. A warrior asked, "Why would the Creator send a foreigner instead of one of our own?"

Hiawatha called Ole to come before the assembly and removed his cap. "Red Hair is a foreigner, too. Look at him well. Have you ever seen someone with such hair and coloring? He was born on a different world."

Ole had gained some fluency, yet his looks and accent still set him apart. "I have seen what the Peacemaker can do. I will tell you why I believe in him and want him to succeed." His audience waited. Red Hair gestured to his own braids. "Long ago, but within old people's memory, people from my world came to Turtle Island. They were Norse. They looked like me, with red hair like the setting sun, and yellow hair like the daytime sun. They used weapons you did not know, weapons like this knife."

He drew and lifted his knife high to reflect the light. "They used bows with arrows that could pierce shields. Look. He passed his knife to a man who passed it on to the others. "Steel is harder than flint. These Norse people decided they liked it here and wanted to stay. The Algonquin said they would permit them to live beside them if they shared their weapons and animals. The Norse people said no and war followed. The Norse had better weapons but fewer people. At the end, the Norse got back on their big canoes and went away."

"What has this story to do with us?" asked a matron.

"The people from my world told others about this good land. They said there were forests of thick trees with which to build their ships, and more animals than they had ever seen, for food and furs. They will come back with more warriors and more weapons to conquer the Algonquin and take their land. Then, they will come for you. How will you resist them if you are fighting each other?" He sat in his place again and his knife was handed back.

An elder asked, "Why do you take our side?" It was a good question.

"Wolf Clan of Doteoga adopted me when I had no home. You are my new people and have my loyalty."

It was a good story and reasonable. More volunteers spoke of their personal dealings with the Peacemaker. He had earned their trust. More volunteers joined them and the group moved on to further towns and villages.

They carted their canoes between the Finger Lakes. Birch leaves yellowed and maples turned red. Oak leaves turned orange and fell. A hunter's moon floated high and clear between night clouds. Frost was replaced by a delicate web of ice in puddles and near the shorelines of the lakes. They broke through to the clear water to visit more towns and villages, collecting believers in the Peacemaker's vision for them.

Ole began to think of himself as Ole Red Hair. The Greenland District of his youth, the glaciers and the ice cap east of them, the war with the English invaders and the last winter of starvation shrunk to a small place in his memories. The white bears of the north and the Inuit with their dogs that pulled sledges over the frozen Arctic were also becoming hazy. His new life and new name grew stronger as they traveled west.

After the first snow, most of the Peace party went home. They made plans to meet on the western shore of Lake Kanyatarak Warote in the spring. Because they had the farthest to go, Red Hair and his townsmen stayed with their leaders to help them through the winter.

Deganawida told those who stayed with him, that they would soon reach Erie, a lake called after the tribe who lived there. They would camp in Seneca land, the westernmost of the Longhouse nations. Jekonsaseh sat in the prow of Deganawida's canoe facing back. She pulled her squirrel cape tight against the snowy wind. Scout paddled, followed by Red Hair, Crooked Arm, Beaver Tooth and Fisher.

They came to land and set up their shelter by lashing the canoes together. The younger men prepared hominy mixed with fish in a cooking sack suspended over their fire. While Scout, Turtle Claw and Crooked Arm hunted, Red Hair remained behind with the younger men to guard their leaders.

Six Pebbles dropped another white-hot rock into the cooking sack and waited for the water to stop hissing. While the food cooked, there was time for stories. "Red Hair," he said. "Tell us how you first became a warrior."

Red Hair scratched his scalp. "You have heard my story. Englishmen heard we were all dead. They came to take our iron knives, our furs and other things. We had to learn war skills and fight them. After the battle, we made our enemies give us their ship because my country had become too cold and empty for us. Imagine a canoe large enough for all the Peace party to ride in. The ship had sails tied to masts for the winds to fill and push." He used gestured to try to explain.

The boys nudged one another. He didn't know if his words had been unclear or if they doubted him. "My father decided my family would go north instead. He knew the people of the north and respected them. We asked them to give us a home. The Naskapi trade with them and call them Eskimo."

"Raw fish eaters?" someone asked. "We've heard of them."

"With the refugees, the Inuit community grew too big. They crossed the frozen ocean in winter to their Western hunting ground. Dogs pulled us on sledges." The boys looked at him suspiciously. "Toboggans?"

"Never mind what you call it. How long was the crossing?" asked Six Pebbles.

Red Hair strained his memory. "The ocean is smaller in the north. We stopped to hunt, but two handfuls of days, twice."

"After you left the raw fish eaters, you came south through Algonquin country. How many of them did you kill?" asked Fisher.

"I didn't stay to count them."

This impressed the young men. "Did you take their scalps?"

"It was not my custom. We were in a hurry."

"How was the hunting in your old country?" Red Hair wondered if it was possible to describe dairy farming and decided against it. He described the seal and reindeer hunts.

Scout, Turtle Claw and Broken Arm returned before dark with one slender deer and a goose. Deganawida remarked that battle and the smell of fire from burned villages and cornfields had spooked the herds even here, but there were stragglers. Turtle Claw agreed, "People will go hungry this winter."

Jekonsaseh said, "If my father continues to burn cornfields, what hope is there for peace? He forces people to starve or submit to him." It was the first time Red Hair really looked at her directly in some time. No one had been eating well lately so why was she rounder? Hiawatha added more food to her bowl.

She rested her hands on her belly. Red Hair had been keeping his distance from her, embarrassed by what they had shared, and the channel that existed between them. He did not want her to be obligated to him out of remorse. She was revered, and had powers he could not begin to understand. Still, she was one of their leaders. Wouldn't she have told him if she was with child? Afraid of the response, he looked away so he would not have to meet her eyes.

They left their fire burning to keep predators away. Deganawida sang their evening song before they settled down for sleep. He did not stammer when he sang. This song assured his followers and defenders they would long be remembered in songs and ceremonies. Before they slept, Six Pebbles complained. "The land here is too flat. It doesn't feel like home. I miss my mother."

Wrapped in her squirrel skin mantle nearby, Jekonsaseh told him he would see her again the following summer. When he returned, he would be a man with all a man's privileges and honor, but now, he needed to rest. Used to obeying women in the longhouse, the boy closed his eyes.

No words passed between Ole Red Hair and Jekonsaseh. They seldom talked together, which widened their estrangement. They traveled in Onondaga land now. He hoped they could avoid meeting her father's warriors. Being near the sorcerer worried her. Red Hair attempted to think of other things so his worry would not increase hers.

He awoke early and went to the lake to shave. His beard made him look too foreign, and they would soon have to request shelter. He mixed some grease he had been saving with cold ashes and spread the concoction over his beard and mustache. It prepared his skin better than grease alone and washed off more easily. Ganeo-gaono warriors devised this method for when they shaved their scalps.

He worked quietly. Fisher found him face forward over a flat rock, using his reflection to slant his steel knife edge against his cheek. He used short, quick strokes and dipped his knife to clean it and resume. Fisher checked his fish lines, not wanting to startle him and cause him to accidentally slit his throat, but he watched Red Hair splash his face and rub away the last of his primitive soap and stubble.

Red Hair rubbed his face and neck dry with a rag. Lastly, he rinsed his knife and dried it on his shirt before he returned it to its sheath. He turned at Fisher's cheery greeting. "Three fish for our breakfast. I'm going back to camp."

An Oneida who had joined the Peace party recently and decided to stay, came to the shore to fill his flask. When he was done, he turned as though he had just noticed Red Hair. "Ganeo-gaono, you with the red hair."

Red Hair had removed his cap. The Oneida did not use the words as a name but as a description. "You want me?"

"The others told me about you. I did not believe." Ole was taller and broader across the shoulders, but the Oneida's arms were well-muscled.

Red Hair met the man's calculated look. "Now you know."

Unless men were friends, a direct look conveyed scorn or challenge. "Are you the offspring of a bear that you shave your face to look human?" Before Red Hair could respond, the Oneida man pointed to the sheath at Red Hair's belt. "Where did you get your white knife?"

Red Hair said, "My name is Ole Red Hair. Is yours *One who is Rude?*"

141

"I'm Cusik of Beaver Clan from Ta-ga-soke in Oneida." The town name meant *forked like a spear* and Cusik actually meant *provoker*. Red Hair had guessed well. "I know about you. You came south through Algonquin land."

"If you know so much, why ask?"

"Deganawida says the Tribes are cousins so we should be friends. I'm being friendly, Cousin Red Hair. Cousins share. Give me your knife."

"No."

"Are you afraid I will keep it?"

Red Hair stepped back. They nearly came to blows when he leaned in and seized Cusik's forearm. "I share good advice. If you don't want to be hurt, Cousin Cusik, don't try to take this knife."

Cusik broke Red Hair's grip and drew his flint knife. Without warning, he lunged at Red Hair who twisted away in time. He darted forward and seized Cusik between his wrist and lower arm and yanked hard. They fell over. The two men grappled until Red Hair had Cusik under his knee. He bent his opponent backward as if to break his neck. It was a wrestling hold his Uncle Scout had taught him.

Scout and the Onieda's townsmen came up to watch. Red Hair pressed his advantage and pulled back his opponent's wrist until Cusik was forced to drop his knife. Moving in, Red Hair got a better hold. With a heave, he lifted the Oneida over his shoulder and tossed him into the cold lake. "Learn manners, Cousin Cusik," he said.

"I will kill you." The Oneida growled. He splashed his way up the gravel bank, shivering and spitting water.

"But we are cousins," Red Hair said, showing teeth. "Let us walk back to camp together to camp. We mustn't disappoint our leaders and behave like unruly boys."

"Do you agree to fight me for your knife?" the other asked, pulling in air.

"I already fought you and won. You should know I have given this knife to my clan mother. I use it on her behalf to protect the Peacemaker so unless you mean to ask her for her knife, I will continue to hold it."

Cusik appraised Red Hair's words and stance. "I only meant to look at it," he said. "There is no reason for anger."

"As long as we understand each other, eat with me. My knife belonged to my father and my grandfather. I don't think you will see another like it. You may hold it, if you like." He held out his hand, fingers curved upward.

"What is that?" he asked, pointing uneasily to Red Hair's hand. "Am I supposed to give you something?"

"No. It is a custom of my first people. If you take my hand for a moment, it means we are pledged not to harm each other. It doesn't mean I like you." Cusik grinned and then clasped Red Hair's hand. The men and boys who watched their interchange tried not to be disappointed.

Cusik said, "I want to hear the story of your knife. Tell me while we eat." The men sat comfortably around the fire, wrapped in their blankets. After Red Hair wiped his mouth and hands, he unwrapped the protective cord from the ivory hilt and let Cusik hold it. "The carvings say my name." Cusik slid his fingers into the grooves. Others drew near to see if magic was involved.

Hiawatha, Deganawida, and Jekonsaseh, across the fire, spoke softly. Hiawatha said, "Red Hair defended himself well. He made a friend rather than an enemy. Don't you think it is time he joined us in council?"

Jekonsaseh said, "No. He is not ready. He understands our goals but he was taught young that one who hears and speaks to the unseen should be feared. He cannot reconcile the two sides of his nature. He pretends not to see that I carry his child so he will not have to face me."

Cusik noticed Jekonsaseh speaking and tapped Red Hair's chest. "Mother of Nations is your woman, isn't she?" he asked.

"She is not mine. I joined the Peace party to repay her for healing me of snake bite. That is all."

Jekonsaseh's hands rested on her rising belly. Her eyes slid regretfully toward Red Hair. Cusik wondered how his strange new friend could counter him so well in words and wrestle with such skill, and yet be so blind.

Chapter 20

Ole Red Hair

Jekonsaseh's long hair whipped around the hood she had pulled down to cover her ears. She faced away from him in Deganawida's canoe so Red Hair could not see her face. The fleet paddled to the southern shore of the most eastern Great Lake. He had not wished for his bond with Mother of Nations, but he did not regret their association. He wanted to keep her safe and prove his worth, but each time he looked in her direction, she was speaking with her brother and uncle or sitting quiet and pensive.

He could not think how to mend the rift between them. He still craved her company, but intimacy between them was no longer possible. She was the well-respected Mother of Nations. She greatly outranked him, as he understood ranking in her culture. In addition, she was a sorceress and therefore supernatural. Red Hair had barely been accepted as a Wolf member when he and his uncle joined Deganawida's enterprise and they began their journey.

This was their second day on the Lake. A brisk wind rolled small waves across the water, but the canoes were well built and their crews knew how to handle them. They were nearing a woody beach on the south shore when flocks of small birds shot skyward, shrieking. They flew over the canoes and disappeared in the distance. Most of the summer birds, the cranes and herons, ducks and geese, had gone to their summer homes. "What caused them to fly like that? A hunting party?" Red Hair asked.

"A lot of hunters," Cusik replied. "Or what is left of a battle."

Deganawida signaled a conference. His men drew their canoes around his white one, sculling to hold them steady when a deeper shadow passed overhead. Crows, ravens, and vultures flew toward what the others had fled. "Carrion-eaters," Deganawida said, "Perhaps we won't be too late."

His men put their shoulders into their strokes and pulled for land. They lifted their canoes from the water and strode toward the sounds of anguish, deep-voiced groans and the higher sounds of women. Bare branches bent over the leaf-covered path. They came to the clearing, but the fighting had ceased. Village women knelt over the fallen men, calling names. "Who won?"

Cusik pointed to the vultures and the crows in the trees, waiting for the living to depart so they could descend to their feast. Injured and dead men lay paces apart between and upon the vacant corn mounds, attackers and defenders together. The earth had been watered with blood.

The Peace party tipped water flasks to those who could swallow. While they worked, Jekonsaseh, Deganawida, and Hiawatha told the women who they were. "We have healers among us. Let us help." The matrons motioned the newcomers to do what they could. Red Hair bent to give drink to a downed warrior. He wondered if the man's war paint, white with red lightning, told a story he did not know how to read. Men tried to mask their pain, it being unmanly to show it. Others with bashed in heads watched unseeing, half alive although they breathed. Nothing could be done for them, but to spare them further suffering.

Women loaded their men on drags to bring them home. A wife who had pulled a spear from her husband's corpse was about to jab it into a helpless enemy. The fallen man was too weak to lift his arms in defense. "Don't," commanded Deganawida. Startled, she obeyed but questioned him angrily. "Don't," he said again.

"Why not? So they can live to kill us another time?"

"We help everyone." The woman scowled, but loaded her husband to bring him home. Deganawida stopped beside the next injured warrior to inspect injuries. "Jekonsaseh, I'll need your help with this one. He took an arrow between his neck and shoulder. The point has to come out. I'll hold him."

She crouched over the fallen warrior with her healer's shoulder bag. Blood had stuck his jacket to his skin. "Use my knife point," Red Hair said. "I keep it sharp." She looked up with thanks. "I'll hold him while you work on him."

Deganawida moved on while Red Hair and Jekonsaseh worked together. She slipped the point under the arrowhead and eased it out. Blood seeped. "It did not pierce a vessel," she said. "He may live."

She cleaned the wound. Someone brought her bandaging, torn hides and strips to hold them in place. "Use this," said the village woman.

Jekonsaseh thanked her. Her mantle was covered with blood from the man's wound. "We need more bandaging anyway." She used his knife to rip out the stitching between the squirrel hides. *Your beautiful mantle* Red Hair thought, remembering lying under it with her. It had been warm, but she had been warmer.

She met his gaze. "It was dead. This man may live." He had communicated without words. Warmth spread across his cheeks and neck when he realized what he had thought. They worked together to save those they could and helped the women bring them home.

The attack had come that morning. The enemy killed the night patrol before they could raise the alarm. The matrons had sent the boys to the nearest Seneca town to ask them for help. Seeing the reinforcements, the attackers fled. Hiawatha thanked Scout for his report. The healers worked by torchlight into the night.

Jekonsaseh was crouched beside a fallen warrior. Someone called her name. She turned and tried to rise, but lost her balance. Red Hair ran to support her. She took a few breaths. "Thank you, Red Hair. Finish this man. I'll go look."

A woman came looking for Deganawida. "Where is Peacemaker?" she asked.

He stood up. "Here I am."

"My husband, Chief Odatshedeh, was lying face down or I would have found him sooner. He is near death. People say you have spirit power. Can you save him?" Deganawida followed her to the fallen leader. Done with his task, Red Hair watched to see what the Peacemaker might do.

The chief was of middle years by the white streaks in his braids, and was heavily scarred. New and clotted blood stained his chest. His breathing was rapid and harsh. Red Hair did not expect the best of healers could save him.

The woman knelt beside him and lifted his head onto her lap. The chief lifted his eyes to the tree above him. Vultures waited, quiet for the moment. Deganawida crouched and tipped his flask to the man's mouth. The man sipped, then took a shallow breath. "Give it to one who can live."

"You will live."

The arrow shaft had broken. When Deganawida pried out the head, the wound bled feebly. He pressed a hide bandage above it. After a while, he offered the chief more water. The man sipped and opened his eyes wider as if to ask why he was still among the living. "Who are you?" His voice had grown stronger.

"People call me Peacemaker."

The chief blinked. "There is life in your touch, Peacemaker, but if you wanted to make peace here, you should have come sooner."

"I, too, wish we had come in time to prevent this."

Deganawida piled furs behind his head to pillow him so he could breathe more easily. The war chief pushed himself to a reclining position and looked around. "Help me to my bed bench," said Odatshedeh. "I don't know how you did it, but I believe you that I will live. How many of our men are left?" he asked his captain.

"Perhaps twenty, if no more die today."

"How many can still fight?"

"Less than half of those. Odatshedeh, you have to rest. There will be no more fighting tonight."

He thanked his second in command. "Who is that woman?"

"Mother of Nations."

The chief grunted. "I should have recognized her. I was injured a few years ago and stumbled into her shelter. She said to expect a man from the north to bring peace." He seized Deganawida's shoulder. "It is you."

"It is me," the Peacemaker confirmed.

Odatshedeh held onto him. "My people," he said in a loud voice. Those who could, came closer. Others looked at him from the bed benches. "This is the man from the north, according to the prophecy. Do as he says."

Jekonsaseh worked over an injured man. Red Hair asked if he could help. "His eye is smashed, and his lower leg is cracked." She dipped a rag into a bowl of cooled hazel water Fisher and Beaver Tooth brought to her. "Thank you," she said. She irrigated the ruined eye and tied a patch over it.

"Can you tell his tribe and clan from his war paint?" asked Red Hair.

"Onondaga South. He is one of Snake Haired's men." She would not call him her father to one of his men.

The injured man's good eye focused on her. "You're not from here. Who are you?" he asked hoarsely.

"Jekonsaseh."

"Mother of Nations! Am I dead already or are you real?"

"I am real." Soon she had set and bound the man's leg. "There is a truce here," she informed him.

"There is always a truce where you dwell," he said. Apparently, the Onondaga did not know of the connection between his commander and his healer.

A Cayuga moved among the other healers, doing what he was told, much as Red Hair was. The man used a black, translucent knife of a sort Red Hair had not seen. He asked what it was.

"Obsidian stone. Traders bring it from the far side of Father of Rivers." They were both free for the moment.

"May I see?" Red Hair held out his hand.

"It is not for sharing."

The words usually went the other way. "I won't keep it." Red Hair noticed his new friend Cusik hovering nearby and thought of something. "My knife is also from a distant country and is as interesting as yours. Look." He drew and displayed his steel knife, flat on his palm, ivory grip first.

The Cayuga allowed Red Hair to examine his knife while he ran his fingers over the steel and ivory. "What is it?"

"Whale tooth and steel."

Red Hair slid his thumb nail gently against the black knife's edge finding it as keen as his own after it had been honed. Cusik had told him about these foreign knives from the west and their tendency to shatter. "Can you sharpen it?" he asked.

"No. If it breaks, glass stone must be knapped again. Where did you get yours?"

"My grandfather brought it back from a war in Spain." At the Cayuga's question, he said, "Spain is on the far side of the ocean." He unwrapped the cord from the grip, revealing the runes that spelled Ole, his Nordic name. These marks protect the one who bears the knife.

Remember that we are under truce." So saying, Red Hair removed his close-fitting cap to expose his hair. The Cayuga drew back.

"You are as unusual as your knife." They handed back the knives and returned to their work. When the last had been attended to, the townsfolk found them beds.

At daybreak, Red Hair, Cusik and the Cayuga went to the lake. Red Hair showed them how he honed his knife on a rough stone. "Let me feel the edge now," said the Cayuga. He touched it gingerly. "I still say mine is sharper."

"It hardly matters," said Cusik. "If Red Hair loses his knife, there is no other to take its place. Obsidian may be had, although one must travel or wait for a trader."

The Cayuga said, "Let the two of us make a contest. I want to see your skill. I won't harm you. Are you willing?" It seemed unlikely the healers would finish their work today. Some of the men had gone hunting. Some antelope or deer might have wandered from the deeper woods around the lake. If food were not found, the Peace party would have to depart. "I suppose," he replied.

Cusik winked to a comrade. "Red Hair, if you accidentally die, can I have your knife?"

"I said it belongs to my clan mother. If I die, give it to my Uncle Scout to return to her."

Cusik sighed but agreed to do so.

"We should know each other's names," said the Cayuga. "I am Maka Tamai which is the first part of a longer name. Call me Condor. It is a large bird with a wing span so wide, a man could lie between them. How do your people call you?"

"Ole Red Hair. You have only to remember Red Hair."

"We found a good place for your contest," young Fisher announced. He and Beaver Tooth had been busy transporting water skins. "The warriors pushed the lake reeds flat and the blood has dried."

Others who had come to wash and fill their flasks stayed to watch. They formed a half circle around the contestants. The lake was to their backs. "Have your contest now, before more water is needed," Beaver Tooth urged.

"They might need us," Red Hair said.

"The injured are sleeping. The women are making breakfast. Let us see how you wield your special knives," said Cusik. "People are already making wagers." The early sun shimmered on the lake, and streaked the dawn orange and pink. Small fish darted in the shallows. A frog jumped in alarm at the sound of men and disappeared into the reeds between the rocks.

Both men unsheathed their knives, one black, and the other when the sun touched it, seemingly white. Condor circled Red Hair, trying to get him to face the sun. It was an old trick. Red Hair jabbed with the point of his blade to keep his adversary back. If he lunged, he would open himself to attack. He must get him closer. He moved halfway around so that the sun favored neither of them. "Come get me, Red Hair," Condor taunted. "Show us how your tribe fights."

Red Hair saw an opening to plunge in his knife. In a real battle, he would have done so, but this was a contest between allies. Instead of going for a vulnerable target, he swung his steel at Condor's obsidian blade. There was a ring and a crack. Red Hair's blade remained whole but the obsidian broke into two shards of black glass.

"Red Hair's blade was best!" exclaimed Fisher, doing a victory dance. "I knew it would be." They were the last words he uttered before an arrow whistled out of the trees and lodged in his throat. The boy crumpled onto the sand, blood welling from his neck.

The small group spun to see their returned enemies who quickly scattered with triumphant whoops. "Kill them," Red Hair shouted. He was too angry to look back to see who ran with him, but he heard yells and the sounds of feet against clumps of snow and fallen leaves. Fisher was like everyone's younger brother. Aside from Runs Fast and Jekonsaseh, Fisher and Beaver Tooth had been the first Longhouse people to befriend him.

His Nordic battle yell flowed back to his comrades. They rushed after him, but he did not look back. He might have been alone for the haze of rage that enfolded him. Two enemy warriors closed in. Red Hair's blade parried the attack. He thrust with deadly intent and results.

The second man leaped at Red Hair, driving at him with his flint. The knife grazed his arm and another slashed his hip, stopping at the bone. At another angle, it would have gone deep and done serious damage, but Red Hair was too full of battle rage to feel. He fought on numb to pain, slashing one's stomach and another's ribs, his blade finding its way to his enemy's heart.

Red Hair was making war against war the only way he knew. Blood spray colored his face and right arm. He could not tell how long it was before weariness stopped him. He felt like he was running through mud when two men seized his arms and one pried the knife out of his hand. He waited for the cut or the blow that would send him to the next world, but none came.

Slowly, the forest and his companions became visible again. The sweet, heavy smell of new blood mixed with the tang of pine, and the wet smell of water weeds. "It is over, Red Hair. We are not your enemy." Condor held one of his arms, and Cusik the other. They walked him between them, for he could not put one foot before the other.

"There is no one left to fight," Cusik assured him. "Beaver Tooth killed his first man. You killed three. We killed the others. You didn't seem to know us. We feared you would turn on us."

Red Hair sagged to his knees, tears burning his eyes as much as his wounds burned his arm and hip. "Fisher was just a boy."

They set Red Hair down to catch his breath. Cusik suggested they drag the corpses from the lake. "They will foul the water." When they were done, Condor brought Red Hair a flask of clear water and told him to drink deeply.

Beaver Tooth was hurt, too. His cheek was torn, but he made no complaint. He was a man now, having killed at least one of his brother's murderers. The cold water helped, but their wounds continued to seep. Red Hair complimented him.

"Fisher won't become a warrior now. I should have protected him better."

"We all should have been on guard. We might have prevented what happened." Red Hair understood the townsfolk's reluctance to heal and bury their enemies. "If the Peacemaker expected us to talk to our attackers instead of avenging Fisher, his vision had no chance anyway."

Deganawida was waiting with Hiawatha when they came in, covered with blood. "You survived," he said. He helped them lay Red Hair on a bed roll. "Someone will see to your injuries."

Jekonsaseh said, "Beaver Tooth, come and show Fisher that you are all right."

Beaver Tooth staggered and looked around, startled. "Fisher fell with an enemy arrow in his throat. Where is he?"

"Here he is." Jekonsaseh cradled Fisher's head. She had stopped the bleeding and bound his throat. "He had wrapped his neck against the cold morning before the arrow found him. It did not go deep enough to kill him. Let him see you. He can't talk, but he can hear. Take my place and feed him." She motioned to the bowl of thin gruel. "Let him lick it off the spoon."

Fisher tried to look brave, but his eyelids creased. "I'll take care of you now," said Beaver Tooth. "We caught up with the enemy. Red Hair killed three of them. I only got one, but I hope he was the one who did this. Cusik and Condor finished off the rest and helped us back. Red Hair is hurt." To the younger boy's questioning glance, he added, "Mother of Nations is tending to him." Fisher attempted a smile.

Jekonsaseh set to work without speaking. Red Hair felt unspoken concern in her soothing hands. She stitched his wound with a bird bone needle. He sucked in air and blew it out, hoping to keep from making a sound. "We had no choice, after they tried to kill Fisher," he said.

"I know."

Cusik told those who had not seen, what happened after the attack. "Beaver Tooth had to avenge Fisher. Red Hair went after them like wildfire before a wind. He said the brothers were his first Longhouse friends."

Chief Odatshedeh asked Red Hair why a man from across the ocean, became one of the Peacemaker's followers.

"He made me believe in him."

The chief was still trying to make sense of it. "Why do any of you follow a Huron? You? You?" He pointed to men at random.

"He asked us to," said Condor. "The Tribes are stronger together. We shouldn't fight each other."

Deganawida turned shrewd eyes on the chief. "Will you help us to defeat the sorcerer Tododaho?"

"I don't know what I can do, but I and my people owe you. You have saved many of us." Condor, Cusik and Red Hair exchanged glances.

Jekonsaseh said to Red Hair, "I will smooth a salve over your wounds to ease the sting. You need food and rest." He squeezed her calloused and wet fingers in thanks before she moved away. He was looking after her when Scout came up to him. "You made a tempting sight, fighting each other and not keeping a look-out."

"I know."

Scout said, "I wonder if we can make peace between the Tribes at all. All of us are too warlike. Maybe that is why the Creator sent us the outsider."

Before Red Hair slept, Hiawatha and Deganawida checked on him. Hiawatha said, "Condor told us you showed courage and leadership today. Praise from a war brother is good, but you must see why we need to achieve peace and soon." He paused, looking to Deganawida. "For the children." He had said the words oddly.

"You mean Fisher? Boys like him?"

"Of course, but your son will grow up in this country, too."

"What?"

Deganawida and Hiawatha exchanged a glance. Hiawatha said, "You have been avoiding Jekonsaseh. Why do you refuse to see what is before your eyes? Rest now, but tomorrow, you and she must speak."

Chapter 21

Red Hair found Jekonsaseh sleeping off her exhaustion in Bear Longhouse. Her sleep was necessary for her health and that of their child. He would not wake her, but he filled his senses with her. The glow from the fire pits gave light enough to his night-adjusted eyes. Jekonsaseh had been too weary to wash. Her face was still smudged with sweat and soot. The smells of fire and hazel-wood and blood clung to her and her clothing as it had when she had cared for him. The scents were not unpleasant. In fact, they stirred him. If this wasn't love, it was witchcraft and if she hadn't brought it about, he wanted to know who did and why.

Although he worked with and saw her daily, he had avoided their mind channel. He never wanted to share her painful memories. She must regret seeing his, too. It was disturbing how his foray into the past affected both of them. In his birth-land, there were Christians that would call her a witch. Here, she was Mother of Nations, and he was the odd immigrant with red hair and freckles. His only use to the Peacemaker was in his strangeness and his knife.

He could see himself as Jekonsaseh must have when he first appeared to her, captive of a runaway canoe, rump in the air and trying to paddle to shore with his hands. Was she remembering that now, and was he looking into her dream? Her blanket rose and fell with her breaths.

He found Hiawatha on the porch. "She's asleep. I couldn't talk to her."

"You could have spoken to her any day. We know you can open your mind to her and ask. She won't object."

If I was a witch like you, I could, he thought, but he wouldn't say the words. Hiawatha had been too good to him, too sympathetic, and the man had suffered for his madness more than he could imagine. "I haven't the right," he said.

Hiawatha was a dark presence with shining eyes. "Actually, you do. Think of her and what she needs from you. Your *orenda* is intertwined with hers."

Red Hair's vague understanding of the term meant unnatural power. If he had such a thing, he had no control over it. He had little control over his thoughts either. They were reminding him of Jekonsaseh's warm body on the island, and of her sadness when she lost her home. He remembered both of them wrapped in each other under her squirrel blanket. He was glad the dark shielded his face, but Hiawatha would know. "She never meant to connect our minds. What if she hates me for seeing her past?"

"She could never hate you." Hiawatha laid his hand over Red Hair's. He was tempted to brush aside such comfort. His humiliation and unworthiness overwhelmed him. He tried to keep his voice low. People were sleeping.

"Think what she is and what I am. Deganawida wanted me to join the Peace party because I'm more of a stranger than he is."

"If being foreign helps Deganawida in his cause, you should be glad. Tododaho's curse turned me into a monster. Deganawida cured me. We tell our stories to help him. You understand our goal. You don't like to admit it, but you have an *orenda* to match Jekonsaseh's. That is why healing you connected your minds. Why do you think she no longer cares for you?"

It seemed obvious. "She saw my worst memory. I was full of anger at everyone close to me, like no one else mattered."

"You were young. Most children are the same. They think of themselves first. Jekonsaseh was much the same when her mother died. She was angry, too, and with good reason. Her clan threw her out. They disowned her."

Red Hair said, "I saw it in her mind. I saw Jekonsaseh's dearest friend trampled. Her own father who brought her in caused such evil to happen."

"I know. Her dearest friend was my last daughter. I couldn't defend her, or any of my family. My helplessness weakened me and Tododaho used it."

"Forgive me. I did not know who the girl was. I saw the curse come over you like black smoke with claws."

Hiawatha turned his face away and sighed. Red Hair felt a reflection of his pain. "Tododaho killed my wife because she rejected him. He destroyed everyone who opposed him. Those he could not change or kill, he drove mad, like me."

Red Hair heard the horror and shame in his words. He wondered how Hiawatha had put this behind him. "Everyone else calls him the Snake Haired or the sorcerer, but you speak his name. How can you?"

"Deganawida healed me. His *orenda* is strong enough to heal all of us. Do you see that yet or do you still think you are repaying my niece for curing you? You belong with us."

"What if this power itself is wicked?"

Hiawatha pulled him closer, as if to look into his soul. He had never understood the idea of a soul either, unless it was the part of himself with which he experienced dreams. Hiawatha must be no mean sorcerer himself. Even if his intention was to help, it was unnatural and frightening. In the North, he had learned to block such intrusions from the Inuit shaman, but it took all his strength.

Hiawatha spread his fingers on Ole's forehead. The warmth of his touch relieved some of his stress. "May I?" he asked. Red Hair nodded and tried to relax. The older man's probe was gentle; relaxing. He had been sleeping off the snake's poison when Jekonsaseh broke down his defenses and bound them to each other. Gentle or harsh, meant or accidental, it must be wrong for one human to enter another's mind.

He was about to object when Hiawatha removed his hand. "I think I understand you better now, Red Hair," he said. "Our different ways have confused and frightened you. I daresay I would be confused if I found myself in your world. Let me tell you something. Jekonsaseh will not mind. There was a time when she feared that her power must be evil. She inherited it from her father, you see, and his goals made him cruel."

Red Hair found his eyes were closing, although he listened. "When she was in a Huron village and learning how to heal, she saw an older boy tease her brother because he could not speak properly. A tree root rose at her wish. The older boy fell into a bramble bush. Instead of being glad, Jekonsaseh was afraid evil had entered her to be able to do such a thing. Her father would have used her to help spread his new Law. He arranged for her to marry one of his followers in a different community. She ran away. She meant to end her life."

Red Hair leaned forward. "What stopped her?"

"Her teacher and a boy called Thinker. You know the boy. People call him the Peacemaker."

"Who was Jekonsaseh's teacher? You?"

Hiawatha blew out his breath. "Certainly not. That was during the years I lived under Tododaho's curse. People called me Mohawk, the Algonquin word for man-eater. They were right. Your adopted tribe is named that by the Algonquin."

"I have heard of it. Tell me about her teacher."

"He is called Hidden in Mist. I never met him myself." He gave a small laugh. "Hidden in Mist taught her how to heal. Deganawida pulled her back from the brink, but Hidden in Mist taught her how to overcome her father's influence. She said her teacher passed through madness himself when his wife was killed in an accident of war. This is why he imposes peace on his domain and his river enforces it."

Red Hair was about to ask why Hidden in Mist did not confront the Snake Haired himself, but Hiawatha guessed what he was about to say. "The guardian has no power away from his river. He can't help us." Hiawatha tilted his head toward the misty moon floating behind thin veils of clouds. A few stars gleamed through the gray. "Go inside now and get some sleep."

The longhouse was darker than the night. Red Hair found his assigned bed bench by counting the glowing fire pits and the lodge poles. Tucked into his bed furs with his head pillowed on his arm, he fell into an uneasy dream. His conversation in the dark must have set his imagination loose. In the dream, he floated over a troubled river.

Only half asleep, he remained aware of his location in the longhouse. His dream self floated more rapidly than the canoe. The forest on both sides of the river receded. The river broadened as it flowed. A stunning white light ahead, whiter than clouds, drew his attention. The light parted like a curtain, exposing a torrent of falling water and a deep gorge. Rainbows hovered below him where the sun smiled on the water.

There was a narrow path and a rocky shelf on which sat an old man. His hair was as flowing and white as the downward rush of the river. Beside him sat a small family. Gliding closer, Red Hair saw the man was himself. With him sat Jekonsaseh holding an infant with green eyes and a smattering of orange hair on a pink scalp. He touched the child. It gave him a toothless smile, but the couple did not seem to see him. The old man puffed on his pipe and met his eyes. *This can be yours, you know,* the image said.

Can be; not will be. It did not seem strange that the man saw him and could speak to him. He was the Guardian. Hiawatha said his power was limited to his domain. Red Hair realized what the dream showed him was far from guaranteed, but it was good. There could be nothing evil about fathering a child with the woman he loved. He would do all he could to make his dream a reality.

He awoke to the smell of corn gruel simmering over a hickory fire. Resin spiced the air. A town woman invited Red Hair and Beaver Tooth to take a portion. "Then take a bowl for the little brother who lost his voice. Add water to it."

Fisher still slept, his throat wound swathed in bandages, but their approach awakened him. "We brought you food," said Beaver Tooth. They piled furs behind him to help him sit. Beaver Tooth held a spoon to his mouth. Fisher swallowed and groaned as the thin gruel touched the rawness of his throat, but at least he had made a sound. After he took all he could, they helped him with other necessities.

Jekonsaseh was seeing to her patients. She felt Fisher for fever. "You will heal," she told him. "It is good you wrapped your neck against the cold that morning. It prevented the arrowhead from going further." She complimented his effort to eat. "Until your voice comes back, Red Hair can teach you the hand signs he used in the north." He nodded. "Good," she said. She cleansed his wound, changed his dressing and moved to her next patient.

Red Hair followed. She suggested that her assistant go with one of the other healers. "This one needs more training." The woman walked off. "Come, Red Hair, and I will explain what I do as we go."

They stopped at the bed bench of the warrior who lost his eye. She carried two flasks. "The first is hazel water for washing; and the second is water simmered with willow bark and strained. It tastes bitter, but it cools the blood and relieves pain. I gave you some on the island."

She washed the man's eye socket and patted his face dry. Then she poured a dose of willow water into a clay cup. "Drink it all," she said. The man took the cup in both hands and drained it. "Rest now. I'll see you again." The man seemed less grim and more hopeful when they moved on.

Red Hair carried her pouch for her. "Thank you, Red Hair."

"I want to learn to heal."

She gave him a searching look. "It is a good way to begin. Hiawatha told you about my teacher." She smiled at the memory. "I learned with him for three years. We wintered with the Huron, but we always returned to his river and his cave house behind the Falls. I learned Algonquin, and healing and more."

He thought of the old man he saw in his vision. Jekonsaseh looked at him, surprise in her dark eyes. "You have seen him."

"Only in a dream."

After that, they were easier together. They did not speak of their estrangement. After they treated their patients and made them comfortable, the Healing Society visited in their False Face masks. Children peeked out from behind their mothers, frightened by the horrible carved faces, but curious. Jekonsaseh explained that men and women were behind the masks. Blowing ashes from past council fires over the sick was meant to scatter evil spirits.

Red Hair collected the bloody rags in a basket and brought them to the lake. He washed and wrung them out and hung them on low branches. Then, he washed as well as he could. The water was cold, but the chill helped clear his mind.

He had rubbed himself dry and gathered up the damp rags when he saw Jekonsaseh emerging from the next cove. She gathered up her long hair in both hands and squeezed out the water, leaving it loose and damp over her shoulders. She wiped water off her shivering arms. Before her attendant covered her, he saw her that her nipples were large and rosy, the areolas darkened and enlarged. Her belly stood out proudly. She crossed one foot over the other to dry her feet. A town woman handed her a new cloak, plain but warm, and they started back.

Deganawida asked permission to make a ceremony before he and his volunteers departed, to hasten healing in the injured and send the newly dead spirits on their way. The chiefs agreed to this, but when he said he intended to pray for all the fallen, people objected. Odatshedeh demanded silence. "Without the Peacemaker and his helpers, more of us would be in the next world."

A matron shouted. "I lost my son and brother yesterday. Why allow him to heal and comfort our killers? They will only come back stronger."

"He's a Huron," a warrior sneered. "Herons were never our friends."

Odatshedeh's chest was bandaged and he leaned on a crutch when he walked, but his valor commanded respect. "I say he will make us a ceremony. He is under my protection for what he and his supporters did for us." No one else objected out loud.

Deganawida chose a spot for his ceremony in the center of a vacant planting field. Dry vines crunched and crumbled under his feet. He set out a hide mat and laid a pouch upon it. Lifting both arms to the sky, he invited the Elder Brother's attention. Next, he invited the newly dead, both invaders and defenders to his ceremony. It made some anxious looks around. Children squinted, trying to see the ghosts.

The Peacemaker took three strings of white and pink wampum from the pouch and laid them out so all could see. He lifted the first and wrapped it around his left hand, letting the fringes hang evenly on both sides. His stammering disappeared when he chanted, and his use of the Longhouse speech had improved.

He said, "When a person grieves, tears blind his eyes so that he cannot see the way to healing. With these words and this wampum string, I remove your tears." He laid the first string back on the hide and lifted the second, holding it wide before wrapping it around his left hand as he had with the first. "When a person loses someone dear to them, sorrow blocks his ears so he does not hear words of consolation. I remove the obstruction to your ears so that you can hear."

He laid the second string beside the first, and lifted the last string. "When a person loses a loved one, his throat is stopped up so he cannot speak. With these words, I remove the obstruction from your throats so you may speak and breathe freely." He set the last string beside the other two and sang of hope and unity to come.

Ole Red Hair's inclination to obtain vengeance for every hurt, and his general feelings of mistrust relaxed along with the tightness in his throat. He inhaled deeply. He blinked away tears and found his vision sharp enough to see gray shapes sliding through the air, seeming to touch eyes and ears and throats with spirit fingers.

Oddly, the spirits stimulated sympathy in him rather than dread. The attackers had been victims too, of one whose authority could not be opposed. Red Hair understood now why the Peacemaker was making this journey. Belief in him made him stronger until he was strong enough to confront the Snake Haired.

He looked around him and saw his friends. "I'm sorry about your black blade," he told Condor. "Perhaps you can find another knife like it."

"I pushed you to fight me," Condor replied. "It is my fault my knife broke. I understand that now and don't blame you." Up and down the planting field, people asked for and received forgiveness. Men and women smiled uncertainly to those they had squabbled with and received goodwill in exchange. Resentments fell and blew away like crisp autumn leaves.

Deganawida spoke again. "We will bury the dead. See each fallen warrior as your friend, even one you yourself killed. We grieve for them and send him to their ancestors in peace."

"What about the men we left near the lake after they tried to kill Fisher?" Red Hair asked doubtfully. "Were they our friends?"

"Fisher is alive after all," said Hiawatha. "Burying them will help you heal."

"Let us do it," said Beaver Tooth. Fisher walked with him to the lake. Red Hair and his friends, seeing them go, followed, as well as many others. Their enemies' bodies lay scattered by scavengers and half-eaten. The villagers and volunteers chased off the birds and foxes and gathered up their remains.

When they reached the burial ground, they had to work to uncover earth for them. Deganawida said, "War makes enemies of us; peace makes us brothers."

Later, Odatshedeh invited Deganawida to speak with him privately at his bed bench. The chief's wife handed over hominy mixed with fish, and cups of dried and crushed blueberry tea. It was her obligation to feed their guests, but she worried they were depleting their stores. "We thank you for your healing, but why did you ask us to feed our enemies?" she asked. "We will not have sufficient food this winter."

"My reason will become clear next summer. As for food, I will send food to replace what we ate." She nodded skeptically, but left the men to speak alone. When she had departed, Odatshedeh closed his eyes and the furrows between them deepened. Deganawida asked, "You don't believe I can end this war, do you?"

"I believe you think you can, just as I believe you will try to find food for us. You healed me. I admit you are an extraordinary healer, but I am not convinced you can vanquish our enemies. The Snake Haired has had years to strengthen his power. As strong as you are, you are young. How long will we feel tranquil once you are gone? If we hunger this winter, will my people remember you kindly?" He did not wait for an answer. "When the snow melts, war will resume. To end it, you must go to the Snake Haired's lair and kill him in his den. Even you must see this."

Their eyes met. "Tododaho will end the war himself when I go to him. He will give up his plan. I have dreamed it."

Odatshedeh allowed his stark disbelief to be seen. "Will you make another ceremony?"

"I intend to talk to him."

"You do not give me confidence," Odatshedeh said coldly, "We were once a larger town. Now, we are fewer and live in fear. My wife says our last harvest was poor. She's afraid we won't have enough for winter, but I asked her to prepare parched corn for you and your followers. Here it is." He handed the heavy bag to Deganawida who received it sadly. "I wish you success, Peacemaker, but leave us."

There was no more to be said. They meant to visit several more villages and towns in southern Onondaga and Cayuga before the snow became too deep. They had best get on their way.

The volunteers traveled on snowshoes to the next town. Deganawida and Hiawateh's words stirred them enough that they agreed to send corn to Odatshedeh even though they lived under Tododaho's Law. They would not let the Peace party stay so the travelers moved again and set up a small village for themselves.

Red Hair found his leaders in discussion around their fire pit. He crouched nearby to get warm. Jekonsaseh and her companions spoke softly, not trying to exclude him but not inviting him to join them either. Red Hair wondered if the three of them were following a false vision. The healings and promises might lead to nothing. Between Onondaga and Seneca, they were seldom invited to speak. The fear Tododaho had generated was too great in this region. In the final confrontation, if they lived long enough to see it happen, would they be able to save anyone at all?

Chapter 22

O datshedeh slept fitfully, awakened by small sounds that autumn night, mice and insects fighting over fallen kernels of corn under the hangings. He touched the squirrel skin dressing over what should have been his death wound. He had expected to be among the spirits Deganawida released, but instead, he was alive and here. Deganawida was a gifted healer, but as for being a prophet, Odatshedeh could not believe it. A prophet should be an elder and a former warrior. The young man from Huron was no warrior. He had never known injury. Why would the Great Spirit have sent him to the Tribes?

Odatshedeh had lost friends and brothers to Tododaho's ambition. They were once a walled town but they had been driven out. Now they were a few dozen families trying to survive and escape domination. He wished he could believe in the Huron's vision, but the young man had no plan beyond spreading his message and hoping to subdue their enemy in some mystic way. Death should be met bravely, not explained away with pretty wampum belts. Fantasy did not win battles.

A wind gusted through the longhouse, shivering the bark shingles. Odatshedeh glanced toward both entry curtains, but the reverberations had ceased. Someone had gone outside to relieve himself, no doubt, but Odatshedeh felt a warning, a quiver of unease. He slipped on his moccasins, slid the strap of his war club over his wrist and wrapped his fingers around its grip to look around.

Nothing seemed out of the ordinary between the longhouses or in the plaza by the unlit Council hearth. He had been tense since the battle and the Peacemaker's visit. The sentries assured him no one had entered the village. Pacified for the moment, he returned to bed and tried to sleep. Between sleep and wakefulness, he heard a low voice say his name. *Odatshedeh! Heed me. You want to believe in the Peacemaker.*

You should have gone with him to be convinced. Help him persuade others to believe in him. They will heed your authority.

Odatshedah sat up and set his feet over the side of his bed bench. Nothing out of the ordinary was there. Mind tricks, he thought, but he still felt a presence. "Who spoke to me? Show yourself." A pale image of an old man with white hair that circled his head like smoke or mist, sat in the air before him. The braided corn husks tied to the rafters of his longhouse were visible through the image."

"What are you? Who are you?" he insisted. His whisper seemed too loud. People would accuse him of speaking to himself. He tried not to blink for fear the old man would go up the smoke hole. He already wavered like a reflection on moving water. The sky above the smoke hole changed to violet-shaded gray. *I am the Guardian.*

Odatshedeh reached for the solidity of the lodge pole and wrapped his fingers around it. "The guardian of what?"

Of Niagara. The voice was in his head, not his ears. The Guardian's eyes shimmered from violet to blue to green, like the morning star sometimes before morning swallowed it as it was now swallowing the night in shades of gray. Odatshedeh's tired eyes closed and he slept.

When he stirred, his wife was crouching over the fire pit. At his movement, she straightened and came to feel his skin for clamminess or fever. She did not trust his miraculous recovery to be permanent. "You are cold," she said, and tucked his blanket more closely around him." I suppose that is better than wound fever. I'll build up the fire."

"Wait," he said. "Did a stranger enter the house in the night?"

"No one came in, but you went out. I thought your mind must be wandering in fever. I stood on the porch and watched for you. You returned to bed and talked to yourself for awhile. Then you slept again."

"You watched?" She gave him a small smile. He felt bad that he had disturbed her. "I was not talking to myself. The spirit of Niagara visited me." He paused. "I wonder. If enough people accept the Peacemaker's vision and have faith in him, will it help him prevail against the Snake Haired?"

"I don't know how these things work, but I know your mind. You are thinking of joining him, aren't you?"

He touched her shoulder affectionately. "I am. The spirit said I can help."

His wife lifted an eyebrow. "I don't think the Snake Haired will send warriors this way again soon. I can't see why they attacked us at all, unless it was to convert or kill you. Our enemy would prefer you to be on his side." She hesitated. He gestured for her to speak her mind. "Are you well enough?"

He pulled her closer and stroked her hair. She was self-reliant, his little wife. "At the rate I am healing, I think so. The guardian spirit said my authority might make a difference. Let the women chose another war chief as they would have done if I were dead or too injured to lead them in battle. I might be able to help end this war."

She filled his bowl with gruel and currants and dipped out a cup of hot water simmered with dried willow bark. "This is the last you will eat at home. The tea will reduce your pain. Wear your warmest clothing. I will pack you trail food."

Odatshedeh tracked the volunteers over the snow for four days until he found their low shelters. They were not much more than deer hides stretched over tilted canoes built up with walls of snow. Deganawida found him. "You changed your mind and found me. Welcome. Let us duck inside where it is warmer to talk."

Odatshedeh obeyed. "Four nights ago, I had a spirit visitor. His hair was as pale as daylight on mist and his eyes were all the colors of the morning star. He called himself the Guardian." He touched his chest. "He said once I was convinced, my influence might help you. I owe you my life."

"You owe the Creator your life. I'm only one of his messengers, as is the Guardian. If you stay with me, you may meet him."

"Who is he?"

"My teacher and friend. When I was a boy in Huron country, he shared his wisdom with me."

"Is he Huron, too?"

Deganawida smiled. "No. He came from the West." Jekonsaseh brought him a bowl of stew. He thanked her.

"I would like to meet him someday."

"Perhaps you will."

The Peacemaker and Mother of Nations seemed to say something to each other without words. Odatshedah waited respectfully until they were done. "I want to learn from you. Will you accept me, even if I can't believe in you with my entire heart?"

"I value your honesty. Know that I will never lie to you. I must eventually confront the Snake Haired. Most of my followers have gone home for the winter, but we will meet in the spring. They will stand behind me the day I confront Tododaho. If he kills me, you may be next. Join me only if you support my mission." Odatshedah waited for Deganawida to put his mission into words. "I intend to bring about a treaty for peace and a new Law for the Longhouse Tribes to live by. The tribes will be equals. Men and women will have different roles but their roles will be equally important. I won't impose the Law on you. You will vote for it yourselves."

No more thought was needed. "It is good."

"Then match your hand to mine." Deganawida held his palm out and Odatshedeh matched it.

The band hoped to winter in a town on the west shoreline of frozen Lake Oneida before the snow became too deep. They slogged southward over the leaf-clogged ice and camped in the lee of a small hill. The heavy sky smelled of more snow when a newcomer arrived on snowshoes with a heavily-covered face. "Who are you?" challenged Odatshedeh.

"A friend to Red Hair. Is he here?" He pulled his fur scarf away from his mouth and nose. Red Hair came forward, peering intently. The newcomer said, "You can shave and cover your hair, but you can't hide from me."

Red Hair closed the space between them. "What are you doing here? How did you find us? How is Ingrid?"

"If you mean my wife, Dreamer is out to here and tired of having me underfoot," said Runs Fast. He reached his hand in front of his belt. "I decided to join you and the Peacemaker. I excel at negotiating, if not at fighting." He smiled to Turtle Claw and Scout, and after them, he complimented Fisher and Beaver Tooth on their growth into men. "Dream Weaver ordered me to find you and make sure you were well. Mother of Nations, Greetings!" She lifted her hand. He grinned all around. "Am I accepted?"

Deganawida told him the risks and asked for his palm which he matched without question. "Now that I'm one of you, I have something private to say to my friend Red Hair. This won't take long."

When they were alone, Runs Fast said, "Are you and Mother of Nations together again? Don't growl at me. Dream Weaver wants to know."

"That is not her business or yours either. Until my status is closer to hers, we will work together and be friends. I will respect and protect her like any man here."

"But she is having your baby."

"That is not for you to think about."

Runs Fast gave a short laugh. "First you lay with a woman and *then* you become friends? Healers don't become mothers by accident. They know what herbs to take. She must like you more than you think."

Red Hair grabbed his friend's arm in warning. "We speak respectfully about Mother of Nations."

"Of course we do, brother-in-law. I nearly forgot. Here is a gift. The matrons told me to be sure the Peacemaker's volunteers had enough to eat." He drew a sack of ground corn from under his coat and swung around a brace of frozen, gutted squirrels and rabbits from over his shoulder. "Are we friends again?"

Red Hair hugged him. "Let us go back inside."

Hiawatha filled Runs Fast in on their situation. "You tracked us, even over the frozen lake. So might others with less friendly intentions. Many communities voted to stand with us, but we are still outnumbered. North Cayuga belongs to Snake Haired but we expect to find refuge in Seneca country. Tonight, we will cook the food you kindly brought us." The men ate, and huddled for warmth near their fire. They pulled their cloaks closer around themselves and prepared for sleep.

It was deep winter outside Tyo-den-he-deh, but inside the walls of its longhouses, the people kept warm and fed. Tododaho's messengers threaded their ways between towns and villages and threatened any who offered hospitality to his enemies. They kept fear of their master alive, even in winter, as women kept embers covered in ash to live until morning when they could fan them to flame again.

Runs Fast made clandestine forays to communities to feel out the chances that the Peacemaker's group might be made welcome. The women were nearly always on the side of peace, but they dared not defy Tododaho's Law. Some left food where he could find it and bring it to camp.

Jekonsaseh slept nearest the fire and ate first, but Deganawida was not surprised when she came to him. "My child will be born before another moon is complete. I need more food, the warmth of houses, and women's care."

"I hoped we would find refuge by now." Her hands were cold. "Hiawatha and I will ask for shelter on your behalf at the next town. They will take you in." Her face fell. "I won't ask for us. We will be together again in the spring."

The next community was a snow-covered town silhouetted against the gray winter sky. The sharpened saplings of its palisade bristled out of the drifts. So their party would not appear threatening, Deganawida asked his followers to remain behind in the forest cover while he, Hiawatha and Jekonsaseh crossed the white planting field. Voices drifted from behind the wall.

A woman inside who had peeked through the opening said, "Mother of Nations is with them. We will not deny her." An old woman emerged clad in winter fox pelts. Men followed. A white tail warmed the lower half of the woman's face and deep wrinkles nearly hid her eyes.

Hiawatha spoke first. "In the name of the Three Sisters, we ask refuge for Mother of Nations."

"Old Mother," added Deganawida. "She is with child and in need."

The elderly woman said, "You must be the Peacemaker." He met her eyes. Men muttered protests behind her. She spun around. "Be cowards if it suits you. I'm too old to be afraid," she said. "I expect I will join my ancestors this winter with or without his help. This is Ga-ah'na of South Onondaga." She gestured to Deganawida and Hiawatha. "You may stay at the guest house."

A younger woman came up beside the elder and said with dignity, "I am Otter Clan Mother. My mother has retired as our matron, but she speaks for me. I welcome Mother of Nations to my house. For her sake, you may come in and be fed too. We will feed you again in the morning and then you must go."

"There are more of us, but not a great many," said Hiawatha. "Are we under a truce of the Three Sisters?"

"We are. Tonight and in the morning, we promise you safety. Then, you must be on your way."

Deganawida beckoned to his watching men. They carried their canoes to the wall and propped them vertically against the palisade. "Follow me." Otter Clan Mother led them to the guest house and promised them they would soon have fire, food and blankets.

"Mother of Nations, come. We go to my house now."

"I thank you. Otter Matron, you should know I belong to Bear Clan."

The woman took her hand. "Otter is your birth clan so you will sleep in my house and under my protection." She smiled at Jekonsaseh's confusion. "Gossip flies faster than eagles. You were expelled from Otter house unfairly. It is time you had women of your own kind to care for you. Sadly, we live under your father's Law in Ga-ah'na. Even under the Three Sisters Truce, I can't do more for your friends."

A veteran warrior entered the guest lodge. It was round, a wigwam rather than a longhouse, and during these years of war, infrequently used. Women came with hides over the bed benches, swept the hard earth floor clean and lit a fire the single hearth. They left enough tinder to keep it burning all night. The warrior asked, "Which of you is Deganawida?" He looked at Chief Odatshedeh.

"Not me. I am one of his followers."

Deganawida rose to his feet. "Here -- here I am."

The man snorted. "You? You are the Peacemaker? You're hardly more than a youth. I am Chief Onoji of Otter Clan in Onondaga. By Lord Tododaho's order, I command Ga-ah'na. An odd man travels with you." He looked over each of them and stopped by Red Hair. "How did you get your colors?" he asked.

Red Hair got on his feet. He was taller than Onoji. "Ask the Creator."

Chief Onoji took a backward step and addressed himself to Deganawida. "Mother of Nations believes in you and your dreams." Hiawatha moved to his friend's side and the other men closed in. "You are a Huron and have no business among the Tribes. You should go home if you want to live."

"That is not for you to decide, Chief Onoji," said Hiawatha.

Onoji grinned. "Can't the Huron speak for himself?" he asked.

Hiawatha said, "The Peacemaker is learning Longhouse speech. He prefers me to speak for him."

Several entered the guest lodge just then, among them Otter Clan Mother and the old Otter woman with two faith keepers. "We are here to be sure our truce is observed," said Otter Clan Mother.

"It will be." Onoji looked over the guests. "You are Longhouse men, but you follow odd leaders. One is a Huron and the other is a fiend that killed and boiled men in his stewpot. Are we to take him for a human again, now that he has parted with his monstrous ways?"

Instead of replying, Hiawatha opened mouth slightly to show his incisors. Red Hair found he could believe the stories that were told about him to frighten children. The people moved back to give him room. Hiawatha said, "Your master is to blame for what I became. The Peacemaker made me clean again. He can make you clean again, too, after the needless killing and suffering you have forced on the Tribes on his behalf. Tododaho's time as anyone's master is nearly over."

"You dare to say his name? You and your Huron beg for food behind a pregnant woman. Your time on earth is nearly over. Winter and hunger will kill you and your volunteers before the winter is out."

Hiawatha said, "We here are under the protection of the Sustaining Sisters. Do you defy them?"

"I do not. You will have food tonight and in the morning, but your men should know the risk they take by being in your company. Submit yourselves to Tododaho and his Law. Persist in opposing him and you will die."

Onoji gathered his mantle around him to depart when Hiawatha asked, "How much longer will your master be evil? He grows older and his snake grows heavier by the year."

"My lord awaits the birth of his grandson." The smoke from the fire pit hung in the room. Deganawida waved his hand and the smoke lifted.

"When you speak to your master again, tell him we will meet in Gano'wages. Neither I nor Hiawatha will bring a weapon. I will explain my plan for the Tribes and he will agree to it."

"You can speak for yourself when you want to," scoffed Onoji, "but your words prove that you are a fool. You will die under Tododaho's war club. Hiawatha will be next. Then, the rest of your followers will die."

He motioned his people to leave, but the bent, old woman of Otter House approached Deganawida and gripped his arm. "I will touch the prophet before my spirit leaves my body."

"Come away, Mother," warned Otter Clan Mother, but the old woman refused.

The faith keepers added their pleas. "Don't call him that. Come away."

They reached for her, but the old woman shook them off. "Let your vision enter us, Peacemaker. Before I die, take what power I possess to destroy the Snake Haired and repair the harm he has done." She stroked his cheek. "Let my children and their children know that I touched your face." She finished speaking, and with a small sigh, she collapsed. Deganawida rushed to catch her. He prevented her body from hitting the floor, but her life was already gone.

"Mother!" wailed Otter Clan Mother.

"I will carry her to her place." No one challenged Deganawida's right to do so. When they arrived in Otter Longhouse, he laid her on her bed. Her daughters saw the respected elder dead. As one, they came forward to arrange her limbs. With a silent look to Jekonsaseh, Deganawida and his men walked out.

~~

At their next camp, the older men set out to hunt, Red Hair and Runs Fast among them. There were few left in camp when two young men arrived and asked to speak with the Peacemaker and Hiawatha. The two emerged from their shelters to greet the newcomers. Hiawatha looked at them closely. "I saw you in Ga-ah'na. You are great grandsons to the elder of Otter House. Why did you want us? Has Jekonsaseh's child been born?"

"Not yet," replied the taller boy. "I am Magpie and Wader is my cousin. We wanted to see you for ourselves. After the elder's words, we were curious. We never met a reformed monster or a Huron who prefers peace to war."

"Now you see us, what else do you want?" Hiawatha inquired.

"We were thinking of joining you," said Wader. "We thought the Huron might be right and Snake Haired's Law might be wrong. Will you take us in?"

Hiawatha said, "Aren't you afraid of Onoji?"

"We are." said Magpie earnestly, "But still, we came."

"How brave of you. If you want to join me, you must renounce your former master."

Magpie's eyes flicked to his cousin's. "We can't speak in the open. Our master in the north is a far-listener. He will think we betrayed him and punish us."

Hiawatha heard the unevenness of their breathing. "Who are you more afraid of – Tododaho or Deganawida?" They did not reply. "If you come with respect, hold up the palm of your hand and touch it to Deganawida's to pledge him your loyalty."

Wader stepped up, extending his palm. Deganawida touched it and drew back. "Run, Hiawatha," was all he could say before Wader seized his arm. Magpie swung his war club and Deganawida collapsed to the ground.

Before Hiawatha could move to defend himself or shout for help, Wader brought up his war club and smashed it into Hiawatha's head. Without a sound, he slumped forward onto the already bloody snow. "Hit them again. Make sure."

At his words Fisher, Beaver Tooth, and others hurried around the shelter. "Run," shouted Magpie. By the time they reached Hiawatha and Deganawida, the cousins were disappearing between the trees. The men returned to find the brothers holding their leaders to them, trying to warm them and weeping.

Chapter 23

B abies were placed in their cradleboards and hung up to sleep.
Toddlers were given a last suckle and tucked into their blankets.
"It will be cold tonight. Here's another blanket," said Otter Clan Mother,
setting the folded deer hide beside her. "Did you have enough to eat?"

Jekonsaseh was sated. Her stomach would not hold much this late
in her pregnancy, especially after the months of scarcity. "Too much. He
takes all the room." She adjusted the hide behind her more comfortably,
stretched her neck and shoulders and gave a grateful smile to her hostess.

"Why do you say 'he'?"

"It feels like a boy." Her lids creased. In a few moments, she opened
them and found the women staring at her.

"Have your pains started?" Otter Clan Mother asked.

"No, but my muscles tighten here. It doesn't stay long." She reached
around to touch her lower back.

"That's what comes of treating only men. You know little about
women's bodies, even your own. Stand up." The matron felt Jekonsaseh's
abdomen, pressing around the bulge of the baby with both hands. "He
is getting ready. It won't be much longer, I think, but he's too high to
come tonight. Lie on your side."

She adjusted the hide so her patient could maintain the position
more easily. Jekonsaseh had not enjoyed a woman's care since she had
escaped her father. She pictured him and sighed at her helplessness. This
town was under his influence. They would surely bring her and her
baby to him at Tyo-den-he-dah as soon as she could travel. Thinking
of the cold night, she deepened her consciousness and sent it into the
dark. A scene appeared before her. Hiawatha and Deganawida had been
attacked. They lay near death in the snow! She could not hold back a
gasp.

"Is it the baby?" asked Otter Clan Mother."

"Not the baby," she said and tried to find air. The house women started toward her. She lifted her hand to stop them and tried to think. If her brother and uncle were dead, she felt sure she would know. So they weren't dead, but they must be gravely injured. She sent silent words to the strongest powers she knew. *Elder Brother, Hidden in Mist, help them.*

###

Fisher and Beaver Tooth sat in the snow holding Hiawatha and Deganawida within their mantles to share their warmth. Only the faint lift and fall of their chests suggested a chance that they could recover. Red Hair could not bear that these men should die. He had the barest knowledge of the gods of his adopted country and how to talk to them, but he lifted his head and looked around to the sky and the forest. Everyone said there were spirits everywhere. He wondered why the men were looking to him. He was no priest and could never be one. In his experience, priests were always full of lofty words. Red Hair's thoughts were too simple and direct to appeal to any powerful spirit. He thought, *If there is a spirit or god who can hear me, please help them."*

Many days journey north and west in the protection of a Huron town, an old man awoke. All the power of Niagara had been caught in the grip of winter. With a start, his inner eyes presented him with a vision of Deganawida and Hiawatha hurt and near death. Their friends tried to keep them warm but they bled from head wounds.

Two voices called loudest; a man and a woman, apart but together. Jekonsaseh was one. He did not know the other voice, but it was a man. He felt the oddness of him. *Good Mind.* thought the old man, *Elder Brother, hear me. You set him a task. He must live to fulfill it, so heal his body now. Open his eyes. Thinker, you have more to do. Don't just lie there frightening everyone. Breathe.*

Encircled by his followers, men who esteemed and loved him, Deganawida opened his eyes and gasped. He felt his wound. His scalp healed under his fingers, the edges of the gash knitting together. His men nudged one another in wonder. "He has come back to us," said Odatshedeh. "The Peacemaker lives."

Deganawida saw Hiawatha lying still. He bent over him and felt his cold cheeks. With one hand on Hiawatha's scalp and the other above his heart, he said, "Master of healers, restore him to health. Our friends have been anxious about us." He breathed warm air into Hiawatha's mouth.

Hiawatha blinked rapidly and took several deep breaths. "My head," he said breathlessly. He looked around at the circle of men. "I floated above our campsite. I thought I was dead." His voice grew stronger. "You breathed life into me."

"I only helped. Elder Brother healed both of us because of the requests of these men and others who love us."

Somehow, Red Hair sensed his feeble prayer had helped and was glad. He wished he could help Jekonsaseh, too. "Thank you," he said softly in case the spirit people still listened. *Keep Mother of Nations well too, please.*

Before they broke camp, Deganawida spoke to Red Hair privately. "Be easy in your mind. Before our journey is over, you will be with your wife again." Red Hair had not heard that word in relation to Jekonsaseh before. It was a good word. He was about to say so, when the Peacemaker added, "And your son."

Caught up in her thoughts, Jekonsaseh did not mark the entry of two young men into Otter Longhouse. They walked directly for Onoji and whispered. She turned her attention to them and stretched her powers to listen. One said, Deganawida and Hiawatha are dead, felled by our war clubs. We pretended to want to join them. They never suspected what we planned until it was too late. We left them in the snow with their followers crying. No one chased us."

"Good work," said Onoji. "You will be rewarded. I will tell the chiefs." So saying, he gave Jekonsaseh and Otter Clan Mother a hard look and went outside.

Otter Clan Mother did not bother to cover her shock and anger. If the Huron were what he claimed to be, he could not be dead. In any case, it was beyond her authority to deal with. She faced her grandsons with disgust. "You brag of your stealth, Wader and Magpie. It doesn't take great bravery to club someone who isn't looking."

Magpie folded his arms. "Onoji said our master wanted them dead. Neither of them are warriors, but how could we know they weren't being guarded? We were brave and we did as War Leader Onoji commanded. The Snake Haired will honor us for killing his enemies." He seized his cousin's arm and they did a victory dance around the fire pit. "He will make us war chiefs. We will command other men."

"Do you think you will live long enough to claim honors?" Otter Clan Mother asked when they were done. "Your great-grandmother accepted the Huron as Peacemaker. The ground is too hard for her burial. Her body is under rocks, but her ghost dwells in this longhouse. She heard of your treachery from your own mouth. Wait and see how she will punish you."

Wader tried to shake off his sudden misgivings. "She shouldn't have praised the Huron." His voice came higher than he expected. Pretending not to notice, he cleared his throat.

Otter Clan Mother said, "My mother chose death over the tyrant's domination. I expect she is as ashamed of you as I am." Her rigid posture dared them to contradict her.

Magpie said, "Take care, Grandmother. Are you prepared to die, too?" A wind gust swooped down a smoke hole and rattled the walls. It lifted ashes and moaned down the hall in swirls of smoke. Gray ashes curled about them like angry spirits. Children whimpered and babies fussed in their cradleboards. Someone opened the door curtain to wave out the smoke.

"The witch is trying to scare us," said Wader, eying Jekonsaseh.

Jekonsaseh lifted her hands innocently. "I am only an unfortunate captive waiting for my baby to be born. Living women have no power. Did the wind frighten you, young warrior, or was it the old woman's ghost?"

"Before you condemn yourselves with your poor manners, remember you are in my house," Otter Clan Mother said. "No new Law changes that."

"It does. Warriors decide things now," said Magpie.

"Until you beg forgiveness for that outburst, you will sleep outside." Years of following their grandmother's orders and the ghost-like form of the smoke and ash had stripped their defiance. Wader and Magpie tied on their coats and left.

Onoji, who was walking between houses, saw them huddled and shivering under the porch eaves. "What are you doing out here?" he asked.

Magpie said, "Grandmother ordered us out."

"She no longer rules. Come with me." He walked them back in and down the long room to Otter Clan Mother. Jekonsaseh felt his gaze brush her as he passed by, but she refused to acknowledge him.

"Feed them," Onoji ordered. The matron huffed with disapproval, but moved off to obey. "That's better." He looked to Jekonsaseh at last. It was to escape marriage to him that she had defied her father. Had she been the compliant daughter he was led to expect, the child she carried might have been his. "Mother of Nations," he said.

He had addressed her directly. "Chief Onoji."

"You may wish to forget you were promised to me, but I remember. Your father will soon have you and your child." As he did not ask a question, Jekonsaseh did not speak. "I won't harm you," he added more gently, "but neither will I allow you to defy us or return to your friends. The Huron and your uncle are dead. Their followers must now submit to our master."

As second in power only to Tododaho, Onoji would let no woman intimidate him, especially this one. "After your child is born, our men will bring you to Tyo-den-he-deh." The red-tinged clouds above the smoke holes cast odd, moving streaks across the pressed earthen floor and bark walls. Onoji wondered if this portended anything.

Jekonsaseh spoke, not to him but to Otter Clan Mother. "I would like to give an entertainment tonight. I offer a story in honor of the old woman of Otter House. It might please you to stay and hear it too, Chief Onoji." The invitation confused him for she had turned a polite invitation into a challenge. She gave him a quick smile. "A story may soothe our spirits and hers."

They held one another's eyes for a moment, not having meant to. "You may tell your story," he said.

"Thank you. May the children of the other houses come?" she asked.

From childhood, Onoji had deferred to the house matron when it came to matters of family. It was a hard habit to break. He looked to the matron.

Otter Clan Mother said, "Sadly, few children have been born in these war years. We can fit them all in as well as their parents. Granddaughters, go to the other houses. Announce that Jekonsaseh will give us a story tonight after supper, in my mother's honor. Daughters, prepare enough treats for us and our guests."

Onoji could hardly keep his eyes from Jekonsaseh. She was delicate in her pregnancy, with narrow arms and legs, but her serious mouth and her deep eyes reminded Onoji of her father's. A man might easily lose oneself in such eyes. Under the new Law, a man should not feel that way about any woman, whether mother, matron, or wife. Thanks to Tododaho, men held authority in Onondaga. Commander of men that he was, he wondered how to deal with their prisoner. She would need watching. He went out to post guards.

Jekonsaseh beckoned the women to make a circle around her. Her voice did not carry, but each woman heard her clearly. "As we mourn the wise woman of Otter House, we also honor her valor. Would you like to see your rights over your families restored?"

No one dared answer such a direct question.

Otter Clan Mother said, "What are you planning, Mother of Nations?"

The question was reply enough. The determination in the faces of the circle silently spoke the women's feelings on the matter. "You will see. I'll need you to lend me your inner strength if we are to succeed, tonight."

"Is she going to do something special?" asked a lame girl, her eyes bright with excitement. She had remained behind when her cousins ran to invite the other children. Jekonsaseh's half-smile said it was a possibility.

"How?" whispered a woman.

"Encourage my lead and increase my power."

When the girls had returned home, Jekonsaseh called them to her. "The first part of my story is for you." They sat, hands on knees, leaning forward. "Do you know that otters are the bravest of animals?" One of the smaller girls giggled. "It's easy to think the bravest must be wolf or bear, but when you're big and fierce, you don't need to be so brave. Because we Otters are small, we are brave in a different way. I will explain." The girls smiled and leaned closer.

"It happened like this. When the world was covered with water, Sky Woman found a hole in the clouds, so she leaned over to see what she could see. Some say Sky Man pushed her, but we'll never know. In any case, she fell. It took many days for her to get all the way down, but there was no earth for her to land on. She would drown in the Great Ocean.

"The animals took council to decide how to help her. An eagle suggested one of them dive below the ocean to find the mud at the bottom and bring some of it up. Turtle agreed if someone could bring up a bit of earth, she could enlarge it and hold it on her back. That would give Sky Woman a place to live. Although the eagle thought of the plan, she wasn't brave enough to attempt to follow it. No bird dared such a dive. The fish could reach the earth under the ocean and so could the turtle, but the fish couldn't come up and the turtle couldn't move for the plan to work.

A brave otter knew she could hold her breath long enough to get some earth so she dove all the way down. She found the earth, but she needed her paws to swim. She carried some mud in her cheek and spread it on the back of the turtle."

"I know. That's how the world started," said one of the bigger girls.

"You are exactly right. Great flocks of birds held the hair of The Woman Who Fell from Heaven so she would fall slowly and land safely. Every time she walked around the turtle shell, it doubled in size until it became Turtle Island. Now, Sky Woman was pregnant before she fell to the earth. When she was ready, she gave birth to Mother Earth. When Mother Earth grew up, she married West Wind and gave birth to Twin sons, our patient Creator and his impatient Younger Brother. Let us not think of him now. The important thing to remember is without that otter, there would be no Earth. Because we otters are the bravest, be brave. Obey your mothers tonight. You will see why."

The girls enjoyed the story and agreed just in time because families from the other clans were just arriving. They filled Otter Longhouse and settled down on their blankets for the story. Men stood together near the entry curtain and puffed on their short-stemmed pipes until the tobacco glowed red. The Clan women had greased the fire stones and popped corn. They set bowls of the treats by their guests.

"I brought shelled walnuts," said a visitor from Bear Clan.

"I brought sassafras root tea steeped with maple syrup," said one from Snipe Clan. She and her women set down pots of it.

"Here is my guest gift – three bowls of dried plums," Turtle Clan Mother announced, "enough for all."

"I have more," said Otter Clan Mother. "I'll bring it out." When everyone was ready for the entertainment, she signed for quiet. "This story is in honor or my mother's spirit. Give heed to Mother of Nations."

Jekonsaseh sat the edge of her bench and asked for a storyteller's drum. An old man brought out his drum and beater. He tapped it, re-stretched the skin, and tightened the bands. "Use this, Mother of Nations. What story will you give us?"

Jekonsaseh tapped the drum to let it get used to her touch, and then tapped it four times. "This story begins after animals forgot how to speak with humans. There was once an Otter girl. She was in her eighth winter when her mother fell off a cliff and died."

This was not the usual kind of story. The children looked to each other uneasily. "This girl was not like most girls. She saw her mother's ghost and asked her why she died. The mother told her, but it was a secret so I can't tell you that part. Because the girl's Otter grandmother and aunts saw her talking to a ghost they couldn't see, they didn't want her any more. She asked her mother what to do. The ghost told her to go and live with her father. So the Otter grandmother brought her to Bear Longhouse."

"She couldn't," a girl protested, looking nervously toward her grandmother. "Children can't change clans. Her aunts had to take care of her."

Jekonsaseh agreed. "You are right. They should have, but they didn't want a ghost talker to live with them. The girl's father in Bear house asked his mother to adopt her. It was unusual, but she agreed. So, the Turtle girl grew up in Bear Clan."

She set down the beater and the drum, and sipped some tea. "We will have refreshments now." She took a dried plum and chewed it slowly. "I have not had one of these since I was little!" she exclaimed. "I forgot how delicious they are."

"They were my mother's favorite," said Otter Clan Mother.

Jekonsaseh said, "Plums remind me of the plum pit game the Creator played with his twin when they were young. They made a game board and tumbled the pits for the best positions. Some say the Younger Brother cheated, but he lost anyway."

"We know that game," said one of the boys. Several of them seized extra plums and plopped them into their mouths to chew off the fleshy pulp. Their mothers began to protest their greediness, but Jekonsaseh lifted her hand. "The new Law says mothers don't rule warriors and these boys are going to be warriors." The boys laughed and took more dried plums.

A sister complained that she wanted one too, but her mother told her to keep still. She must keep in mind that boys came first. She could have walnuts or popped corn. The girl turned sullen eyes on Jekonsaseh who met her gaze with a tiny nod. Knowing she was doing well, the girl continued to complain while the boys took all the sweet plums.

Jekonsaseh returned to her story. "At first, the Otter girl was lonely because she didn't know anyone in Bear Longhouse but her father. A Bear Clan woman called Sweet Water took pity on the girl and decided to be her aunt. Her husband, Hiawatha, came from Turtle Clan. They had five girls. Laughing Water was the same age as the formerly Otter girl. They became good friends."

A child called out. "Is that the same Hiawatha who came with the Peacemaker when they brought us Mother of Nations?" Onoji stood and would have interrupted, but Jekonsaseh sent him thoughts of restraint and motioned for him to sit down again. He did so, but couldn't understand how his protest had dried up on his tongue.

Jekonsaseh reminded her listeners an interrupted storyteller might forget the words. "The girl's father thought so well of himself that he decided to make all his clan's decisions. Soon he was making all his town's decisions. He abolished the council's right to disagree with him. This went well, so he decided to spread his Law throughout Onondaga and then, all the Tribes. He went to war with those who didn't obey him. Hiawatha objected, but the girl's father's *orenda* had grown so powerful by then that no one could tell him what to do. Hiawatha's wife died and then his girls died, until only Laughing Water remained. The Creator sent an eagle to protest the father's behavior, but the father ordered his men to bring him his bow. He clouded their eyes so they did not see Laughing Water standing in the porch. The men trampled her. Laughing Water died and the father shot down the eagle."

Amid the gasps of horror and astonishment, Onoji found his voice. "This is not a real story."

Jekonsaseh tapped her drum lightly. "It is a real story. I should know. Do the children want me to continue?" She turned to them.

"Yes," shouted a boy. "Tell more," echoed other voices.

"Take care, then. Remember who is master here." Onoji warned.

Jekonsaseh rested both hands over her belly. Life was growing in her. According to the earlier Law, it gave her authority over Onoji and the men in the house, but she spoke meekly, saying, "I remember."

"Then go on," said Onoji.

"The girl's father consoled the mourners, but misery weakened Hiawatha's *orenda* so the father's curse could twist his mind. Thus, he punished the girl's uncle for opposing him. Hiawatha no longer saw men as men but as their clan totems, otters, turtles, snipes, wolves and bears. He ran away to live in the wild places.

"The men who had trampled Laughing Water had not meant to kill her any more than Hiawatha meant to be cursed. Everyone was sad, but no one was sadder than the Otter girl, because her father had changed. The Younger Brother's snake slithered toward him. He reached down to invite it up to his shoulder. It made itself comfortable there and rested its head on the father's scalp. Except when the father slept and the snake hunted, the two remained together.

"People began to call the father Snake Haired. He became feared as a far listener who could send his power against his foes. Let the old woman's death be a lesson to all of you."

"No more!" exclaimed Onoji.

"Don't you want to know what happened after that?"

"I know what happened," Onoji said, but his protest was overridden. His authority had been sapped away as sap pours from the maple when we tap it in the spring. He could not understand how it had happened.

Jekonsaseh finished her cold tea. "The next day, Snake Haired told his daughter she was to marry a man who was loyal to him. The man lived in a different town. He meant for her to persuade the matrons there to keep his new Law. 'I'm too young to marry,' said the girl.

"'I know best,' said her father. "He is a brave warrior and a good provider. I will bring you to him this winter." The girl dared not argue. She bowed to her father's command, but she waited until he and his warriors left for war.

When the leaves had begun to fall, she took her blanket and a bundle of trail food. She visited the cemetery to tell her friend's ghost that she was running away where no one would force her to marry the wrong man. Failing that, she would end her life. Laughing Water's ghost urged her to keep living and to try to cure Hiawatha, but the girl knew she wasn't strong enough. What was she to do?"

Pine cones snapped and sputtered in the fire pits. A boy called out, "Wasn't she afraid to go near her uncle?

"She was, but the ghost seized her *orenda* with its cold fingers. 'Listen to me,' it said. "Go west to a powerful river. There is a mystery there that is hidden in mist. The other ghosts say so. The guardian of Niagara will show you how to be stronger.'

"The Otter girl promised to try. Laughing Water's ghost let go of her so she could move again. She had to walk far before dawn." Jekonsaseh played a finishing beat on the stretched skin of the water drum. Because of the water, the note lingered.

"Is it over? Did she get there?"

"What else happened?"

"Did her father find her and bring her back?"

"Did she find out what was hidden in the mist?"

"Did she marry her cousin?"

"That is enough," Onoji demanded. If Jekonsaseh named the proposed husband, he would be laughed at. "Storytelling is over. Go home to bed, all of you."

"But the story is not finished," said his son. "I want to hear the rest of it." Onoji glared until the boy pulled on his boots and sleeping furs, and joined the line leaving Otter Longhouse.

A man who had stood in the shadows pulled on his coat and wrapped his mouth and nose with his scarf until only his eyes showed. He exited with the others, but he circled to the far side of the longhouse. Once the clearing was empty, Runs Fast left the town and hurried back to Deganawida's camp.

That night, the boys who had been greedy with the dried plums moaned on their bed benches and ran outside frequently. Next time, they might listen to their mothers. Jekonsaseh promised the Otters she would finish telling her story on the second night, if the spirits and Onoji allowed.

Chapter 24

The old healer showed no anxiety. "There was nothing wrong with the dried plums. My sister brought them from Turtle House. She and Jekonsaseh did not meet until we entered Otter House." He kept his smile inside where Onoji could not see it. "We gave the boys binding potions. They got sick because they ate too many of them. Had they obeyed their mothers and not been greedy, they would not have suffered. As for Mother of Nations, are you frightened of a simple woman?"

"She is not simple."

Onoji told the man to go back to his potions and rattles, and to tell the next healer to enter. "Was there anything off about the plums? Tell me the truth. I've eaten dried plums and never suffered for it."

"Greed made the boys sick. They ate too many. Snake Haired's Law does not allow mothers to reprimand or command their sons. We did better under the old Law, when men presided over hunting and war, and women ruled the homes."

"This town surrendered to Tododaho. You will keep his Law. Wasn't the old woman's rebellion and death enough to convince you?"

"It was enough," she replied and turned away sadly.

"Women were made to produce food and babies," Onoji mumbled to himself as he walked between the houses and the palisade. Why should he feel troubled? Jekonsaseh was a rebellious daughter. This was no ordinary story she was telling. She was encouraging insolence. Proper stories gave boys lessons in courage in hunting and war. They gave girls industry in growing and preparing food. Should he have asked to hear the story before she told it? Why did she pick this town to ask for refuge? He scratched his scalp between his braids.

He could hardly wait for spring to come so he could get back to war. Deganawida and Hiawatha were dead. Without them, the resistance would end. Jekonsaseh's presence made him long to crack heads. It was for the best that he did not marry her. The thought made him shudder. His wife was a decent woman. On the other hand, she had not spoken last night when their boys ate too many plums.

He needed the company of men to sort this out. There was no question that he would bring Jekonsaseh to her father. Lord Tododaho would subdue her and train the child. If Onoji proved his loyalty and ability, he would be given a command far from the witch. Onoji wished he knew which of Deganawida's men was hers. They could kill him or take him captive to make her conform to her father's Law.

A hazy half moon was visible between the trees. When the people finished their evening meal, they filed into Otter Longhouse for the rest of the story. Onoji waited outside with three men he trusted for their maturity and intelligence. They had fought with him against Cayuga Nation last summer. He praised them and gave them their orders. "I value your judgment. Mother of Nations' story is defiant, but she is persuasive. We cannot let her plant dissention. We three are enough to keep order. After her baby is born, we will bring her to her father. If you have questions, ask now."

Tawanyas of Otter Clan had been chief here before Onoji replaced him. "My wife says Mother of Nations is within a month of giving birth. She needs women now. I wasn't there, but my wife says the story did not challenge our master directly. The children were entertained on a dreary winter night. How is that bad?"

"You weren't there. She is subtle," said Onoji. "That is why I want you to listen tonight. Too many men feel obligated to Mother of Nations to hear the danger. Her words are like a witch's enchantment."

Deer Chaser of Wolf Clan said. "I have benefited from her kindness, myself." He lifted the corner of his shirt to show the scars below his ribs. "Perhaps you should wait for spring before you bring her to her father. You do not want to endanger Mother of Nations or her child."

"We will go in easy stages and let her rest," Onoji said.

"What will you tell Lord Tododaho if she or the baby dies?" Onoji gave Deer Hunter a sharp look. "She is old to be bearing her first child. I would not like to give her father bad news."

"Nor would I," Onoji admitted. "Could you tell which of Deganawida's men is her husband? We can kill him or take him captive to enforce her obedience."

Jagged Scar of the Turtles scratched his chin under his scarf. "None of the Huron's men seemed close to her, apart from the accursed Hiawatha and the Huron himself. Could it be one of them?"

Deer Hunter scoffed. "Hiawatha is her uncle and the Huron is her brother. Obviously, they are not truly sister and brother, but she would not lie with him. Relatives, even by adoption, can't marry."

"That was the old Law. I'm of Otter Clan and so is Jekonsaseh," said Onoji.

His friends shook their heads in disgust. "You couldn't have married her. You are related."

"That is true under the old Law but not now. I'm glad she ran away. Who would want that witch for his wife? Last night, Jekonsaseh told her own story although she did not give names. Listen tonight, but be on guard. Don't let her cloud your minds."

They entered. A young woman bade them welcome. "Will you take some refreshment, my lords? Mint tea or popped corn? I'm afraid the boys finished all the plums last night."

Jekonsaseh and Otter Clan Mother paused at the porch. "Go in first and I will come shortly. You know how it is when the baby presses."

There was an old oak outside the stockade. A man hid in its low branches, but Jekonsaseh felt his attention. No one watching would have suspected anything. She made no obvious movement, but whispered to Runs Fast, "I am safe. My father's men intend to bring me to him. Do not interfere." She smoothed out her long skirt, and returned to Otter Longhouse.

When her audience was settled, she positioned the water drum, closed her eyes and invited her story to flow into her mind. *Lend me your strength*, she sent to the women and girls. They had helped increase the power of her *orenda* the night before. When Onoji would have stopped her, he found himself speechless. She struck the drum four times. "This continues the story," she said, and even the boys became hushed.

"When we stopped, the girl had just left her cousin's ghost. She began her trek west, trusting the damp fallen leaves to muffle and cover signs of her passing. She thought about the man her father intended her to marry. Her father told her he was a good hunter and a brave warrior, but he was of Otter Clan. Since she was also of Otter clan, marrying him would break the Creator's Law.

"The journey from Tyo-den-he-deh to Niagara was long, but the girl had faith in her friend's counsel. She came to the beach of the Great Lake. She had never seen so much water in one place. It seemed to go on forever so she asked the lake's spirit to send help to her.

"A fisherman saw her and paddled close. He asked who she was and why she was alone. Who could stop him if he wished her harm? But her muddy and troubled face troubled him and he held back. Her eyes were dull by then – for she had not seen or spoken with anyone for many days and nights. The girl feared to speak for he might guess who she was. He asked again why she was alone and where she belonged. The girl pointed across the lake. 'There. Take me,' she said.

"She sounded like a simple child, not a young woman. After some thought, he told her to climb in. While he paddled, she barely looked at him. He offered her a raw fish and she ate it. She was very hungry. At last, she was nearing the Niagara River to seek out Hidden in Mist. Her cousin's ghost said he was the spirit of the waterfall. Have you heard of him?" Jekonsaseh looked to the children.

"The legends say he is very holy," said a girl.

"Did she find him?" asked another.

A boy asked, "Did the man with the canoe guess who she was?"

"The man did not ask her who she was again, but he offered to bring her to his family and have his wife feed and care for her. She did not reply so he kept near the shore. They covered a good distance. It saved her more than three days of walking. At last he said he could go no further and must get home before dark. He brought his canoe to the bank and she continued on her way.

"She entered a wild forest where ivy and brambles climbed the trees and wood flies buzzed and bit her ears. This was the kind of place Younger Brother might like. That is where she found her accursed uncle. He sat in a small clearing by a fire. She called him by name, but he didn't remember it. His ragged clothing was stained with sweat and blood for he thought no more of washing than a wolf, and he had no companions to clean him as wolves clean each other with their tongues.

"Her uncle had killed a traveler recently and had butchered him into portions as we would butcher an antelope or a wood bison. He munched on a roasted arm while the head, bones and organs simmered in wide cooking bowls for soup. The muscles hung in neat strips where they smoked above the coals to preserve them for winter."

"Ai," groaned her listeners. The more tender-hearted wept openly at the traveler's fate. "That's terrible!" protested the lame girl. "Say it didn't happen."

"Hush," said her mother. "Don't interrupt a story. Mother of Nations, please, go on. What did the girl do?"

Jekonsaseh could see the horror again in memory and her voice shook as she fought to keep speaking. "She called to him. 'Uncle,' she said loudly. 'See me.' He looked in her direction and blinked in disbelief. 'A talking otter?' he asked. "How is that possible? No. Wait. It's a bear. What are you -- an otter or a bear? Hold still. Why do you keep changing?'

"Another girl would have run, but the girl said, 'I can't hold still and I can't stop changing. Would you be kind enough to kill and eat me, too? I'm young and tender, and would taste better than what you are now eating.'

"Her uncle backed away from her. He tripped over his fire log, landed on his backside in hot ashes. He grew angry. 'You are trying to confuse me. There's no such animal as a bear otter. Go away!' He thrust out the arm at her. 'This is my forest!'

"'I will go,' the girl said sadly, and she did. She had tried to help him as she had promised her cousin she would, but it had done no good. All she wanted next was to find the Niagara River. When she grew hungry, she dug for roots or picked berries or found grubs under rocks. She ate missed ears of corn and slept under the leaves or in a tree. Sometimes people saw her and called for her to stop, but she only asked the way to the white river. They pointed and she trekked on.

"Her face became streaked with mud and her appearance like that of a forest demon. Tales began to be told about her to frighten children. The day came when she arrived. The Niagara splashed and tumbled angrily over rocks as it gathered speed. She followed it until she came upon the more regular of two cliffs. The river plunged over it and descended powerfully to the broken boulders at the bottom. The high and powerful falls sent up droplets that hovered in the air like clouds. Would she find Hidden in Mist here? If not, she intended to leap to her death so her father could not claim her. What do you think? Did she jump or live?"

"She has to live!" shouted a girl. "Let her live."

Even the boys called out that the story girl should live. Men puffed on their pipes, making them glow in the dim light since the fires had burned low. Only the three older men near Onoji remained solemn. They knew what she was doing but could not interrupt. "Tell us what happened," said Otter Clan Mother.

Jekonsaseh sipped her cooled tea. The fires had burned down to embers. The room waited. She looked to Onoji. Was he still her enemy or had her praise changed him? She beat her drum softly. "Niagara is truly a place of power ruled by a powerful spirit. The girl felt like she could be a drop of water in the river. She could fall and become part of something greater. She would be with her cousin again. She pictured herself falling, and floating away. Her spirit would soar up to the clouds.

"Perhaps the clouds or the mist heard her thought. The sun touched the mist below her and two rainbows appeared. She had seen rainbows in the sky, but never beneath her feet. She had found something hidden in the mist, rainbows and beauty and mystery. She didn't need to face her father again, nor the man he intended her to marry. Her answer came to her."

"What was the answer?" demanded a girl.

Jekonsaseh beat her drum. "A boy ran up and took her arm. 'Don't!' he said. She stopped looking at the rainbows and looked at him. He had intelligent eyes and a thoughtful mouth. He pulled her back from the edge. It was peculiar that she understood him since he didn't speak Longhouse. She assumed the Spirit made it possible.

"'We knew you were com-coming,' said the boy. 'Hidden in M-mist has pre-prepared sup-supper for us. Come and say hello to him.'" Jekonsaseh stammered and stuttered when she spoke for Deganawida. "The boy walked them to a steep path beside the torrent and she saw the Spirit of Niagara."

Her listeners' mutters grew louder. A child shouted, "The boy was the Peacemaker, wasn't he? He talks like that. I'm right, aren't I?"

"You are right. His name means Thinker in Huron."

"And Mother of Nations was the girl! Did I guess right?"

Jekonsaseh admitted it and the children congratulated themselves. "Be quiet," demanded Onoji. They fearfully ceased their chatter, but he only said, "Let our storyteller finish the story."

She felt the tingle of power projected by the girls and women of Otter House. She drank it in, amplified it, and sent it back to everyone in reach of her voice. Even those too young to understand a storyteller's magic hushed.

"Thinker led her down the narrow path. On a shelf before a cave sat a man with gray hair hanging loose over his shoulders. He rose and held out his hands in invitation. She closed the distance. At his gesture, she sat beside him.

"He smoothed her hair and shoulders. 'I live here,' the man said. His lips moved this time, but the falling water covered the sound of his words. She felt them, instead, like she felt the rumble of the Falls. *I'm called Hidden in Mist. Thinker and I have been waiting for you.* He nodded forward. *Niagara and I belong to each other. It has taken my hearing and given me this instead.* He touched his head. *You hear my thoughts because I wish it.* She asked how he knew she was coming. *Red Wing, my ghost wife, told me.* Hidden in Mist would not call her a witch for hearing ghosts. He heard them too.

"The girl recalled her cousin's words. *I hoped if I found you, that you would help me. I ran away from home.* He waited. *My father would have made me marry a man of my own clan. My father was trying to change the Law. He killed my aunt and cousins and cursed my poor uncle for speaking against him, but he was good to me when my grandmother threw me away. I don't know what to do. Will you pity me and help me?'*

"She feared Hidden in Mist would not respect weakness, but she couldn't help the tears that leaked out of her eyes and slipped down her cheeks. They mixed with the drops of mist. Perhaps if she told him she cried for others, not only herself, he would not think her weak. *The Ho-de'-no-sau-nee Tribes are at war. Many people have died and the herds ran away. The Tribes don't have enough to eat and children don't obey their mothers.*

"*That is bad, but I can't fix it from here. I have no power away from Niagara. Tell me about your uncle. What is the nature of his curse?*

"'He thinks men are animals and cooks them for his food, but he doesn't know what he's doing. When I saw him, he didn't know me.' She stopped trying to be brave and let her tears come. He wiped them away.

"The boy called Thinker patted the girl's arm to get her attention. He said, 'When I'm old enough, I'll c-cure your uncle so he'll know you again and s-stop being mad.' He was only a boy, but he seemed very confident.

She said, 'If you can do that and end my father's war, too, I would be glad.'

"The boy said, 'Wait until I grow up and you'll see what I can do.'

"The girl said, 'I will stay here until then and go back with you. I can't go home or my father will force me to marry the wrong man. I'm not strong enough to defy him.'

Hidden in Mist took her chin, turned her to him, and spoke directly to her mind. His words said, *You will be. I will teach you. We will go to the Huron villages where you will learn to listen and to heal. When you learn all I can teach you, you will go back to the Tribes to prepare them for when Thinker comes to stop the war.* When he smiled to her, the sun lit his face and his eyes twinkled like many-colored stars. The girl and the man exchanged their real names, but except for the boy, no one else heard."

"The girl came home and she is in this house!" shouted a girl. "You can say the names now because we guessed."

Jekonsaseh looked out from her bed bench over the children, their parents and elders. "You are right. The girl is a woman now and she is back with her own people. Hidden in Mist is Saiyen-gu. The girl is Jekonsaseh, and Thinker is Deganawida."

The lame girl said, "Hiawatha was here so that means Thinker grew up and cured him. Isn't that so, Mother of Nations?"

"It is. Now you know all the secrets, but the story isn't over. The Tribes still have to make peace. If you have faith in the Peacemaker, it will happen." Jekonsaseh beat her drum again. On the fourth beat, she held the drum-skin still.

"Jekonsaseh told us the story of Jekonsaseh," said the lame girl. "We heard it before anyone, even though it is not finished." The guests thanked their hosts, bundled up against the cold and left Otter Longhouse. Jekonsaseh set down the drum and waited for what Onoji and his men would say to her. The clan matrons waited with her.

Instead of coming directly to her, the men spoke to each other. Onoji protested loudly. "That is not why I summoned you. How dare you suggest this? Have you no fear of what he will do to you?" He walked out alone, wondering how his plan could have gone so wrong. A gust of wind shivered down the center line of the longhouse and sparks rose from the fire pits as he opened the curtain and walked into the night alone.

The three remaining men came to Jekonsaseh and the matrons. Tawanyas spoke on their behalf. "Thank you for tonight's entertainment, Mother of Nations," he said. "We three are ready to follow your commands. In the morning, we will escort you anywhere you say."

Chapter 25

Onoji

In the old days, a treaty could be revoked by the clan matrons, but that was before the new Law. The old woman of Otter House must have known Tododaho could hear her. Was Onoji as courageous? He kept walking. Going to the Snake Haired was risky, but had his lord wished, he could have felled Onoji where he stood.

He had guessed that Jekonsaseh had power, yet he had underestimated her. Somehow, she had forced him to let her tell her story. Some had the power to see or hear from afar or to cause things to happen. Onoji had only his senses and weapon skill. As it turned out, they were not enough. He would make no excuse. He had to go north. Lord Tododaho might appreciate details about Jekonsaseh who was, after all, his daughter.

Swinging his arms helped propel him and keep him warm. His hips swayed in a rocking motion as he placed his snowshoes. Without much thought, he avoided stumbling over dips and obstacles, leaving his mind free to ponder what he could have done differently. Even three elders on his side had not been enough to prevent the woman's influence. Even pregnant when she should have been at her weakest, she proved stronger than all of them.

Onoji did not want to think further ahead than his arrival at Tyo-den-he-deh, his lord's stronghold. He would tell Tododaho the facts as he understood them and accept the consequences. He crossed frozen streams and ice-encrusted brambles. Brittle twigs snapped under his weight. The cold was better for travel than snowfall or rain as it kept him from slipping or sinking. Fatigue numbed his tired arms. He hoped he would have no need to use his war club. It remained in its holder on his belt, but he doubted he could close his hand around the grip.

He scooped up snow and let it melt between his tongue and his cheek. Swallowing it frozen was dangerous. His pemmican was hard, too. He held it against his cheek to soften it and kept walking.

Before twilight dulled his vision, he found a large oak with thick branches groined to the trunk. He unlaced his snowshoes and tied them together around his neck, and climbed into the crotch of the oak to sleep until daybreak. He braced his feet, wrapped his scarf around his face, and pulled his deer-hide cloak around him to hold in his body heat. It occurred to him that he might freeze. If he did, he would not have to face his master's wrath.

He left his fate to winter's spirit and sucked in air through his scarf to warm his throat. The oak bough felt hard and rough against his back. He adjusted his cloak again when he felt the depression of a squirrel hole. As long as he was resting, he thought of making a fire to roast it and warm up. He reached in and discovered scales.

From what he could feel, it was likely a rat snake that slipped into its winter sleep. He might eat it to save his trail food, but a warrior did not need a full stomach. Besides, his master honored snakes. This one would live to see another spring, he thought as he set it down again.

Frantic squeals above him informed him of a small creature, maybe a mouse, in the grip of an owl. One never heard their wings. He wondered if owls were favored by the Elder or the Younger Brother. Something heavy and nearby broke through the brush. He looked down to be sure it had not begun to climb after him, and tried to tighten his fist around his war club. Thankfully, the sounds died. A bear might have left its den to discover what smelled good. He hoped it was too sluggish to come after him. A wolf wouldn't climb. Either way, he was probably safe if he kept still and did not freeze.

He imagined the many ways Lord Tododaho might kill him. Would he use shaman spirit power to stop his heart? Would he choke him or cause his brain to burst? Onoji would try to die bravely, as a warrior should. He shifted on the bough, doubling his cloak against the hardness and cold. At last, he slept.

The sky hung grey and low when he awoke and climbed down. He took care of bodily needs, ate and drank, and then strapped on his snowshoes to resume his journey. To warm up, he covered the ground at a stride. Soon large flakes drifted down to blanket the forest. They quickly coated his cap and mantle. He wondered if he resembled a walking snowman or a ghost.

At the end of the second day at dusk, he arrived at Tyo-den-he-deh's planting field which rested dormant under the thick snow. Winter was not supposed to be the season of strife, yet strife continued. A sense of power came from the walled town. Its many longhouses were protected by the palisade walls, but he should have seen watchers. Smoke rose from smoke-holes behind the wall.

He walked with care to avoid pitfalls. He knew the approach, but his master might have changed it. Warriors often kept vigil from platforms where, in summer, children threw stones to frighten the birds from the corn hills. He had to suppose he was being observed, but saw no one. It was eerie. His leggings and moccasin boots, his long shirt and knee-length cloak were torn and damp with sweat and melted snow. Duty and dread were uppermost in his mind.

The clouds opened and several stars appeared in the new night. Snow fog enshrouded the forest as he approached the palisade's opening. He must identify himself before they took him for an enemy. He lifted his hands to show that he held no weapon and said in a carrying voice, "I am Onoji from Ga-ah'na." Someone called down for him to wait. Onoji lifted his eyes to a figure above the wall with his bow half-drawn. "I'm alone. I must speak with Lord Tododaho." Soon, two men exited and approached him. "Where are your patrols?" he asked.

"Tyo-den-he-deh is protected. Come inside."

There were watchers, but he hadn't seen them. "His daughter has been in Ga-ah'na. I can give him details."

"Are you sure he doesn't know the details?"

The question made him feel insignificant. He might as well admit the truth. "I came to admit my failure and accept his judgment, or be available for his use."

"Brave of you," commented the townsman. "Walk between us. He is expecting you."

At the largest longhouse, his escort pulled aside the hide curtain and motioned him to enter. Onoji removed his snowshoes and left them hanging beneath the eves with his mantle. The heat from the fire pits tingled against his cheeks and arms. The evening meal was over but his mouth watered at the lingering smells. He sniffed roast bear, squash, beans and onions. He must be light-headed to hope for a warm meal before Tododaho pulled his soul from his body and scattered the fragments. Why waste food on a condemned man?

The inhabitants watched him silently as he stopped before the Snake Haired, bowed his head briefly, and lifted his eyes. "I meant to control her, to bring her to you," he said flatly. "I summoned an elder, a war chief and a shaman to help me. She turned them into her dogs. I left them panting to serve her." He tried not to flinch when Tododaho came forward or when he placed his large hand over Onoji's shoulder.

"You are loyal and bold, but you are no match for my daughter." Did his master sound proud? He had not expected that. "With her son's *orenda* to draw upon in addition to her own, it is small wonder the others fell to her. That you didn't, speaks well for you. I see I will have to deal with her myself." "But aren't you angry?" Onoji told himself he was a fool to ask.

"Actually, this is better. She will bring me my grandson to me in the spring. She will also bring me Deganawida and Hiawatha."

Onoji startled so badly, Tododaho chuckled. "But they are dead."

"Your young men were not as thorough as they thought." He turned to a woman across from them on her bed-bench. "Deenah, bring Onoji food and dry clothes." She hurried to obey. Tododaho returned his attention to his guest. "Deenah is Bear Clan Mother and my sister. Hand me your boots."

As Onoji had not been invited to sit, he held onto the nearest lodge pole to draw them off and handed them over. Tododaho inspected them and his lips drew back. It took Onoji a moment to realize the expression on his master's face was a smile.

Tododaho turned to another woman. "Find this war chief moose-hock socks to warm his feet and dry moccasin boots for the morning. His are ruined." The woman took the ruined boots to measure them against others. "You can tell me more after you eat and warm yourself, Onoji. Sit down." He patted the place beside him.

Tododaho was a solid presence, ruthless and determined but fair, as Onoho, Onoji's father, had impressed upon Onoji when he was a boy. His father was one of their master's first converts outside of Tyo-den-he-deh. He had agreed that the clan matrons had too much power. Men should not have to report to them and wait for their approval over treaties and appointments. Onoho had trained Onoji to war before he died.

Gray streaked the Snake Haired's dreadlocks. A sleek black snake rode his shoulders and rested its head among them. At Onoji's approach, it leaned toward him and flicked its thin tongue to taste his scent. "What do you think, Brother?" Tododaho asked the snake. His voice sounded like a serpent's scales moving. "Is my servant loyal? Read his secret heart."

The snake examined Onoji. Its head zigzagged from his face to his upper torso, and then moved around to lick Tododaho's ear. "My serpent brother says what you lack in spirit power; you make up for in loyalty and weapon skill. You should eat now and rest. We'll talk later." Despite the favorable verdict, Onoji wished he could have avoided the snake's examination.

Deena led Onoji to an empty section on the bed bench. One of her women brought him a steaming bowl of braised rabbit with dumplings. Another brought clean, well-made clothing, a breech clout, a shirt and leggings. "Here is a mantle. It belonged to my husband. He died last year fighting in north Seneca."

When he set aside the food bowl with thanks, Deenah brought him two bowls of heated water, a lump of ash soap, small rags for washing and large ones for drying. She backed away, drawing his privacy curtain. He peeled off his hide shirt and leggings, and finally unwound his breechclout. When he was clean and dry, he pulled on the new clothing. The warmed moose-hock socks were an added comfort.

For fourteen families and seven burning hearths, the house was entirely too silent. In his youth, houses were full of talking, couples loving behind their curtains, story-telling and children's questions. The war had made his people glum, but he was not here to question his master. He crossed to Tododaho's bed-bench and waited.

"You are still uncertain of me." Onoji didn't trust his voice, so he gave a small nod. "You have always been loyal. Sit beside me. It should have been your son in my daughter's womb. You have fathered two boys."

"Yes, two sons and a daughter." Onoji thought of his sons. They were nearly old enough to fight. Would they live through another summer of war?

Tododaho spoke. "You did your best. Not everyone is as gifted as my daughter. Although you resisted her influence in Ga-ah'na, you couldn't oppose it. Hiawatha was my cousin and once my friend. He became my enemy when he tried to thwart my plans. He works against me now, with my new enemy. The two of them joined forces with my daughter, so now there are three. I will deal with them."

Tododaho seemed in a contemplative mood. Onoji wondered why he was confiding in him, but he continued to listen, fascinated by what he was sharing. "Twenty years ago, I brought Jekonsaseh into this very longhouse, outcast and alone. I asked my mother to adopt her into the Bears, but I should not have had to ask. Under my rule, she would have been mine. You let the Huron and his men into your town, and you let them go again."

Onoji took a breath. "They asked in the name of the Three Sisters for Mother of Nations to be cared for. The old woman of Otter House invited them all in. Otter Clan Mother backed her up. I made sure it was for one night only. I made them leave in the morning."

"Yes. It is too bad Wades the River and Magpie could not complete their task. It was a worthy effort, but there were other powers at work. The Elder Brother has not given up yet, but we will succeed." Tododaho stretched and shook his head, causing his dreadlocks to wave and twist like actual snakes, but there was only the one. It waved its smooth head and hissed. Onoji backed away.

"Onoji," Tododaho said kindly. "Put away your worries. We will visit South Onondaga and plan our spring campaign with my other chiefs. We will finish taking Seneca and Cayuga before midsummer. You will take a large force to the river and then west. I will lead our northern combined forces to Cayuga where Tawanyas led the breakaway warriors from Ga-ah'na. They will try to reunite my daughter with my enemies, but we will circle around and defeat them."

Onoji was amazed at how Tododaho could foresee so much. No one could defeat his master. "Tell me now, Onoji, what you thought of my daughter's husband."

"It did not seem to me that she had one. All the men were committed to her, but none more than the others. She must have lain with a warrior who shared her shelter last summer."

Tododaho smiled indulgently. Onoji felt like a cared-for but dim-witted child. "Tell me about the foreigner."

"The foreigner? He kept furthest from her. He is called Red Hair. His skin color is unnaturally pale. His nose is of a different shape than ours and his chin is more rounded. His hair is red as an oak leaf in autumn. Someone said he came from across the ocean. Hiawatha said Wolf Clan Mother adopted him at Doteoga, a Ganeo-gaono Town on the south bend of Wide River before it flows out of tribal lands."

"Good. You have helped me see him." Tododaho eyes moved as if he watched someone and listened to him speak. "I don't know his accent. Maybe he did come from the other side of the ocean. He is going hunting. I'll wait until he's alone." He met Onoji's horrified gaze.

"Yes. He is her husband. None of her friends will be able to help him. Once Red Hair is dead, Jekonsaseh will lose heart and come to take her place at my side where she belongs. Hiawatha's anger at me will destroy him as it did before. Without him, the Huron's power will shrivel. When he is powerless, he will kneel at my feet and tremble before I bring my war club down to smash his skull! If I had him here now..." He curled his fingers as if to squeeze the life out of his enemy. At his low growl, heads peeked from bed curtains. They pulled back in quickly.

The shaman's smile showed his pointed incisors. Onoji's skin crawled as when lightening filled the air. "Jekonsaseh will be punished for her rebellion, but she will come home to me." Onoji held himself steady, but his trembling hands betrayed him. "Don't let it concern you. Go to your bed bench."

Before he closed the curtain, Onoji looked down the room. The fires had burned low. Shadows within the longhouse loomed larger and appeared to climb up the walls. So strong a power hovered around them, babies were afraid to cry. He consoled himself that before another winter, his master would have extended his Law over all Five Nations. The Longhouse wars could end. In a few years, the Tribes would expand their territory into Canada from the Huron north of the Lakes to the Algonquin northeast of the Wide River. Jekonsaseh would take her proper place as her father's helper. As for him, his name would be remembered as Lord Tododaho's faithful captain. He could put his mind at rest about the red-haired foreigner. He would be destroyed.

Onoji wondered whether Lord Tododaho still intended to give Jekonsaseh to him as a second wife. He hoped not. The thought of Jekonsaseh on his bed bench, of touching her, shriveled his manhood like ice water.

He tried to get comfortable. Sleeping had almost been easier in the tree. It was unseemly for a warrior to fear a woman, but it was so. Onoji turned over. His master stood near the central fire pit, his face intent, with reaching arms. His hands were empty, but Onoji suspected his master could see through walls and into the distance. Tododaho swayed. His stiff dreadlocks moved about his head like ten or more writhing snakes. His fingers were curved like a raptor's talons, grabbing for something. The fingers tightened around something that wasn't there, at least nothing that Onoji could see. He felt a sliver of his master's power, vicious even at its edges, and it terrified him. He would not want to be Red Hair when Tododaho's power penetrated his mind to destroy it.

He turned away and bundled into his blanket. The banked fires down the centerline of the longhouse suddenly flared. He had to look. The sky above the smoke holes darkened as if the stars had gone out. The brightness died and the hum of fear that had filled the room subsided with the flames. The magic had ended. Onoji turned his face to the wall and hoped for the oblivion of dreamless sleep.

Chapter 26

Red Hair followed the deer tracks, but the wind and drifting snow threatened to obscure them. Even his own were soon covered. He wouldn't be here at all if the camp had food. The shadows were growing. He must succeed before dusk or not at all. He bent a narrow branch to point the way back. He needed to keep a firm hold on his bearings.

His companions' snowshoes crunched the frozen snow just beyond the trees. He checked the final thicket and found it empty. They had had poor hunting luck these last few days. He admitted defeat and began back. None of his companions were visible between the bare trees and black branches. He blew out his cheeks in frustration. The snow was falling faster and a winter mist was rising, the kind that obscures the trees faster than a blizzard. There was the broken branch. Had he bent this one, or had someone else. The white ash had taken a different shape.

He stopped beside a mid-sized oak at the edge of a clearing and sniffed for the scent of their campfire. The smell of wet snow covered other smells. It was unusual to find so large a clearing as this. A village or town must have been here once and been burned to the ground. He couldn't recall the last time he saw Runs Fast, Condor or Cusik. His last snowshoe impressions were covered over. He had to hope he was walking toward instead of away from his friends. A line of paw prints showed him a wolf had crossed the meadow recently. He saw a gray tail before it vanished behind the trees.

The long shadows blended together into night. A hazy half moon became visible behind the mist. It should have risen in the east, opposite the setting sun, but by now the white snow and sky made directions impossible. A pervading feeling of being lost and alone overcame him.

He should stop in a thicket to get out of the snow before he wandered aimlessly in the night. He wouldn't eat at all or get much sleep, but it was better than sleeping exposed.

He turned back to see if he could find the deer thicket he passed. He had taken a few steps when pain stabbed his temple. He fell onto his knees and then forward into the snow. A rumble like thunder filled his ears and flashes crossed his vision. A wind gust scoured his face with ice crystals. Then the wind ceased and the air grew still.

Twelve-year-old Ole Halvardson rubbed the snow from his face. He pulled his scarf up to cover his mouth and nose, and breathed in warm, damp air. He kept on his knees for a while wondering how he had fallen. He was slightly dizzy and his head still hurt. He felt his hair for blood, but his mitten came away dry.

He had gone out to hunt hours before. The family would be getting worried. He looked around for his brother but didn't see him. The lad must have wandered off. He heaved himself to his feet and looked around. Sparks and swirling lights circled the sky. Nothing seemed normal. Uneasiness quickened his heart and cold was making him sluggish and uncoordinated, but he must keep moving or freeze. He lurched forward, hoping he might find a homesteader to offer him shelter for the night.

He managed to pull off one of his mittens with his teeth and pressed his cold fingers against his hot eyes. Another shower of sparks pulsed behind his eyelids. These were not the familiar Northern Lights, but cold suns. The wind and snow, or his tired mind, must be playing tricks on his eyes. He squinted at the gray sky over the meadow and prayed for Odin to part the clouds. As if in reply, a breeze whipped up and flung bits of ice against his cheeks.

He covered his aching eyes for a moment, and then pulled on his mitten. He squinted to clear his vision. There was the star he wanted. No wonder he was lost; he had been walking east, not west toward the District. He turned around. His snow shoes caught on something and he slipped forward, but he caught himself this time. The damp snow felt like a feather quilt, quite warm actually, as if he was home in bed. His next to last thought was that it did not hurt to freeze to death. His last thought was that no one would know he had died, but he no longer cared.

He awoke to sunlight blazing off the melting snow. He rubbed it off his cheeks and slapped his mittens against his thighs to knock away the clumps. He wondered how he had lived through the night, but he was glad to see the sun again. It would help him find his way home. All he had to do was walk toward his shadow until something looked familiar. He pushed himself to his knees and then to his feet.

The terrible pain in his head was gone now, thank the gods, but he was hungry! He felt in his pocket for his last piece of goat cheese. Instead, he found chunks of half-frozen meat. He popped one into his mouth and sucked it until it softened. He didn't remember bringing meat. "You'll get a warm meal soon," he told himself. "There must be a homestead housewife who will give you soup." His voice was too deep and he was too tall. Something had changed his perceptions. Not knowing what to make of it, he wrapped his scarf closer over his cheeks and mouth and trudged on.

The rising sun colored the snow a bright orange pink. Pink even touched the snow- covered trees, but what trees these were! He had never seen trees so tall and thick. A hot spring must have melted the permafrost. A small herd of dark, shaggy cattle lowed and pawed away the snow between the trees to graze. The last District cattle had died several years earlier, but here was a pocket of them.

A cow left her companions and walked over to him, blowing steam-like breaths from her great black nose. Her calf followed at her heels. Ole had to wonder how these few had escaped the slaughter when Greenland's grass was no longer sufficient for the large beasts. However, appeasing his hunger came first. Warm milk would sustain him for now. Getting home might take longer than he expected.

A large gray dog trailed the cow and her calf. It eyed him warily, but kept its distance. That was fine with Ole. Hungry dogs could be dangerous. He approached the cow, hoping she would let him milk her. She was larger and shaggier than most. "Good girl," Red Hair soothed. "Spare me some milk and I'll help you find your home. We must be near the glacier. Your owner will be glad to have you back."

She regarded him with large, brown eyes, but flinched. Perhaps she'd been lost longer than he had. He continued to talk to her. When she calmed enough, he smoothed her shaggy wool, then knelt and reached for an udder. "I'm sorry my hands are cold," he said. Her breath puffed in and she snorted and shook, but she allowed it.

He had no pail so he squirted the hot, rich milk into his mouth, swallowed, and pulled again. The calf nosed its way beneath its mother to drink from the other side. There was enough room for both of them. "What do YOU want?" he asked the dog as it came nearer. "Move back. You'll scare her." The dog backed away.

When he had had taken enough, Ole got to his feet and looked another time at the dog. He stepped toward it. The dog pulled back its black lips, showing fangs, and growled. Why would it suddenly become aggressive? Perhaps it feared he might steal its charge. The rest of the herd seemed to have wandered off.

"Let us find our way home together," he suggested. "Will you answer to Gray?" The dog tilted its muzzle. The pale half moon hung opposite the sun. The two cast overlapping shadows. The dog sat and whined, and then scratched its ear with a long hind leg. Ole whistled his shepherd's whistle. The dog perked its ears, stopped scratching and got to its feet. "What, Gray?"

It came closer and stopped just out of reach. Ole held his knuckles out, fingers curled as was prudent with an unknown dog. "As long as we will be traveling together, let's be friends." The dog side-stepped his hand, but when he persisted, it licked his fingers. "That's a good dog, Gray," he said. "Let's go. I want to find a house."

They were among the trees now. He wrapped his fingers in the cow's woolly neck to lead her, but spoke to the dog. "Tell me, Gray. Did you ever see anything like this? Grandfather says in the south of his old land, there are forests. I think this must be one of them. Did your master send you to find his herd? You lost the rest of them."

They were walking westward as far as he could tell. He must have miscalculated how far east he had gone. They came upon another meadow and then a stream, bumpy with roots and stones. Water bubbled to the surface of the thinning ice. After a while, he felt someone watching and turned to see. A boy of about ten watched him from the flap of a travel shelter. The child whistled sharply and a man emerged. Both of them stared at him leading the cow with the dog at his side.

He stared back. They were Skraelings, northern barbarians that called Greenland home before the Norse arrived. He didn't know their speech well enough to ask where they were. He tried Norse. "I'm lost. Can you tell me the way to the District?" The man smiled, and said something to the boy, but Ole did not hear. "The cathedral? The big stone building near the fjord? Where is it?"

"What language does he speak, Father?" the boy asked. "Do you think he's Huron?"

"His hair is red as fire. He holds a bison cow with its calf and a wolf follows him like it is a dog. You've heard of the fire heads and the white granite men?"

The boy nodded. "Of course, but not both in one. He casts two shadows, one from the moon and one from the sun."

"He might be a western shaman wearing white paint with red mud in his hair. Let us hope he keeps going."

It surprised Ole that he understood their words. They were afraid of him, which seemed odd. He walked a bit farther. Behind him, the father said, "If the red hair's *orenda* is strong enough to tame a wolf and a bison, be glad he is passing us by."

Ole looked back. The father lowered his bow and said, "He travels toward Niagara. Let Hidden in Mist deal with him." He motioned the boy toward their shelter. "Let us take it down and leave this part of the forest. We'll hunt somewhere else."

Ole pondered what the man meant. Who would deal with him? All he wanted was to get home. His father and step-mother might give him up for dead. His brother and half-sister might try to find him and encounter the same strange place he had come upon. Everything seemed odd, even himself. "I have an idea, Gray. You go home and I'll follow you." The dog tilted its muzzle. "Let us hurry. Wolves hunt at night."

The dog seemed to grin. Then, Ole heard wings. Against the startling blue sky and thick tree trunks flew a dark bird. "Don't snap at it, Gray," he commanded. "Ravens are sacred to Odin, King of the gods."

The canine stretched out tensely and watched the circling bird, but the cow pawed away the snow and bent to graze. Her calf moved in to suckle. Ole took his share. The warm milk helped fill his stomach. Before long, some kind housewife would give him a solid meal.

The bird settled on a branch. "Do you carry a message?" he asked, wiping his mouth. The bird folded its dark wings and eyed him. Ravens were known to be wise. Some said they could talk. "What is your message?"

"Follow me," said the raven. It crouched and leapt back into the sky. "Follow me," it repeated and shot ahead.

"Not so fast. I can't fly." He grasped the wooly shag of the bison cow again and pulled it along. She nudged her calf until it shook itself and got to its feet. The bison with her calf and the wolf continued with Red Hair to follow the hawk. Where in the world was he and what had become of Greenland's West District?

They walked for a long while. Red Hair stopped to catch his breath. He should have found signs of humans by now. He rubbed his aching legs and discovered his pants were not patched goat hide, but something else. The cow swept away at the snow with her shaggy head and hooves and grazed again. Her calf lay down again and closed his eyes. "Yes, I'm tired too, but I don't want to spend another night in the open." Red Hair and continued with just the wolf and the hawk.

He needed to follow the raven. "I wish I knew where we were, Gray," he admitted. The air grew warmer as they walked deeper into the forest. "I must stop," he said and sat on the ground, his back against a tree. "You look well-fed. Can you find us something to eat?" The wolf trotted off. A flock of grey birds settled above him on a hickory bough, making unfamiliar calls.

The hawk rebuked him with annoying shrieks. "I had to rest. Where are you bringing me, Raven?" After a while, he stood up and followed the annoying bird. It soared forward, and then waited. This was becoming a pattern. It remained in sight, returning for him when he fell behind.

"Where are we?" He was becoming disturbed at the sound of his voice which still sounded older than it should have. "If I'm dreaming, why do my legs ache and why am I hungry?" He looked at himself as well as he could, and rubbed his legs again. "What are these?" He inspected his moccasin boots and snowshoes. Flickers of memory returned, but his bladder was full. "All that milk," he told himself, and looked down, confusion growing. Could he have slept for years?

He removed his mittens and fingered his deer-hide shirt and coat, and his fur-lined hood. When he rubbed his cheeks and chin, his fingers met a new growth of beard, not soft as in youth, but rough against his calloused fingers. "Did I cross the rainbow bridge into Asgard?" The bird circled back and scolded him for delaying.

After a while, Gray found him. He carried a half-eaten rabbit in his mouth. This, he dropped before Red Hair. "Good boy. Thank you," he said. The dog backed away, licking blood off his muzzle. "No time for a fire. Raw will have to do."

He ate until he was sated before he noticed that the knife was using to slice the meat belonged to his father. "How did I get this?" Bands of sinew surrounded the grip, obscuring the runes with his name. It had once belonged to his grandfather's father who had carved the runes of his name into the ivory. His ancestor, also called Ole, had won it in a Viking raid in a warm country he called Spain.

Water gurgled in a nearby stream. The ice had melted. Red Hair wiped his hand across his face. It came away with blood. He was smeared with blood from his meal. He knelt at the stream to wash.

Patches of snow still covered the rocky banks, but fern curled up at the water's edge, and early watercress swayed as the water flowed over them. Red Hair cupped his hands to bring the icy water to his mouth. The stream might lead him to a homestead where he could get answers. He walked on, following the raven.

Dark came and he slept again. When he awoke, he found the raven and Gray had been guarding his sleep. He didn't need his snowshoes anymore. The raven led him down the stream. It grew wider until it became a river that tumbled and churned as it splashed around boulders, bubbling and splashing like the fjord in spate. There was no river like this at home. The glacier must be melting. This was a most unusual spring. The river grew wider. It troubled itself into backwards-flowing waves it dropped over the edge of and disappeared in a roar of sound.

Ole crept up carefully and looked out through the clouds of mist. He could not see the bottom, but the lower lake was bordered by blue spruce trees. In the distance, the other half of the river rushed down an inward-curving cliff. The water foamed below him like new milk. Three rainbows danced where sunbeams lit the mist.

The raven flew down the cliff. "Do you expect me to climb down there?" Ole asked. "Are you sure? What do you think, Gray?" The wolf crouched and whined, then trotted down the narrow descent. Ole decided he could no longer be in the land of men. The rainbows proved it. Gods must live here.

He followed Gray cautiously. It would not be good to lose his footing. Drops of mist clung dampened his clothing and dripped from his lashes and cheeks. The roar of the water hid other sounds, but he picked up fragments of words. Finally, he was able to grab an entire sentence.

He looked around to see who had spoken. The man must be hidden by the mist. If Ole found him, he could ask where they were. Halfway down behind the narrow path that led behind the Falls, he beheld a stone ledge. A white-haired man sat watching him descend. The raven soared out and across the face of the waterfall. It pumped its wings and spread its talons as it glided down to perch on the man's leather-sleeved arm. It walked up to his shoulder and rubbed its head against the man's cheek.

Under the old man's touch, the raven's beak shortened and curved. Its body and plumage expanded, and its blackness lightened to a speckled brown. "What did you do to Odin's raven?" Ole shouted.

Gray leaned against the man's knees, but it was no longer a dog. It was a gray wolf. Started, Ole would have moved back, but there was nowhere to go. "What is happening?" he demanded, trying to be heard above the flood.

The man's face seemed to shine. It was Odin, as he imagined him, but with two good eyes and no beard. This couldn't be Asgard. "Who are you?" he demanded. Then he realized this was no way to approach a god. "Can you help me?" he asked.

Ole felt, rather than heard him say, *I can. I am called Saiyen-gu. I have been waiting for you.*

"What kind of name is that?"

It is Iowan. That was my name on the prairie. The people hereabouts call me Hidden in Mist.

The words seemed familiar and unfamiliar at the same time. "What people? Where are we? What place is this?"

The old man pointed above them and then opened his hand, fingers down, to indicate the falling water. *This is Niagara. Come with me. I will answer all your questions.* The wind lifted Saiyen-gu's white hair. It blew about his head like wisps of cloud on a brisk day. Ole shouldered his pack and followed Saiyen-gu into a cave behind the granite wall.

Something simmering in a clay pot gave off a fragrant steam that made his mouth water. Saiyen-gu filled a bowl of food and handed it to him. *Here is water to drink with your food,"* he added as he set down the folded bark cup.

208

Saiyen-gu directed Ole to remove his tattered moccasin boots and coat. *I prepared a bed for you. We will talk again after you rest.* Ole washed, and then wrapped himself in the indicated furs. His full belly, the warmth around him, and three days of travel did their work. Before he could remember his questions he was asleep.

Saiyen-gu sat beside him and gently pressed Ole's temples. *Open your mind to me. Allow me to straighten your thoughts and retrieve your lost memories.* The soundless voice penetrated his consciousness. *Tododaho tried to kill you, but your* orenda *was too strong. It protected you. When you were young, you were Ole Halvardson. You lived in a country without trees, and at the end, without food. You are no longer young. When you awake, you will remember everything.*

Red Hair's last ten years returned. He had followed what he had taken for a raven and a dog. The raven became a hawk. The Icelandic cow became a different sort of bovine with a shaggy head and sharp horns. Whatever she was, she had let him take her rich, warm milk. He had walked for three days with a dog. It was not a dog but a wolf. How was any of this possible?

He woke up and turned his head. The old man was watching him. The wolf crouched at his feet to be scratched between its ears. The land of Ole's ancestors was gone. He remembered that now. He lived in a new world with trees and strange beasts. Sorcerers and witches, ghosts and spirits abounded. A man was going to bring peace to tribes at war. He, Red Hair, had vowed fealty to him.

He closed his eyes and saw a woman. Her dark eyes full of trouble, her breath hissed painfully between her teeth. He felt the echo of her labor as her muscles clenched, pushed and clenched again. She was bearing his child. *Where are you, Red Hair?*

He sat up abruptly, sleep dashed away. His anguished cry pierced the crash of the falling water outside the cave. "Jekonsaseh!"

Chapter 27

Gano'wages was a large longhouse town. Its Otter Clan Matron a small, efficient woman. Luckily for Jekonsaseh, she had delivered many babies. She examined her patient again, counting between her contractions and feeling for the baby's position. Sunlight slanted down the smoke holes and etched the frown-creases between her brows deeper. One of her daughters handed her a damp hide scrap to wipe her hands.

Jekonsaseh shifted on the hide mattress to find a more comfortable position. She pressed both hands against her lower back. After a moment, she sighed, took away her hands and stretched her shoulders. "The child pushes here as he has done before. It stopped."

"It won't be long until before it starts again. You are almost ready to grip the ropes. You've tended injured warriors, Mother of Nations, but you know less than many of our girls. Have you even seen a child born?"

"When I trained to be a healer, I saw several births in the Huron villages, but I didn't assist. I didn't know enough. As you say, my work has been with battle injuries, but shouldn't the pressure be here?" She touched her belly.

"It can come either way. It is good your men brought you to me. You're old to be bearing your first child. It won't be much longer before your real work begins." She commanded her women to bring necessities to the birth lodge. "The next time your back tightens, tell me."

Jekonsaseh recalled stories of women working in the corn, moving aside when their pains began, scooping up their babies into a sling across their breasts, and continuing their work while the baby suckled. She mentioned this.

Otter Clan Mother admitted it sometimes happened. "They were younger and had not half-starved themselves before they admitted they needed help." Another pain made Jekonsaseh grit her teeth to keep from crying out. "That is why we will assist you. I won't have it said that Gano'wages lost the famous Mother of Nations to childbirth when she might have lived. Let me see." Sitting back, she announced to her women, "Mother of Nations will soon be a mother in truth. When the pain stops, we'll go to the birth lodge."

Two girls went with them. "They are two of my granddaughters," explained Otter Clan Mother. "They will help us." While they arranged Jekonsaseh over the ragged hides, Otter Clan Mother kept up a steady stream of chatter intended to teach.

"Are they training to be healers?" Jekonsaseh asked after she caught her breath. "They are thinking about it, but they will be mothers someday. Giving birth is a woman's test. It is like war for a man. Men have been known to turn tail and run from war like frightened deer, but the Creator made us differently. We have no choice but to be brave."

Tawanyas and his friends watched Jekonsaseh being led to the birth lodge. Men were not permitted near it. The best they could do was to ask the Three Sisters to give her an easy time, and to wait.

One of Otter Clan Mother's daughters struck sparks with flint rocks and built up a small, steady flame. The lodge would soon be warm enough for mother and child. More women arrived with bowls of heated water and rags. It might be a long wait.

During the day, women stopped by but did not linger. Jekonsaseh bore her pains valiantly through the night and into the next day, but she was growing tired. About noon, she gazed westward with pained and weary eyes. "Red Hair, where are you?" she asked.

Otter Clan Mother did not know who Red Hair was, but assumed it must be Jekonsaseh's husband. "If he were in Gano'wages, he could not enter the birth lodge," she said. Unsure her patient heard her, she told her granddaughters to continue to rub Jekonsaseh's back.

Jekonsaseh seemed to withdraw further. She continued to speak softly, eyes lifted to the smoke hole. "Red Wing, tell Saiyen-gu and tell Red Hair to send me strength." Red Wing's ghost touched her forehead and abdomen with comforting spirit fingers and nodded. She understood, having given birth many times. She would carry Jekonsaseh's message. With a relieved sigh, the laboring woman watched the ghost depart.

"She speaks to spirits and asks for help," said Otter Clan Mother. "Keep holding her arms and sharing your strength with her. Daughter, is the root tea cool enough?"

"It is," she replied. She tilted the cup to Jekonsaseh's lips at the end of the last contraction. Jekonsaseh sipped the medicinal tea. She had nearly taken it when it might have stopped this child she bore from beginning, but Lili had been watching. The Creator and Earth Mother must want her to have this child.

She forced herself back to the present and the birth lodge. Otter Clan Mother and her daughters and granddaughters crowded around. She spoke hoarsely. "If I die, cut my baby out and find someone to nurse him. Keep him away from my father."

Otter Clan Mother assured her that would not be necessary. She would live to hold her son, but Jekonsaseh was not sure. The effect of the tea manifested. Her muscles contracted strongly. She rose to her knees over the birthing hide once more, and pulled the rope taunt with both hands. Her efforts availed her at last. Otter Clan Mother's waiting hands eased her son's head and shoulders out. With a twist, the rest followed and the child was with them. "Catch your breath now, Jekonsaseh," she said.

She cleared the baby's mouth with her fingers and used a hollow reed to suck the nostrils clear. The infant gasped in a breath and yelled. "He is perfect," she announced. "Look." She held the infant where Jekonsaseh could see.

One of her daughters tied the cord with sinew and severed it with her flint knife. "It's nearly over. One last push and you can rest."

One of her women washed the babe with warm water and dried him. She set dried moss between his legs and wrapped him snugly in a small deer hide. At last, he was placed in his mother's arms.

Jekonsaseh trembled in exhaustion but she smiled to the women and girls, grateful for their help and grateful to be alive. Her son rooted and attached his mouth to her nipple. His sucking caused her muscles to push again to expel the afterbirth. At last the pain subsided. One of the women wrapped the afterbirth and took it away to leave in the forest while her sister washed the new mother.

Jekonsaseh touched her son's damp, sparse and gingery hair. His scalp was pink. His tiny lips and tongue made loud sucking sounds. While he drank she felt him all over and counted his fingers and toes.

If only Red Hair could see what they had made. "Do you have a name for your son?" asked Otter Clan Mother.

"I want to call him First Son, for luck," Jekonsaseh replied. "My husband believes in luck. First son might be an older brother some day." Some future day, these tiny hands with their curled fingers and fragile nails would be large and strong enough to nock an arrow to the bow string and draw back a bow. Would it be food he hunted, or men? After a while, First Son's mouth relaxed and his head dropped in sleep. Warm and clean, in the absence of pain, Jekonsaseh and her son slept.

###

The last snow drifts melted, new oak leaves reached the size of mouse ears, and the seed corn was planted. Children accompanied their mothers, singing songs of praise to the Sustaining Sisters all through the Tribal lands, but at Gano-wages, one field was left unplanted. Tododaho had responded to Deganawida's offer.

The corn was knee-high, the beans were ripening in their pods and the pumpkin blossoms were turning to new fruit when Deganawida's followers from each of the Longhouse nations arrived. When Snake Hair arrived, if he gave the order, his warriors would slaughter all those who opposed him.

Deganawida and Hiawatha crossed the town to talk to Tawanyas, Odatshedeh, and the other chiefs under the council oak. They wore no war paint. Neither did their men, but Gano'wages' warriors were prepared to defend their town. They were painted for war, their faces white. Suns, clouds, and lightning-bolts decorated their faces and shoulders. Full quivers leaned against archers' shoulders, and their bows were in hand. Those without bows held war clubs. Each man kept a sheathed knife at his belt.

Side conversations between the warriors ceased. "Why do they carry weapons? Are they planning to fight our visitors?" Deganawida asked, nodding to the townsmen.

"Visitors?" Odatshedeh faced the peace leaders. Ever realistic, he expected a final battle could be the only outcome. Even after the attack that had nearly killed them in the dead of winter, the two refused to admit they could fail. "How do you label our enemies visitors? If we are not prepared to defend you when the Snake Haired arrives, he will kill you. Not everyone here is as sure as you that this will end well. We will fight him and his company of warriors until they or we are dead."

"Have you no faith in me?" asked Deganawida. "I thought you did."

"We agreed to let you have your parley first, but it may not be enough. I intend to stand on your side and protect you. If it comes to a battle, either you or Snake Haired will prove the stronger and the war will end. In any case, I will not fight again."

"If I am the stronger, I won't need your protection. Believe in me and I will win. If you and the others do that, it will be enough."

Patrols had been posted along the trail to watch for the Snake Haired and his company of warriors. It would not be long, today or tomorrow. Jekonsaseh's son rode a sling across her chest as she walked to the council circle under the oak. The oak was clothed in early summer green. She nodded to the townsmen and the Peace party that contained more of Deganawida's followers than could stay within the town. They had erected shelters around the palisade. "The meeting will prove the rightness of your words, brother," she told Deganawida.

"It will. Your babe is growing. His grandfather should be happy. I hope there will be enough food after the conference. Everyone will be hungry."

The men looked to each other doubtfully. "I expect there will be fewer of us after the conference," Tawanyas said. He squinted into the sun, just visible behind the trees. "I'll send out some of my men to hunt. We don't want to deplete the town's reserves. The patrols will signal when our enemy arrives."

The hunters returned with a stag and some turkeys after sundown. The women set to work to prepare the meat. Pots were set to boil the chunks with onions and roots. "It seems we must wait a little longer," Deganawida said.

More friends arrived the next day. Many had not seen each other since the first snows of late autumn. Another day passed without the Onondaga arrival. Jekonsaseh sat with the clan matrons before the All-Clans fire, nursing First Son when the two brothers from Doteoga saw her and came over to see the child.

"Fisher! Beaver Tooth!" she said. Beaver Tooth had filled out over the winter and looked much more the warrior, with muscled arms and chest. He could fight, as he had proved, but his hopes lay with his leaders.

Young Fisher had reached his full height. He still had the shape of a boy, and had not yet regained much of his voice since his throat wound. He grunted approval when Jekonsaseh held up First Son to show off the boy's strong legs. The infant, finding his legs free, kicked and crowed. "He will be a good runner like you," she said. Fisher pumped his hand and smiled.

"Let's hope he has the chance to grow strong. We will need warriors," said Beaver Tooth gravely. "But not against the other Longhouse People, I hope," he added when his brother glared at him.

Condor and Cusik, Turtle Claw and Crooked Nose, Scout, and Odatshedeh of the Oneida murmured agreement. Runs Fast had returned from Doteoga and the birth of his daughter. He said nothing could prevent him from seeing how it would turn out. Only one of their old companions remained absent. Fisher's throat had healed enough so that he could manage a whisper. "Has anyone heard from Red Hair?"

"We will see him again," Jekonsaseh replied. "I expected you would talk again, and see? It has happened. While you were silent, you used the Eskimo hand signs he taught you. You learned to open your mind to thoughts. Not everyone can do that. When the discussions are over, you may become a shaman or a healer. Your brother will assist in the important work you will do." Fisher glowed under her praise and Beaver Tooth said he hoped they would live through the discussions.

They turned at the sounds of children singing. Deganawida had been rehearsing them to provide a special entertainment for their guests. "They are our witnesses to future generations," said Hiawatha. "They will remember and tell the tale of our meeting to their children, and they will pass it on. We will need delegates from all the Tribes to serve on the Central Council. We decided that Chief Onoji should represent Onondaga for his loyalty. Of course, his town's clan mothers will have to ratify his status."

"Onoji?" Tawanyas turned on him angrily. "He is bringing the Southern Onondaga against us." It had not escaped his notice that Deganawida and Hiawatha spoke with confidence. They fully expected Deganawida's vision to succeed, and that the matron's authority would be reinstated in the Confederation of Tribes.

Hiawatha replied calmly. "After Tododaho and his men acknowledge the Peacemaker's victory, Onondaga cannot be left out. It is in the center between the eastern and western tribes. It will be their honor to light the All Nations' Fire for our council meetings."

"All Nations' Fire!" Odatshedeh exclaimed. "None of this has happened yet. Has the Peacemaker foreseen that we will live through the meeting?"

Deganawida's mild eyes seemed aglow in confidence, but he tilted his head modestly. "I can only hope. More hunters are returning with game. Women, do your best to prepare food for our visitors for there will be many of them."

"Your Huron brother will not give a straight answer. Will we live through the talks?" asked Otter Clan Mother of Jekonsaseh.

"Chief Odatshedeh just reminded the Peacemaker that he can't see into the future. We must have faith. Tododaho and his men should arrive tomorrow in the early afternoon." People looked to each other. The three shamans agreed that they could not tell what would happen, yet they seemed sure of when the Onondaga would arrive. None of the patrols had yet seen the enemy or reported their position.

Hiawatha said, "All of Ganeo-gaono and half the Cayuga communities accepted the Peacemaker, as have the Seneca communities west of the Genesee River. That leaves most of Onondaga and those Oneida who are determined to fight for Tododaho unless we defeat him. I have faith our Peacemaker will prevail."

"I hear your words," said Chief Odatshedeh, "but you don't know the Snake Haired. The snake that whispers in his ear won't let him accept a peace he does not control. For what our enemy did to you, Hiawatha, and sending boys to ambush you at your camp, any sane man would wish him dead." Listeners murmured agreement.

When Hiawatha did not reply, Tawanyas looked to Odatshedeh. "Last summer, you and I faced each other on opposing sides. Today, we are friends, united by the Bringer of Peace. Anything is possible."

"If we live," added one of their men.

That began a new round of discussions when a higher voice interrupted. "Women, we have food to cook and preparations to make." The matrons led the women to their work, but the men's discussions went on as the sun descended.

The next day shortly after breakfast, runners came in to report that Tododaho was approaching Gano'wages with a great show of strength. The children climbed onto rooftops and platforms to watch them emerge from the forest.

Jekonsaseh exited the stockade to watch for them. She had not seen her father in more than ten years and wondered if she would know him when she saw him. He would be taller than most of his men, and his hair should identify him. Would he recognize or even notice her among the women of Gano'wages?

Instead of the expected host of warriors, two men left the forest and walked arm in arm through the fallow field toward the town. Was the taller man her father? What would people say when they saw the snake on his shoulder looking out from his twisted and dreadful locks of hair? Would he frighten the children? They seemed less frightened than excited. Then, she felt something else and she knew. Her heart beat faster.

"I never saw a man so old!" shouted a boy. "His hair is like clouds. Look at the younger man. He's even stranger. Who ever saw such colors? His face is pale and his hair is like fire."

"Let me through, please," she said. People moved aside. Deganawida turned to the arrivals and jumped up in delight. He ran to embrace the old man. "Why have you come all this way? You never leave Niagara except in winter."

"Someone had to bring this red-haired traveler back to his wife and son," he replied, wrapped in his son's welcoming arms.

Red Hair stared at Jekonsaseh as if she were the first fresh water he had seen in days. The couple touched hands and cheeks and breathed in each other's breaths as if each could absorb the other. "I feared I would never find you," Red Hair said. "I forgot who I was for a time. I thought I was still a boy in my father's country. Hidden in Mist sent out a bison, a hawk and a wolf to find me and bring me to him. Half of my memories were taken, but they came back when I heard you call my name."

"You heard me from Niagara?"

He smiled. "I heard you in my head when you were bringing our son into the world. You were right. I must have some *orenda* power after all. Let me see him."

She pulled around the carrier so Red Hair could see their baby. "I call him First Son." She undid the ties and placed the boy in Red Hair's arms. "First Son, this is your father."

He held the boy awkwardly, but turned him this way and that so he could look him over. The boy looked right back. His eyes were already turning hazel. At last he set the babe in the crook of his arm. The women laughed when the baby rooted. Finding no breast, he began to squall. "You'd better take him back."

"He can wait a little. Saiyen-gu!" She pulled her teacher's hands to her cheeks and breathed on them. "Thank you for bringing Red Hair to me. Come inside, both of you, and we will feed you. I stay in Otter Longhouse now. I finally was able to forgive my Otter Clan Grandmother after Deganawida's forgiveness ceremony."

As they walked, she introduced them to the chiefs and matrons. Hiawatha watched their joyful reunion. There would be more than one reunion soon. Chief Odatshedeh was right in that he must confront the man who had destroyed his family and cursed him. Deganawida had cured him of his insanity and his brutal melancholy, but on seeing his tormentor, would his madness return? Tododaho had killed his entire beloved family and left him a monster to wander in the wildest part of the forest. Could there be enough forgiveness in the world for that? If not, Hiawatha feared he would revert to the predatory beast he had been.

Chapter 28

This was the year Tododaho meant to solidify his power over Tribes Cayuga and Seneca and lead his combined forces east. Tribe Oneida could not stand against them. Tribe Ganeo-gaono was the toughest, but even they had to surrender to his greater numbers. With numerous flint deposits, it was rich in weapons and fire stones, but flint was not their master weapon. That was their reputation. Their perennial foes, the Algonquin, called them Mohawk, Eaters of Men. The name had taken over and they took pride in it. Onoji did not know the truth of it, but even they could not withstand the combined might of the other four tribes. With Tribe Ganeo-gaono his to command, Tododaho would be Turtle Island's most powerful ruler of all.

It irked Onoji that his master had not only agreed to talks, but let the Huron trespasser name the place. It would delay them at best and they might try to kill his master. Lord Tododaho decided to camp overnight and enter Gano'wages Town rested.

He had a council fire lit. His chiefs gathered around him to plan their strategy. One who had fought against Gano'wages described the town and its largest field which was to be left fallow for the conference.

When each man had spoken his thoughts, Tododaho turned to him. "Well, my trusted Chief Onoji. You met the Huron last winter and had words with him. What do you think he will try when we meet?"

Determined eyes challenged him to say something original. While the others were speaking, Onoji studied his master. Tododaho's hair was gray now, his arms and chest knotted with scars. Age had strengthened his *orenda*. More than three thousand hardened warriors huddled beneath the trees, watching for weakness, to flush it out as a dog flushes a bird out of hiding. Those closer would repeat for the farthest. Around the council fire, Tododaho's officers turned to him. He said, "Even if he doesn't, his followers want to destroy you."

"Of course they do." Tododaho's laugh was taken up by three thousand throats in ripples of sound as the words were passed back. The laughter died with a gesture from Tododaho. "Everyone knows that. I want to destroy Deganawida and his supporters. What is his plan?"

When they quieted, Onoji added. "I expect his loyal followers to rush you when you kill the Huron. Once he is gone, there will be no one to stop them, no one else they will obey."

Tododaho lifted his hand to end the exclamations. "He makes people obey him. That is why I agreed to meet him for he might turn out to be a worthy opponent. We will talk first so I can study him. As for his men, that is why I want you and my other captains in the field with me." He looked at them. "Be alert. When I raise my war club to kill the Huron, watch his followers. Kill anyone who rushes forward. We will give the town a chance to pledge themselves to me. If they insist on fighting, kill their warriors and burn down the town, but try to capture the clan mothers and Jekonsaseh alive. Women must be taught their place. Eat lightly tonight and rest. Tomorrow we shall feast on Gano'wages' corn and meat."

The sun was overhead when Tododaho's company arrived at the field. They spread out many deep in the outer three quarters of the field. Those in the fore sat, those behind knelt and the further warriors stood. Two years had passed since Deganawida first came to the Tribes with his message of peaceful unification. The warriors muttered to each other that those of them who survived the imminent battle for Gano'wages would soon have a story worth the retelling.

Red vertical lines decorated the shaman's cheeks and chin, and snakes appeared to writhe from his scalp. Onoji beat a small war drum and followed a few steps behind among the five captains. Tododaho stopped at the carefully arranged hide mats and his men formed a semicircle behind him. He motioned and they took their seat as he did, war clubs laid across their knees.

Deganawida's followers and the townsfolk took the field edge nearest the town. If battle erupted, they would defend themselves, but they were vastly outnumbered. Deganawida and Hiawatha entered the field followed by Gano'wages' chiefs, elders and clan matrons. When they halted, the witnesses positioned themselves.

Two were shrouded in robes with hoods that covered all but their eyes which remained in shadow. One was a young woman, too young to be a matron. Something about her pricked Onoji's interest and seemed to draw his master's as well.

Onoji could only wonder, but Tododaho reached with questing spirit fingers to see the woman more clearly. She blocked his probe. Deciding no woman was worth the effort he sought knowledge of the man, but again ran into resistance. Whoever they were, their spirit colors had blended. Only together were they strong enough to resist him. He must direct his attention to Deganawida and Hiawatha. Onoji ceased drumming.

Our final test and my final test, Hiawatha thought. *We triumph here or it is over.* Age had frosted his hair, but although creases lined his thoughtful eyes, they were steady. He was ready to sacrifice himself if that proved necessary to end the evil that threatened all of them.

Deganawida spread his *orenda* like a cape to envelope them both. *He won't curse you again. If he proves stronger, we will die together.*

Tododaho acknowledged Hiawatha first as the elder of the two men and a member of the Tribes. "Cousin," he said.

"Cousin," agreed Hiawatha.

Tododaho sensed their friendship was stronger than a blood bond. For a confused moment he resented seeing another so high in Hiawatha's affection. He wondered at the odd thought, reminding himself he had no need for affection. Affection was a liability. His power would lead the Tribes to victory. It was time to speak to the Huron. "Deganawida," he said. "I have come."

"I th-thank you. You have questions. I will answer them." Tododaho's men smiled, thinking their lord's challenger showed apprehension.

The stutterer wanted him to begin. He knew just what he wanted to say. "Tell me this then, Huron," he said. "Your tribe dwells north of the Great Lakes. You came a long way to interfere in my business. You want the Longhouse Tribes to be at peace. That is also my wish after they accept my authority. You are not needed here."

"The Good Mind says I am."

"Who are you to speak for the Elder Brother, Huron? Different spirits watch over your people. Are you prepared to die for your vision?"

"If I m-must, but first we agreed to speak." He nodded to Hiawatha who retrieved something folded from his pack and handed it to him.

"P-please, be good enough to examine this belt. One of our women wove my dream into a picture with dog hair thread and quahog and whelk shells." With both hands, Deganawida unfolded the belt and extended it to Tododaho.

The background was purple with two white squares on either side of a stylized fir tree. Each square was connected to the others and to the tree. Tododaho turned the belt over to inspect both sides. He lifted it so his men could see and describe it to those who were further away. Then, he laid it across his knees. Tododaho asked, "Was it made by the young woman who sits near you?"

"No. Another wove it."

"Purple is the smallest part of the shell while white is plentiful; yet the background is purple and the design is white. What is the meaning of it?"

"Purple is most precious and sacred, as is the belt. The squares are the tribes, united with the Peace Tree on a field of trust. Trust is above all in value."

"There are five tribes, not four."

"The center shows the P-peace Tree which will be in Onondaga. The Tribes will meet under the tree. The belt shows the future you and I will bring to them."

"You and I? There is no you and I." His snake wrapped its tail around Tododaho's left arm for balance and dropped its head for a closer look.

Hiawatha, watching Tododaho, said, "The squares on the left are Seneca and Cayuga. Oneida and Ganeo-gaono are on the right."

Tododaho shook his head. "Let the Huron speak for himself, Hiawatha. Speak slowly, boy. I will hear you out." He could afford to be gracious.

Deganawida took a slow breath. "You, Lord Tododaho and Hiawatha are the first two lords of Onondaga. Onoji is third. The rest shall be chosen by your matrons. All Longhouse delegates will meet by the Peace Tree and swear to live in peace with the Tribes of the Confederation and to abide by their mutual decisions. The All Nations Council fire will be lit in Tyo-den-he-deh each year when the leaves turn red or when a special council is called. Onondaga shall be Keepers of the Flame. Your name, as the Confederation's highest Lord, will never die."

"What about your name?"

"Except when recounting our story at the Council, I do not wish my name to be spoken. After the first Council, the Tribes will not see me again."

Tododaho covered the shape of the tree with his right hand. "They will not see you again after today, except to bury you." He fingered his war club with his other hand. "Do you think I will spare you after what you have done?"

"Before you use your war club, listen and watch. Because you will be Supreme Lord of the Confederacy, the children practiced a special song and dance for your visit. They await your permission to start."

Curious, Tododaho waved permission. The townspeople parted to allow the children to file into the field. The boys and girls had washed and dressed in their best vests and leggings with their hair braided into neat plaits. They circled the negotiators in a slow dance while they sang the song of peace Hiawatha had taught them. Their voices were young, sweet and high.

When they concluded, Deganawida made a gesture and they returned to their parents. Tododaho frowned. "This changes nothing. Longhouse warriors don't sit at home singing songs and waiting for meetings. Men compete for power and dominance. I face the truth. You make up dreams for a land where you do not belong. It will not end like this."

"Perhaps it can." Deganawida turned and beckoned his nearest two attendants to push back their hoods. Tododaho stifled his emotion, but his dark eyes flickered and his hands clenched when Ole Red Hair and Jekonsaseh came forward. "You may wish to greet your daughter and her husband. The child in her sling is your grandson."

Tododaho seized his war club and rose in a single motion to confront Red Hair. He had been watching Deganawida and Hiawatha too closely to feel the proximity of Jekonsaseh, his traitor daughter. He would address her in a while, but he wondered how the stranger had survived his strongest curse. "You live," he accused.

Red Hair met his gaze. "As you see." He stretched his *orenda* toward Jekonsaseh and their son. His connected with theirs as Hidden in Mist had taught him. Their combined strength urged Tododaho to agree to Deganawida's plan. For a moment, Tododaho wavered. His power and theirs met and shimmered between them, neither breaching the other but locked in struggle.

Jekonsaseh looked up and met his eyes. "Father," she said. Her voice held all the longing of a lost child for an absent parent. Tododaho's war club slipped from his hand and lay, barely noticed, on the earth. "No one here wishes you harm. Would you like to hold your grandson?"

He nearly reached for the infant when he realized what he was about to do. "Get him away from me! If I touch the child, he will die." The snake opened its mouth, revealing fangs. Its narrow black tongue flicked out to taste the child's scent. Jekonsaseh covered the boy with her blanket to protect him from that lidless gaze. "I can never touch him. I must kill this Huron or he must kill me. There's no other way."

Deganawida beckoned Red Hair. "You are wrong, Lord Tododaho. There is another way. Red Hair will show it to you." He spoke gently. "If the Haudenosaunee, The Longhouse Tribes, cannot stand together as one in the future, strangers from Red Hair's world may come here to take Turtle Island away from us."

"What strangers? What kind of threat is this?"

The mutters and questions grew louder. Tododaho directed his gaze to his men and they fell silent. "What strangers?" he repeated.

Red Hair answered him. "My people were attacked by them, after a long and cruel winter. Sea Woman, the Eskimo spirit of Ocean, weakened us. They will use new kinds of weapons ours cannot match. I have one such knife. It is not stone, but of a substance unknown to you."

Tododaho took in Red Hair's nearly blood-red spiky hair, his short beard, his freckled nose and hazel eyes. He made a circle of protection around himself in the air with his hands. "Nothing will harm me," he said. "Show it to me."

Red Hair had honed and polished the steel blade so its edge could split a hair. It reflected the pale sky like a mirror. "This is steel," he said, tapping it with a flint fire stone to make it ring. Tododaho saw his own reflection in the knife. When he backed away from it, the sun's reflection made him squint.

"Move it away from me," he ordered.

Red Hair turned the knife to its side. "Sorry." The snake hissed, following the movement, but Red Hair continued to rotate the knife, being careful not to send the sun's reflection into Tododaho's eyes. "This blade is made by combining iron and carbon, metals found in certain rocks. Under great heat, the metals part from the rocks and become soft enough to blend and shape. I have not found a stone knife here that can equal it, not even the black glass. There are many countries on the other side of the ocean. Men use iron and steel for armor. Your stone points cannot pierce it.

"The men who attacked us came in canoes large enough to carry many warriors. Each man will have such weapons. These canoes catch the wind. When many come, they are enough to fill several towns. These men are greedy for land, slaves, and furs. They will take them. They will take Turtle Island as long as it possesses something they want. Will the Tribes be able to stop them? Look at my knife again, Lord Tododaho."

Red Hair tried to hand Tododaho the knife, but Onoji rushed to prevent him. "He will try to kill you, my lord," he warned.

"He won't. Let him come to me." Tododaho extended his open hand. Red Hair gave him the knife, ivory grip first. Tododaho felt the cool edge, and then, suddenly, he plunged the blade into the ground. The steel did not crack or break but slipped in easily. He pulled it out and handed it back to Red Hair who wiped it off, leaving it as unblemished as before.

"Your people are making ready to come here?"

"Not mine. I am the last of my tribe. They are another tribe called England. Word came to them that we were weak so they came to take our wealth. The last war left too few of us to keep together. We had to ask other nations for refuge. It can happen here too, and will, if you weaken yourselves by fighting each other."

Tododaho stiffened. "Why do you care?"

Red Hair remembered the wounded and maimed on Greenland's beaches. "Tribe Ganeo-gaono adopted me. I would repay their kindness. Let the Five Tribes become one. Accept Deganawida's vision so Jekonsaseh and our son, and all these people, won't lose their homes like I lost mine."

While Tododaho weighed Red Hair's words, his snake reared to follow the back-and-forth movement of Red Hair's knife. Quite suddenly, so fast its movement was a blur, it struck and tried to sink its fangs into the steel. Red Hair pulled back the blade, but the snake's fangs had curved over the edge. There was a peculiar sound, then a hissing and bubbling of blood. The sinewy body convulsed. It gave up its scaly grip on Tododaho's matted locks and shoulders and dropped to the ground. In another moment, it had slipped into the shadows and slithered away.

Red Hair sheathed his knife and stepped back, looking to Jekonsaseh. "I did not plan that," he whispered.

"Elder Brother did. He wins today," she returned. Voices around them lifted in shock and horror as they explained to each other what had happened.

Tododaho's power deserted him along with his snake. He became bent. His hands withered and shook while tremors of pain flicked across his forehead and his hooded eyes. His mouth drooped and his shoulders slumped, bent under the weight of his crimes and his years. His warriors lost the will to fight. Nothing made sense except that Younger Brother had been defeated with the defeat of his snake, and that their leader had lost.

"What have you done?" demanded Onoji.

Red Hair said, "I did nothing." Yet, it was obvious to all that Snake Haired's snake had abandoned him and seemed to have taken his power with it.

"Will - will you allow me to touch you?" Deganawida asked Tododaho in his mild voice. "Perhaps I can help."

Tododaho turned and swayed, unsteady and off balance. His men still guarded the periphery of the field. Onoji and his sub-captains were beside him. Only he had changed. "Why speak to me with respect? I am broken. Touch me if it pleases you. I can't stop you." Rendered helpless at his words, Tododaho's captains did nothing.

Deganawida stroked Tododaho's cheeks with the soft pads of his fingers and sang a song of healing. He stroked the edges of the wrinkled brows, the lips of the drooping mouth and the neck that had become too weak to hold the head upright. "Your hair is unruly, Lord Tododaho. Will you allow me and your cousin to comb out the tangles that weigh so heavily upon you? Without these tangles, your thoughts will become straight and your head lighter." He gestured for him to take his seat on the hide.

Tododaho shifted his gaze from Deganawida to Hiawatha. He sat, but not as before. With bent head, silent tears dripping down his cheeks, streaking red into the white base, he said, "End my life or comb my hair. It no longer matters."

Onoji found he could move again. He began forward to protect his war leader, aiming his spear at Deganawida and shouting a warning. "If you kill him, his men will fill you with arrows."

Deganawida lifted his right palm. "I won't kill him, Onoji. I will comb the tangles from his hair. Move back just a little and watch." Onoji obeyed. "Red Hair? Please hand me the comb you use when you shave your beard." Red Hair handed over his sharp-edged steel knife.

Jekonsaseh sat beside her father and withdrew her son from his sling. "You can touch him now, Father," she said. "Feel our future." The old shaman reached out uncertainly. "That's right." She guided his fingers to the baby's cheeks and thighs. The corners of the small mouth curved into a smile, while Jekonsaseh continued to assure her father. "Your name will continue in this child and many after him as the first lord of Onondaga. Our story will be told as long as our people continue. You will not be forgotten, Father."

Tododaho was so intent on his grandson and daughter that he hardly noticed Hiawatha stretch out each twisted rope of his hair. He barely felt Deganawida slice them through near his scalp. His dreadlocks dropped around him like dead snakes.

While he worked, Deganawida sang his song of peace and strength and unity. His followers and the townspeople echoed the words and the children sang it with them.

Tododaho's warriors crept nearer, trying to understand the extent of what had happened. They saw their feared lord's peaceful and dreamy face. Many of them set down their war clubs and spears, turning to one another in wonder at what it could mean.

At the end, Tododaho sat up straight and felt his head with both hands. "I feel light," he said surprised. He stretched out his neck and wriggled his shoulders. "I feel as if I could float."

Deganawida returned the knife to Red Hair who sheathed it out of sight. Hiawatha and Deganawida placed their palms against Tododaho's scalp. Jekonsaseh remained with him. She took her father's hands and rubbed his knuckles. The baby was in his lap now.

Deganawida knelt to his level. "Lord Tododaho," he said. "Your crooked thoughts have been combed straight. Your men are prepared to follow your commands. You swore you would end your war the day I knelt before you. I do that now."

A thousand and more gaped as Deganawida prostrated himself. The old man looked toward his war club. He might still change the outcome of this day, but his grandson gurgled. Forgetting the club, Tododaho leaned the child over his shoulder and patted his back.

Deganawida rose. "Shall we bring the tribes together, Lord Tododaho? Will you accept my vision of the Great Peace and help me spread it?"

"How?"

"When the leaves turn color, I will come to Tyo-den-he-deh for the first council. Together, we will dig a pit by the largest sweet pine and bury the weapons of the last war between the Longhouse nations." Deganawida looked to Odatshedeh of Oneida Nation. "You said Oneida would accept me if Tododaho gave his approval."

"I did," Odatshedeh affirmed.

"Tawanyas of Seneca Nation," Deganawida said and the man stepped forward. "You guarded Jekonsaseh and kept her safe. Will Seneca agree?"

"I will speak to them. When they hear of today's discussions, they will."

"Scout, Crooked Arm and Claw of Doteoga, delegates of Ganeo-gaono Nation, yours was the first town to accept my message. Go home and give testimony to your tribe. Ask the clan matrons to choose who will represent your country and invite them to the first All Clans Council at Tyo-den-he-deh after the harvest festival."

"We will."

"Cusik of Cayuga Nation. What do you say?"

He came forward. "They will hear and agree."

Tododaho handed the baby to Jekonsaseh. "Hiawatha." His voice sank to a whisper. "Take my war club and avenge yourself for what I did to you and your family. My captains, do not stop this man and do not avenge me."

Hiawatha had come too far with the Peacemaker. Revenge would not return his youth or his loved ones. It would only prove that he had not conquered himself. His eyes held more sorrow but also more gentleness than Tododaho could remember. "What was between us is over," Hiawatha said with unwavering finality. "The future of our people is more important. I won't take your life." The shimmering of tension around the central figures lifted like mist, leaving each of them more distinct and vivid.

Deganawida turned to Jekonsaseh and Red Hair. "Jekonsaseh, Mother of Nations, was the first to believe in me." He turned back. "You, her father, are the last I will ask. Lord Tododaho, do you approve and confirm my message? Will Nation Onondaga be the Five Nations' Fire Keeper? Will your Tribe rekindle our All Nations Council fire each year for its sweet smoke to ascend to the sky?"

Tododaho rose and looked over his warriors. He saw relief that they would not have to slaughter their brother tribesmen. Perhaps now they would be strong to resist strangers from across the sea. "I confirm and accept the Peacemaker's message. Our war is ended. Lord Onoji, tell the holdouts of Tribe Onondaga to accept the Great Peace. Lord Odatshedeh, tell the holdouts of Tribe Oneida. Lord Tawanyas, tell the Seneca towns and villages west of the Genesee. We will meet in the harvested corn fields of Tyo-den-he-deh next autumn for the first All Nations Council."

Onoji took a breath. "It shall be as you say." There would be no slaughter today. The Elder Brother had won and his Younger Brother had gone off to sulk.

Tododaho said, "At the first Council, we will bury our weapons under the roots of the Peace Tree, as the Peacemaker requires of us. Let no one hold back."

Turtle Clan Mother announced that the women had prepared food but portions would be meager. "If our guests brought trail food and are willing to share, we will prepare a feast that will long be remembered." Tododaho's men returned to the forest encampment for their rations and gave them to the women. The warriors broke into groups and began toward the stockade.

Deganawida found Hidden in Mist and embraced him warmly. The old man said, "You know I could give you no help here. You made me proud." The luster of his white hair resembled the sun shining against the torrent he guarded.

Tododaho took in the radiance of the older man's face and hair, and stepped back. "Who are you?"

Saiyen-gu's aged eyes looked over the former warlord. "I'm an old man who lives near a waterfall. In Iowa, the country of my youth, I was Saiyen-gu. Of late, I'm called Hidden in Mist, Guardian of Niagara.

Peace came to the Longhouse Tribes today. After the feast, I will go home."

Hiawatha and Deganawida brought Tododaho to Jekonsaseh and Red Hair. The baby, back in his sling, gave his grandfather a toothless grin and reached out to touch his bald head. The group followed Saiyen-gu into the stockade.

"Hidden in Mist is more than an old man," Tododaho remarked. The Peacemaker met him and they entered the town together.

Chapter 29

Deganawida and Saiyen-gu sat contentedly on their ledge, smoking their pipes. The waterfall beside them roared too loudly to be spoken above, but they didn't need to speak. "How was the council?" sent Saiyen-gu. "Tell me."

"At the end of the ceremonies and discussions and songs, Tododaho buried his war club by the roots of the Peace Tree. He suggested Red Hair drop his gray knife into the pit, too. His knife actually belongs to Doteoga's Wolf Clan Mother. When he agreed to come with me, she charged him to use it on my behalf. I told him it would be best to bury it. Sadly, that knife won't be the last steel weapon to come to Turtle Island. Red Hair finally accepted that he's worthy of Jekonsaseh." He paused before adding, "He was not guessing about the foreigners. Sometimes he sees the future."

Saiyen-gu tilted his head, a silent request for his son to go on.

"They will come and attempt to take Turtle Island, to destroy and change it. He says it is their way. He says if the Tribes keep together, they will survive. They may lose some land, but not all." Deganawida blinked away the droplets that had settled on his lashes. "I wonder what will become of my mother's people. Red Hair couldn't say, but I'm worried for them. With Elder Brother's help, I persuaded the Five Tribes to accept peace. We both know I will never succeed with the Huron."

Saiyen-gu pulled on his pipe and let the smoke curl from his lips and nostrils. "If the Tribes invite them into the Confederation, they would be wise to accept. If not, your grandmother will have dreamed true. The Huron will be wiped out."

Deganawida sighed. "Do you think the Five Nations will be able to keep the new Law throughout their generations? They will be tested."

"No human can see that far ahead. I assume they will tell the story of their founding each year before the All Nations council."

"I suggested it and they agreed." Deganawida looked up to where the mist blended with the sky. It caressed his cheeks, leaving drops like tears. Small rainbows winked in and out of existence where the sun's rays touched the mist. The air itself seemed like clouds, a fit place for gods and ancestors.

"Then you've done all you can. It was good to see Jekonsaseh and Red Hair, and their baby. Red Hair is finally done with his journeys. Wherever he and Jekonsaseh dwell, they will be home with one another. Did they speak of their plans?"

"They will pass the winter in Doteoga with Red Hair's sister Dream Weaver and her family. She married the trader Runs Fast. Those two will make each other happy. After Jekonsaseh births their next child, they will visit Tododaho in Tyo-den-he-deh and dwell there for a while. First Son already talks. His grandfather will be glad to watch him grow and see the new baby before he joins his ancestors. Hiawatha will live on in Tyo-den-he-deh in honor for the part he played in bringing peace to the tribes."

"Good." They smoked in the silence for a while feeling the hidden power around them. "What about you, my son? You dare not return home until those who knew you forget the fatherless boy who went away."

"That is true," Deganawida agreed. "Someone should stay here to watch over this holy place. You must join your own ancestors soon."

Hidden in Mist tilted his head toward Canada across the water, and his wrinkled face broke into a gentle smile. "It's true. Red Wing is waiting. Niagara knows you. It will respect your desire for peace as it respected mine. There will be young Huron wives who have yet to conceive. They will come here where the River's *orenda* increases their beauty and fertility. When they go home, their men will respond and long to possess them. You may yet have many sons and daughters to honor you in your old age. You shall be the new Hidden in Mist."

"It has been a good life for you."

His father agreed with a smile. "When a hard winter comes and the river forms columns of ice, you may want to go north again. See if you can influence the next generations to make good choices."

The past flowed like the stream behind them, over and around obstacles, separating, plunging from great heights and coming together in the future. The Niagara River flowed into the next Great Lake and from there, into the Wide River. It crossed Algonquin country and became a marsh and a gulf. Finally, it poured itself into the encircling ocean that held Turtle Island and all the islands of men. Old and bent fingers touched young ones that were strong and straight. White smoke rose from their pipes and became part of the mist that ascended to heaven.

THE LEGENDS

Iroquois and Huron history and legends have come into the public realm. I used several of these for inspiration in writing of HIDDEN IN MIST. The Elder and Younger Twin Brothers are the sons of Mother Earth, daughter of the "Woman Who Fell From Heaven." Elder Brother was born in the natural way. Impatient, Younger Brother was so anxious to be born, he tore a hole in his mother's side. She died and her elder son buried her. The Three Sisters that Sustain, Corn, Beans and Squash, grew from her bones and Holy Tobacco grew from her skull.

Elder Brother overcame Younger Brother at a game of Plum Pits. As his prize, he created men and taught them to use tobacco in their ceremonies, for its smoke to carry their prayers to heaven. He taught them how to use fire and make weapons for hunting, and he gave them laws. Since Younger Brother lost, he had to go away to live in the wilderness. He was jealous as well as impatient. In revenge, he plagued men with creations of his own -- thorns, venomous serpents and war. He also put water in maple sap which had to be boiled away again to return it to its original sweetness.

Under the green canopy of early America, civil war raged between the Five Longhouse Nations. Tododaho, a powerful shaman, decided to dominate all the tribes and remake their laws as Younger Brother prompted him. Ruthless in his ambition, he set about destroying all opposition. His evil grew with his power and manifested in snakes growing from his head instead of hair. Those who dared oppose him died under mysterious circumstances.

Hiawatha threatened Tododaho's dominance. When even the death of his wife and daughters did not frighten him into submission, Tododaho caused the death of his last daughter, Laughing Water.

Hiawatha's spirit had been weakened by the loss of all he loved and he became a creature of terror. Unaware of himself, he hunted and ate unwary strangers in the wild forest.

Jekonsaseh, a gifted young woman, constructed dwellings on the trails home from battles. She gave refuge to the weary fighter, food to the hungry, and nursed the injured. Some said she healed men only to send them back to kill again, but most said she never turned away the hurt or needy. For her kindness to all warriors, the Iroquois called her Mother of Nations.

North of the Great Lakes a son was born to a Huron virgin. His grandmother dreamed the boy would be the ruin of the Huron and tried to drown him under the ice of a frozen pond. During the night, the babe was miraculously rescued and returned to his mother. The child was called Deganawida, the thinker. Tormented by the other boys for being fatherless, the lonely child spoke with a stutter, but he gained strength from other quarters. He would be the Peacemaker, the Man from the North. He would bring peace to the Five Tribes even at the risk of fulfilling his grandmother's prophecy.

Deganawida's first act in his mission to the Tribes was the curing of Hiawatha. Because Deganawida stuttered and did not yet know Longhouse speech well, Hiawatha spoke to the Tribes for him.

A guardian lived in a cave behind the American side of Niagara Falls. A young woman escaped rather than take the wrong husband. She meant to paddle her canoe over the edge of the cliff. The spirit of Niagara saved her and became her teacher. While she traveled with him and learned healing, she became known as Maid of the Mist. To this day, the tour ship of Niagara bears her name. The Guardian gave her instructions and sent her home to help her people.

Ole Halvardson, last son of Greenland, is my own creation. He was introduced in PICTURE MAKER as a nine-year-old. In DREAM WEAVER, he reluctantly helped his half-sister find acceptance in her mother's tribe. Her journey was ended, but Ole had much farther to go. As one of the Peacemaker's followers, he had to change his nature, learn new ways and define himself. Finding Jekonsaseh and finally Hidden in Mist, he learns what he must do to succeed. Finally where he belongs, he helps when Deganawida defeats Tododaho and forms a new thing on Turtle Island: the Five Tribes Confederation. Today, they are the Six Tribes, also called the Iroquois

Made in the USA
Lexington, KY
10 September 2018